AL.

Ain't Life

by

Eddie Hardin

with Oliver Gray

Sarsen Press
Winchester, UK

Design: Oliver Gray and Judith Blake
Cover design: Richard Williams for Pacific Hill
Printed by: Sarsen Press, 22, Hyde Street, Winchester, SO23 7DR, UK
Published by Sarsen Press

Contact Eddie Hardin at **www.eddiehardin.com**

ISBN: 1-897609-67-1

Eddie Hardin was only seventeen when he passed the audition to replace Steve Winwood in the Spencer Davis Group.

In **ALAB**, Eddie lifts the lid on life in the music business in the sixties and seventies, talks candidly about his battles with the demons of alcohol and provides us with a hilarious insight into the craziness of life on the road with one of the world's most successful and enduring rock and roll bands.

Dedicated to the memory of Isobel Harding.

Thanks to Spencer Davis and John Fisher.

Special thanks to Liz and Emma.

CONTENTS

FOREWORD by Spencer Davis

I have known Eddie Hardin for thirty-six years, since 1967 to be exact, and during that time, we have bounced between the two poles of love and hate for each other.

Now, as we slip into the evening of our lives, we have arrived at a mutually deadlocked acceptance of each other's presence and a warm, fuzzy respect for one another.

I hasten to add, I still keep a wary eye on him!

In various formations of the Spencer Davis Group, he has terrorised the population of the entire European continent (as we speak, this state of affairs still persists), with several memorable forays into the North American continent, wreaking mayhem and havoc wherever he went.

I can still see the faces of some of the hotel staff in various parts of the globe, who, upon hearing the name Eddie Hardin, have felt the icy cold grip of terror overwhelm them to the point of never being able to lead normal lives again.

Eddie's achievements in the Olympics and the sporting world are non-existent, but no one can ever take away his title of being the only holder of the triple platinum medal for wine and cigarette consumption in the universe.

I hand you over to my friend, Eddie Hardin, wherever he and his Hammond might be.

Spencer Davis, Los Angeles, 20/05/03

CHAPTER 1
EARLY DAYS

I have always thought it incredibly presumptuous to devote an entire volume to describing one's life. Now, against my earlier judgement, I find myself embarking on that very project. Okay, so I'm incredibly presumptuous.

Sitting here in Southern France in the scorching heat, my beginnings in South London seem light years away; yet somehow, they're still with me in heart. I was born in post-war Britain in the winter of 1949. My father had served in the Royal Air Force and my mother had served in the NAAFI. Their backgrounds were poles apart, my mother being from Lambeth in South London. Her family were Cockneys, the real thing. My father, on the other hand, was educated at St. Paul's and later joined the Royal Horse Artillery, with which he served in India, where his education was honed into that of an English gentleman, the kind that seemingly just doesn't exist any more. He was considerably older than my mother and had one son, John Harding, from a previous marriage.

His family were antique dealers and lived in Kensington Church Street, whilst my mother's family were actually quite poor people and lived in Methley Street, Kennington. It's quite incredible what difference an 'S' could make in this instance. They really did meet at the NAAFI, where my father had gone to be measured for his new Officer's uniform. At least, that is the story that was fed to me.

My father, like me, I regret to say, had Olympic drinking habits. Also like me, he reformed much later in life and regretted it until his dying day. He actually had a charmed life, living well and in some style on the proceeds of his antique dealing. In his early days, he lived at Remenham Place in Henley-on-Thames and later, he owned a Country Club in Weybridge, which was full of old Colonel types and resulted in his losing a great deal of his fortune. As I understand it, he was pretty pissed most of the time and had little regard for organisation, again very much like me.

His passion was horse riding, and he was obviously a fine equestrian since his days in the Royal Horse Artillery. He kept two horses stabled in a mews off Hyde Park Corner and rode regularly in Rotten Row and, on occasion, to his antique shop in Kensington Church Street. He dabbled in politics in the 50's, becoming an Alderman, which resulted in more financial losses until, in the 60's, he slowed down somewhat under my mother's influence and tended to spend much of his time at home with his absolutely vast collection of antiques. He owned the largest private collection of ivory in Great Britain and, when I eventually became the owner of a 32-roomed mansion in Sunningdale, he furnished it from top to bottom with his collection of porcelain, paintings, ivories and furniture.

My mother's life had been totally different. She came from a huge family, about which I'm still pretty confused. I have aunts who aren't really aunts and uncles who aren't really uncles. For some reason, it was my grandmother's house in Kennington that was the axis point of the entire family. Even my father was forced into the regular Saturday get-togethers which occurred every week without fail. My father hated it and, as I grew older, so did I, but it was an obligation and it continued right up to my grandmother's death. Both my grandparents on my mother's side died in their sixties and I can remember vividly the nightly hospital visits. Hospitals in South London in those days were pretty grim and still very Victorian. The hospitals themselves made you feel ill, just looking at the bleak interiors and exteriors. The progress in this field, even in my lifetime, has been quite staggering.

My mother's sister Maureen, again not a blood sister (Maureen was left on my grandmother's doorstep at birth but was always known as my mother's sister) was my favourite "aunt" and she had a hand in my later career. There was also a smattering of villainy on this side of the family, since I can remember Freddie Foreman (Brinks Matt robbery and many, many other famous escapades). Another "uncle" who attended the Saturday gatherings on occasion was Buster Edwards (The Great Train Robbery) and his wife June. So, all in all, I was exposed as a child to a pretty confused set of rôle models.

There were also constant parties, which were great for me, as I got to stay up until I fell over and also got to learn some great old songs. They always had a piano player who seemed to be able to play anything at the drop of a hat, and the singing and merriment was just fantastic. All this, I suppose, must have had an influence on my music. I actually love the old songs because their chord structures, when played properly, are very ingenious. How these old guys got their fingers round all those tunes still amazes me. There were guys who played in the Fats Waller style, which can be pretty tricky, and others who played like Erroll Garner, which can be quite beautiful. They were just playing at our parties and going back to work on Monday! It was a very, very happy time for me.

My first concrete recollections stem from around 1960 when, as a pupil, or rather a bloody nuisance, at Alleyn's School, I met two people who were to become friends throughout my life. My preparatory school,

Oakfield, had been in Dulwich and, having looked at its website, it seems there were only two distinguished pupils there. Norma Major was one and I was the other!

Memories from this period are fairly blurred, but I can recall my very first day at the school. My mum had made me a bag with a cat embroidered on it, in which to keep my pencils and things. We weren't allowed to use ink, that came much later. In fact, it's a shame it ever came at all, as I would not have been able to put my name on some of the ludicrous contracts I would go on to sign. Anyway, on my first day, I refused to enter the school and sat on the steps outside until lunchtime, at which point Mum was telephoned and I was sent home. I found it very hard to make friends. Indeed, I still do, but once a bond is formed with me, it is never broken.

I stayed at Oakfield until the obligatory 11-Plus, which I failed. However, thanks to the intervention of a teacher who had blind faith in me, I "re-sat" the exam at home that night and miraculously passed. It was obligatory to have passed for me to go on to my next school, Alleyn's, again situated in Dulwich. The other main school in the area was Dulwich College, which I didn't particularly like the look of, although it had a certain kudos which failed to impress me. We were always told by staff at Alleyn's that it was in fact the elder of the two schools and therefore had an element of discreet superiority.

Alleyn's also had a military side. Every Friday, we would all turn into soldiers, with the choice of Army, Navy, or Air Force. I plumped for the army, but found the uniform the most uncomfortable bloody thing I've ever worn. Still, it was fun being given guns and allowed to run about shooting things. We were given charge of the most fearsome weapons. I doubt if this situation exists today, but there were Sten Guns, Bren Guns, Lee Enfield 303's and we even had our own armoury, which was run by a guy of about fifteen! He eventually unsurprisingly suffered some mental problems and blew his head off one morning.

I was sitting through a particularly boring chemistry lesson when I overheard an incongruously distinguished and mellow voice booming from the row behind, telling some story about the formation of an "orchestra". I was interested in following this conversation rather than the one being addressed to me from the front of the room because, at the time, I was dabbling with drums and guitars and, more prominently, the piano.

I seemed predestined to become a pianist. When I was a child, my father had a black Bechstein full grand piano, and for some reason, during the day, I was put underneath it in my cot. I have distant memories of gazing up at the vast undercarriage of the instrument. Later, at preparatory school, there was a beaten up old upright piano at the side of the playing field and we were given the task, for our amusement, of smashing it to pieces. For some reason, I felt I couldn't take part in its destruction.

Anyway, the voice in the classroom continued to expound the merits of various orchestras I knew absolutely nothing about, and in particular that of John Barry who, it seemed, at least as far as the orator was concerned, was the only one in contention with his own vast talent. Out of curiosity, I turned round for a quick glance at the chap who was spouting all this guff. There he was, John Fisher, an almost Dickensian character, totally different to everyone else in the room, which I liked. He just looked odd and, as years were to tell, he was bloody odd. He had a centre parting with black cascading hair and a monstrous Cyrano de Bergerac nose. The poor chap getting the brunt of his banter had not a clue what he was talking about, but I felt there was a bit of common ground between us and so introduced myself. The chemistry lesson disappeared from our thoughts as we instantly became absorbed in general musical conversation. By the end of the lesson, I had, sure enough, joined his "orchestra" and it was decided we should meet up at my house to take matters further.

However, it unfortunately soon became apparent that John had no musical expertise whatsoever. True, he had a great and influential (on me) knowledge of records and composers but technically, he was a non-starter. I played the piano and bashed the drums and he seemed pretty impressed, so I was in. Next came a singer, introduced as N. Twai. His real name was Geoff Warner, but obviously, Geoff was not a star's name so he was re-christened. My own name didn't have much of a theatrical ring to it either, so I was baptised Paul Syphon.

After several rehearsals, it became clear that not only did our leader have no musical inclination, but neither did our singer. Days turned into weeks and we'd get together for what soon became regular shouting matches. But we had some great fun and I got to play endless piano and, as a result, learnt an immense repertoire.

School became an inconvenience, although it served as a good meeting place. Each day, we suffered until the lunch-time break, left for my house and rarely returned. Our repertoire could be called eclectic, featuring, as it did, material by Al Jolson, Frank Sinatra, Judy Garland and The Animals. Day after day, we pounded away, singing, shouting and using various household utensils for extra percussion. This may all sound pretty stupid to you, but the fun and pleasure we derived has remained firmly implanted in our memories. When, one Christmas Eve, we decided to go public, we were assured of a captive audience. This was our hapless parents. The show-stopper was "Pasadena", and the dubious sound of John Fisher's voice will ring in my ears forever.

Aside from music, there was the opposite sex to consider. Well, I did. The others seemed happy to bash away day after day. On music, nothing else. As we were a trio, I found it difficult to leave the others behind, so they came along to most of my courting exploits, which cramped my style somewhat.

I had an au pair taking care of me at this time and it was her job to prepare lunch for me. Lunch soon got scrapped in favour of other interests. Helle taught me the ways of the world and also had a great Elvis Presley collection, which got me into Rock and Roll proper. I was besotted with Helle and went on to spend several idyllic holidays in Norway, where she had a piano, on which I entertained her family in the evenings. They must have known this was not just a cultural exchange. It is true to say that I had no intentions of learning Norwegian, but this was definitely my first love affair and on the occasion that I took Helle to Kings Cross for her solo trip home to Norway, I remember experiencing that horrible empty feeling in my stomach. This happened quite a few times later on in life, but the first time is the one that hurts the most.

I still had a year or so to go at school, but nonetheless began to look for some form of "proper" band to play with. I found it easy to pick up work and my nights were generally spent playing with some combination of musicians. Many of them were far older than myself (I was still only 16) and many of them were also crap. The hours were late and school suffered beyond repair. Come O-level time, John Fisher and I felt it not even worth the time to take the exams, as we knew literally nothing of most subjects. We sat one or two and, on one occasion, John handed in a totally blank piece of paper at the end of the exam. I took music and passed, but for the rest I either didn't bother to turn up or just wrote nonsense. Well, I have to say that what I wrote looked quite interesting to me, in fact far more interesting than the question, but probably not entirely relevant.

We decided to spend our exam time elsewhere. Charing Cross Road was a favourite haunt, just gazing through the windows at the amplifiers and organs. Then we'd go to a soup kitchen off the Strand and listen to Bob Dylan albums. I really liked the Bohemian bit and the atmosphere of these places always seemed very creative to me. In this way, things picked up for me socially no end and I started to get to the outer edge of contemporary music and become acquainted with its players. I was completely fascinated by the whole thing and just wanted to be a success in the business, though I had not the slightest clue as to how to get to my goal.

Running parallel to my initial forays in the music business were my first fumbling forays into sex. After I had recovered from the devastation of the end of the affair with Helle, I began to infiltrate my local scene. John Fisher's father owned a menswear shop in Lordship Lane with a newly converted flat above and, by coincidence, it was to here that I was directed by two very "obvious" local girls, Janet and June. As it happened, I eventually had flings with both of them, on separate occasions! They said there was a "serious" party going on and this was definitely THE place to be. All this was, of course, totally unknown to the passive host, the hapless John Fisher. As it happened, the party proved to be even better than promised. People were dancing, drinking and generally throwing themselves around in wild abandon. This was the time of the beginning of drug awareness, even in South London, and it showed.

One guy, convinced he could fly, jumped from the highest point in the flat and crashed through the ceiling, landing in the menswear shop below. The burglar alarm went off and the police and John's dad arrived, followed by John, who refused to believe there was anything happening there in the first place.

The party therefore came to a premature end, though not before I'd struck up a friendship with the very temporary tenant, Jane Fabian. Jane seemed pretty cool to me, especially as she was into Jimmy Smith and Jimmy McGriff, both of whose records she played constantly. In the circumstances, I decided not to admit to a liking for The Beatles; this would have been very unhip. Bob Dylan you could sort of get away with, but anything more commercial was a no-go.

This was a time when people, to be "in", sought out the original recordings of current hits. For example, it was cool to like Maurice Williams and The Zodiacs' version of "Stay", but definitely not The Hollies' version. I personally much preferred The Hollies, but could never admit to it, because the true purist had to prefer the originals. The same thing applied to "Twist And Shout": It had to be The Isley Brothers, not The Beatles and definitely not The Tremeloes. For me, the Beatles' version was by far the best.

Anyway, Jane was ultra-trendy and even a little aristocratic. She seemed far more worldly than me, although I suppose, in retrospect, she probably wasn't really. It was Jane who introduced me to the mysteries of the suspender belt, but I have to admit that my first impression, with all the straps and confusing bits, was that she had something wrong with her and that this must be some kind of surgical aid. At first I declined to touch anything at all, in case something dropped off. There was also the added fear that she might have been suffering from some secret and unspeakable disease. Nevertheless, I persevered and eventually got to grips with this gadgetry.

During one of our afternoons of passion, we were unfortunately interrupted by John's dad. He was horrified and flew into a complete rage, making me feel unclean and sordid. We were both thrown out on the street there and then, leaving Jane homeless. At this point, my other cohorts, John and Geoff, gave up on me. Their sex lives were non-existent and my developing one was an intrusion upon our routine. Geoff never did bother with the opposite sex, casting the entire activity aside as a messy business on the assumption that all women were brazen hussies. John did eventually seek out a wife, although things were never quite right for them and he ended up taking solace in booze.

As the musical side of our friendship dwindled, other forms of entertainment were devised, such as country rambles, which John and I hated. Geoff would plan impossible routes, we'd get a train to lord knows where and walk back. On most occasions, John and I would find a pub and catch a train home together, leaving Geoff to ramble onwards, alone and disgruntled. The three of us were like the characters in "Last Of The Summer Wine".

Frankly, we were going nowhere, so I suggested we should spend time in restaurants. At least there we could eat better than the packets of crisps and the odd bar of chocolate which we consumed on our rambles. This idea picked up quite well. Breakfast was at Herne Hill Station and lunch was at a third-rate Italian across the road. Of course we couldn't afford this lavish lifestyle, so John was frequently forced to raid the till of his dad's shop to keep us afloat. John has kept me afloat on many occasions since. We started to become a pretty popular trio in the area, largely due to the size of John's nose, which started most conversations with outsiders.

Since those days, it's true to say that I've wined and dined in some of the best places around the world, but nothing has ever compared to those carefree, happy days of toasted cheese sandwiches and cups of hot tea with genuine friends. Our favourite haunt was Nina's Cafe. This establishment was owned by a guy called Frank Jacques who somehow knew a side of my family it's best not to talk about. Frank was eventually to help me in my serious musical career. He turned up at my house one day and shocked me by revealing that he wasn't called Frank at all. This was merely one of his many aliases.

Along the parade of shops near Herne Hill station was a chemist's shop. As we stood at the bus stop, we could see what I thought was the most beautiful woman I had ever seen, serving and dispensing behind the counter. The three of us would stand at the bus stop for hours each day, desperate to go inside the chemist's but never daring to. Eventually, I plucked up the courage to buy some aspirin. It was an act of heroism. I returned to the bus stop with exaggerated stories of my triumph, although all that in fact had happened was that I had bought a packet of aspirin that I didn't want.

How could I impress the lady in the chemist's? There was nothing for it but to get myself into a band. That might do the trick. I started answering all the adverts in Melody Maker and, to my surprise, got back more replies than I thought I'd sent letters.

Thus began my audition period. One of the first was with Tony Jackson, whom I'd seen on Ready Steady Go. Tony had just left The Searchers, who were, at this time, a pretty big band. He was looking for a keyboard player. Boldly, I rang up and, to my complete amazement, he returned my call within the hour, and, before I knew it, I was attending an audition in Carnaby Street in the bowels of some awful nightclub.

Unfortunately, Tony and his new band were, in fact, not very good. I'd practised myself silly and was, I thought, pretty hot. I'd learnt solos by Alan Price to the last note and had a very quick style, which I hoped was impressive. It's easy, with practice, to bluff a solo and make it sound ten times more accomplished than it actually is. It all seemed to impress Tony and he asked me to join. The problem came with my age. I couldn't get a work permit for Germany, where Tony's band was due to tour, because I was way too young. Happily, this turned out to be a blessing, because the band vanished into oblivion after a couple of below average singles.

Next, I auditioned for The Animals after Alan Price left. After all, I could pay his every solo note-perfect. The job eventually went to Dave Rowberry, the problem being that I didn't fit in sartorially. They were all total scruffs and I was going through my "moddy" period. Much later on, I met The Animals socially and they had no idea I'd even been to their audition. Mind you, their guitar player Hilton Valentine didn't seem to have much idea of where he was, had been or was going. I did make a friend of violinist John Weider, who by then was a member of what was called the "New Animals". John told me fascinating stories of their American escapades. He claimed that he used to bring dope back from the States for his Gran!

The Animals, The Searchers ... This may all sound pretty up-market, when most musicians of my age were blundering about in semi-pro outfits. The secret was that I was unnaturally bold and confident and had absolutely no fear of phoning anyone. My long-suffering dad ferried me to and from these auditions, which, I think, had a positive effect on his own social life.

Despite these ambitious attempts to join top bands, I inevitably ended up in a semi-pro band, called, uninspiringly, The Intruders. The other members were adequate, in the sense that they had an idea of which way the guitar should face. Chords were a wee bit more tricky. I once suggested an E flat minor 7th, which was, of course, totally out of the question. On the other hand, we did manage to amass enough material and chords for a five-hour show. (Yes, five hours.)

Our first booking was at a wedding at The Elephant And Castle. The audience of old men and brassy women laughed, drank and vomited throughout. Plus there was, of course, the obligatory fight. I remember thinking that night, after I'd picked up my thirty bob (£1.50.), "This is not how it's gonna be."

In an attempt to obtain proper equipment for us, I went into Vox and Selmers in Charing Cross Road, armed with the impressive claim that we were going for an audition for "Ready Steady Go", which was actually true. In the end, a gentleman called Mr. Lee from The St. Giles Music Centre actually lent me everything we needed. I ended up buying my Hammond C3 from him.

The "Ready Steady Go" audition was our last appearance and it inevitably came to nothing. It was a "Best Up-coming Bands" contest. We weren't Best, and we weren't Up-coming, but soon I got a call from an agent by the name of Norman Jackson, who was a middle-of-the-road type promoter. He offered me a job with another band with the unfortunate name The Sassenachs.

Surprisingly, we worked a lot, lots of corporate events, society bashes and similar crappy engagements. The Sassenachs' bass player was Paul Bennett, who went on to work with Cliff Richard. Paul got me into Little Richard by doing great versions of "Oh My Soul", "Clarabella" and "Long Tall Sally", and I realised that I wanted to sing like that!

At this stage, I was still trying to incorporate music with school and the latter was coming a very bad second. Most of our work was very late at night. On one occasion, after playing at The Café Royal, I finally got home at 8 a.m, as did my father, who accompanied me on all these forays. Once again it was obvious that we were going nowhere. The other members, as ever, were much older than me and were content to slog away on this pretty dull circuit.

At this point, I gave up and resigned from both the band and school and it was back to John and Geoff and our country rambles! The main bonus was that now we could film our adventures, as I'd earned enough money from playing to buy a movie camera and all the accessories. As Geoff had abandoned any hope of any kind of sensible career, he plunged himself into the role of film producer. Both John and I left school but Geoff remained there till his twenties, amassing a grand total of fifteen O-levels. The problem was that they were in groups of three of the same subject.

John, to avoid a similar fate, was sent to a "crammer" in London in a vain attempt to boost his sad lack of qualifications. Poor Geoff, meanwhile, suffered a mild stroke as a result of his ludicrous country rambles. One day, he ran some 20 miles in blistering heat, wearing an overcoat! We visited him in hospital that night.

All of this left me to my own devices, so I filled my days by practising and writing songs, an avenue for which I had a rapidly-developing passion. I'd bought a Brenell tape recorder from my playing profits and began recording demos. Never one to start at the bottom, I contacted Dick James, then the Beatles' publisher, and to my amazement, he gave me an appointment. The songs at that time were pointless, because, unless you were in a band and doing the rounds, nobody was interested. Everybody had become a songwriter and everybody wanted to record their own material, as it was potentially a far more lucrative activity than being out on the road.

When I later joined The Spencer Davis Group, Dick's path and mine crossed again, as he looked after Spencer Davis Music. Graham Nash wanted me and Spencer to sign to Gralto Music, (also handled by Dick James) a publishing company set up by Graham, Allan Clarke and Tony Hicks of the Hollies, but Spencer was astute enough to set up his own company.

However, as I'd been told that a band was needed in order to promote the songs, I decided to form my own group. Again, I started high, and approached Brian Epstein, who surprisingly granted me an appointment. However, the meeting was not with the man himself, but with a colleague, Alan Eisenberg, an enthusiastic homosexual who was apparently taken by my audition photograph. In my naiveté, I made several trips to the NEMS offices next to the Palladium, although it soon became clear that Alan's intent was not entirely musical. I explained the situation to my father, who suggested I make a further appointment, this time taking along him and Frank Jacques (the underworld character mentioned earlier).

The plan was for me to let Eisenberg make his suggestions, leave the room and then return with reinforcements. I arrived at the meeting and, after Eisenberg began his chat-up lines, I left the room and returned with Jacques and my father. Eisenberg was, not surprisingly, devastated by their appearance. Garbling apologies as he dangled some three feet in the air, he suddenly offered all kinds of tours, appearances and recording deals, none of which would materialise. He did, however, suggest I meet a "very reliable chap" by the name of Reg King, an up-and-coming manager with good connections. As Eisenberg slumped to the floor, we wrote down the telephone number of Reg King and left, to a further litany of apologies.

Thus began the Reg King era. This was to become one of the more engaging periods of my illustrious career. Reg appeared at my home one Saturday afternoon, dressed in his own particular kind of "Gatsby" style. He was tailored to the extreme, but overall, he came across as a likeable sort of chap. He had valid contacts within the business and, to be fair, he was the first person in the music business to spot some potential in me.

Within days, three more band members had been chosen by Reg. One of them, Gordon Barton on drums, later went on to play with Thunderclap Newman. I was on Hammond and "bit" vocals. Reg had ideas of what he reckoned a band should look like, though not particularly what they sounded like. I guess we were fairly presentable, both musically and visually. We rehearsed in The Cellar Club in Kingston-on-Thames every single day for what seemed an interminable length of time. I travelled daily from Waterloo to Kingston to rehearse in this booze-stained and fag-burnt club. Ever since then, I've loved the smell of clubs the "morning after".

The rehearsals progressed at a pretty gruelling pace, but the repertoire was developing into one I personally didn't like. I HATED soul music, and we rehearsed Wilson Pickett and Otis Redding stuff, interspersed with Everley Brothers and Buddy Holly material, which, to me at any rate, was much more acceptable than the phony groaning, grunting and shouting of our attempts to emulate US soul.

After we'd become pretty "tight", a strange thing happened: One Saturday, Reg appeared with Keith Moon to jam with us. His style certainly kicked the band up the arse and, after he'd left, we didn't speak to our own drummer for hours! Keith played with Pete York and me some years later, but by then he'd become, to say the least, a little unpredictable.

When our first booking came along, we didn't have far to travel, since it was in the same club as the rehearsals. We had far more gear than was necessary: five Marshall Stacks, the hugest drum kit I have ever seen and a couple of Leslie cabinets for the Hammond L100. It took up pretty well all of the small stage.

We were playing support to The Troggs, who had far less equipment and were very intimidated, if not pissed off, by our mounds of guitars. Our guitarist had an amazing array, blagged by Reg King, consisting of a Rickenbacker twelve and six-string, a double-necked Gibson, a Fender Strat and a couple of Gibson acoustics (which never actually came into play, although they did look impressive on stands) and amps. The Troggs were at No.1 with "Wild Thing" at the time. Despite this, the audience wasn't too impressed with either band and the Troggs were far from wild.

Whatever else happened that night, we managed to create enough interest to get a further booking at "Tiles", a club in Oxford Street, this time supporting Georgie Fame, one of my heroes. I wished we'd rehearsed something along the lines of his material and, after hearing his show, I was even more convinced that Soul was out the window and Jazz and Blues were in. Still, we ploughed on as support band to the likes of Dave Berry and the Cruisers, The Creation (who were a great band), culminating with a support to The Honeycombs. This band had had a dreadful hit with a song called "Have I The Right?" In my opinion, they had absolutely no right to be in charge of any musical instruments.

We, known as "A Wild Uncertainty" may well have been a crap band as far as our repertoire was concerned, but we had the advantage that we could play. We managed to get into a great social scene. The Small Faces, Lionel Bart (who fancied our bass player) and even Andrew Oldham (who fancied anyone) showed interest in us. It was, in fact, Oldham who christened us "A Wild Uncertainty". Doubtless he was taking the piss, but it stuck.

I went, with Reg King, who was impressed by the way Oldham operated, to his suite at The Mayfair Hotel in London, where he was grooming the band Twice As Much for stardom. This was clearly doomed to be a wasted effort. Maybe he fancied them too, but they certainly couldn't do much musically. At this time, there were some very interesting sexual liaisons within certain strata of the music business.

Reg then persuaded Glyn Johns to produce us. This was a mighty step in the right direction, since Glyn was working with The Who, The Small Faces and The Rolling Stones and now, (fanfare of trumpets): A Wild Uncertainty! (If only I could write that smaller).

With Glyn, we recorded a couple of tracks at a studio called IBC in Portland Place, which were released on the aptly-named Planet label, run by Shel Talmy. Arthur Greenslade made some contributions to the arrangements, although to this day, I can't detect anything that was either necessary or relevant. Our dubious record, an Everley Brothers song called "Man With Money" was, with the aid of my dad, "bought" into the lower reaches of the charts. In those days, this was pretty common practice, as I'm sure it is today. The price determined the placing in the chart. I think we reached Number 25 or 26 at a cost of £500, so you can work it out pro rata from there, right up to the Number 1 position, which, of course, was also available.

The advantage was that, once you were in the charts, the workload increased, as did appearance fees. You also had media interest, albeit entirely unmerited. But, if the band actually was good, a hype like that could provide a useful launching pad. After all, everyone else was doing it.

At this stage, I experienced a phenomenon known as "song nicking". I had written a song with our bass player, who had some kind of, um, relationship with Lionel Bart. Oddly, this song soon afterwards appeared on a Lionel Bart LP. The album was entitled "Isn't This Where We Came In?" No, this wasn't where I came in, because, needless to say, my name appeared nowhere in the credits. I challenged Lionel about this matter and he said, "Don't rock the boat, Eddie, I promise you'll get your royalties". Did I? Did I heck.

I started to go to lots of shows around the London area and saw Jimi Hendrix in Bromley at a very small pub venue. These were early days for Jimi. Alan Price was also doing the rounds with The Alan Price Set, and he continued to be a great influence on me, along with Zoot Money and Georgie Fame.

Transport was a serious problem. All forays to gigs were made by tube and mainline trains and it was then that I swore that, if possible, I would never, ever travel in this way again, a policy I've managed, on the whole, to maintain to this day. Mainline trains I quite enjoyed and sometimes they provided the opportunity to meet girls. One or two little affairs began between Bromley South and Waterloo, but we won't go into that.

The first of us to have a car was Geoff. On the condition that we made contributions to his petrol costs, he ferried us to and from anywhere. Unfortunately, he however made it a rule that, wherever we went, it had to be on an authorised public transport route. We even had to stop at the bloody bus stops. At the end of each trip, he had to take an hour's break, which he told us was what his Union stated as statutory. When I later became part of the Spencer Davis Group, Geoff's system was a little frustrating.

I had an ambition to became a car owner and soon achieved this aim, albeit without a licence, so I was basically the owner of a useless lump of metal. Geoff took on the role of chauffeur but only on his aforementioned conditions of following the correct public transport routes. My first car was a Mini. I bought it from new and had the whole thing converted, with black electric windows, leather seats, Wilton carpet, a record player and a stunning 8-track player with four speakers. We all loved travelling in that car (no wonder). Shortly after this purchase, I eventually got my own licence and was at last free of all bus routes. It was a great feeling and London finally became a smaller place!

John was, and still is, incapable of driving. Some do and some don't; he don't. On one occasion, my Mini was being serviced and I asked if I could borrow John's car (which he had, even though he had no driving licence). Jumping at the chance of a friendly driving lesson, he agreed, on the condition that he should be in complete control. I had to travel with him from Dulwich to the centre of London and I foolishly sat beside him, although I'm not convinced that he'd actually driven anywhere before.

After about twenty minutes, he managed to switch the thing on and we set off from his house. Within less than a hundred yards, he had hit five parked cars. His poor father, dying from cancer, heard the clatter of twisted metal and ran from the house to find us sitting amidst a pile of debris, being verbally abused by five demented car owners.

There was a fourth, previously unmentioned, member of our circle. He was Steven Patrick Cameron, affectionately known as "SPC". He was soon to become the next motorist amongst us. SPC was very "old school" in his attitude to life, a Bertie Wooster character who had no time for the modern world. He lived in a dismal block of early Victorian flats in Camberwell, called Evelina Mansions. His mother was a cheerful old Londoner who kept her apartment immaculate, although somewhat spartan. We were all welcome en masse at any time of the day or night. Every Christmas, due to my new prosperity, I took her two bottles of Harvey's Bristol Cream, which she did her best to drink on the same night.

We were never aware of SPC's father, who was never mentioned, and it wasn't clear if he was dead or alive. SPC had a sister, Janet, who had a boyfriend of long standing, who, every night without fail, would arrive at Evelina Mansions and take his position next to Janet and hold her hand. He never spoke and neither did she. This went on for four years, until she finally dumped him and suddenly married a school friend of ours whom she hardly knew.

The family pet was a budgie. No doubt inspired by the example of

Janet and John, this creature had chosen never to fly, nor indeed ever to venture from its cage. On one of the frequent occasions when I visited Evelina Mansions, I suggested we should try the bird at flight. The flat was on the 12th floor, so my idea was to throw the budgie from the window, the theory being that it would flap about and return to roost. This all went terribly wrong. It couldn't fly at all and just fell to the pavement below, throwing the flat into pandemonium. I was branded a budgie killer and John's lip curled menacingly. My argument was that the bloody thing was useless anyway and probably relieved to be released from the tedium of its life. The following day, I bought the family a more mobile budgie.

SPC did his best to maintain a certain standard of current technology within Evelina Mansions and, by mail order, purchased all kinds of useless items. His stereo was a Rima. It was bloody awful, with a cabinet about five times too big for its electrical content. Beside this monstrosity stood a dreadful acoustic guitar (mail order), on which SPC would strum tunelessly to Roy Orbison songs. SPC's private quarters within the apartment were also a disaster. I had started to re-decorate a house I'd just bought and had tins of various colours of paint left over. I donated these to SPC, who ended up with probably the first ever psychedelic bedroom.

His wardrobe was also mail order and he wore what were called Godzilla boots, along with hideous licorice coloured jeans. During the day, SPC would work at Monarch, a sweet warehouse in the Walworth road. This always came in handy at Easter, when there would be ample Easter eggs he'd "forgotten" to load.

Financially strapped, he set about finding himself a vehicle both grand and cheap. After a long search, he found a Lanchester, verging on vintage, which was the perfect choice for him. He took us all along for expert appraisal (we all knew absolutely nothing about cars) before he parted with his £20. We drove to Forest Hill and there it was: a hand-painted, sickly green heap. SPC went into raptures over it, pointing to the ripped leather interior and the crystal radio set hanging out of the dashboard. He haggled the price down to £15, but he had to be convinced that the vehicle was at least mechanically sound. The owner had no doubts and pointed out that "They don't make 'em like this no more". Indeed they didn't. And I'm not sure they ever did.

No key was required, since it was the old push button method: completely thief proof, as SPC pointed out. John, Geoff and I stood on the hill as SPC drove off on his test drive. As he progressed up the hill, we noticed pints of oil pouring from the sump. Minutes later, SPC coasted silently and ignominiously back down the hill. Undeterred, he bought the car and took it home on a low loader, this journey costing three times the value of the car.

"A minor problem, easily fixed!" said SPC.

£300 later, the Lanchester was in motion, but, bearing in mind that in those days you could buy a new car for around £600, it wasn't the soundest of investments. Nevertheless, SPC seemed to enjoy endless happy hours of motoring in the vehicle, not the least of which were spent every Saturday, taking his mum shopping, both of them sitting several feet higher than the other motorists. There was always a certain look of apprehension on SPC's face as he sat behind the wheel.

On the music front, I was disheartened with my lack of progress, considering that I'd tried to become an Animal and even a Searcher, to no avail. It was at this point that my aunt and uncle, Maureen and Freddie Foreman, (Freddie Foreman has written his own book, "Respect", which will make things clearer!) began to take a keen interest in my career and even suggested taking over my management. I was a little dubious, as they really knew nothing about the music business, although they did know a lot of people in it. I had a horror of being detailed to play at their private parties, of which there were many.

Freddie, in hindsight very astutely, suggested we should by-pass the normal channels and manufacture, own and control all our product, from the master tapes to the publishing. I spent days finding new songs, doing the rounds of all the publishers in Denmark Street, and finally came up with three that I thought were pretty good. I had no faith in my own songs at this time, although in retrospect, I wish I had!

We appointed Arthur Greenslade as musical director. I'd met him via Reg King and he'd done arrangements for the Rolling Stones and various other Andrew Oldham projects. He was a great guy, but, to me, his arrangements, even then, sounded dated. Today they sound like a sort of caricature.

Uncle Freddie arranged a lunch at Simpsons in the Strand, where we had our preliminary discussions. Arthur was typical of most musicians and maximised the prospects of being paid handsomely for very little work. He was an East Ender, as was Freddie, so they had quite a lot in common and most of the first lunch was spent discussing the East End! Freddie had also introduced me to Mike D'Abo (then with Manfred Mann) and we both got on pretty well. I spent quite a lot of time with Mike, who showed genuine interest and played me hundreds of his songs with a view to my recording some of them. Mike unfortunately also started me on my dangerous passion for red wine.

I finally selected a D'Abo song, plus a composition written by me during the Wild Uncertainty days and a song written by John Cameron. Of the three, the only decent one was the D'Abo tune. Arthur Greenslade wrote the arrangements for a small string section and brass section, with me on piano and organ. Olympic studios (where Hardin & York would later record "For The World" and most of "The World's Smallest Big Band") was booked for a Saturday evening and we all set off in Freddie's Mercedes for my first "proper" session.

It was a pretty wild night weather-wise and, on reaching Barnes, we got totally lost and, to cap it all, the car broke down. I was well aware of the cost of studio time, but Uncle Freddie seemed unconcerned and I was impressed when he got out and single-handedly pushed the car with four passengers in it! Eventually, we arrived at Olympic, where Freddie began unloading endless cases of booze for the assembled musicians. This was convenient, because musicians have no qualms about eating and drinking absolutely anything that's free.

The results of the two 3-hour sessions were pretty average, and I preferred my efforts with Alan Whitehead, recorded in The Old Kent Road at Maximum Sound (later owned by Manfred Mann), again at the instigation of Freddie Foreman. In fact, this tape still exists and is a kind of forerunner to Hardin & York, just Hammond and drums. Whitehead was the drummer with a band called The Loose Ends at the time, and later became a founder member of Marmalade. He now makes a supposed fortune running table dancing/lap dancing clubs, or whatever they're called.

So, at last, we had a master tape. Sadly, no one knew what to do with it. And in fact, no one ever did do anything with it!

Freddie owned a casino in Balham at the time. It had previously been the home of Lord Nelson and Emma Hamilton, and this venue had become a haunt for musicians, in particular Paul Jones (of Manfred Mann), with whom I immediately got on very well. It was Paul who mentioned that Steve Winwood was contemplating leaving The Spencer Davis Group and would I be interested?

I was not a particular fan of the SDG at the time, but they had just been voted the biggest band in the world, so I'd have been pretty dumb not to be interested. It was such an unlikely dream that I didn't even give it any consideration. Paul Jones, however, managed to arrange an audition for me, and yet another uncle, John Fitzgerald, was appointed roadie for the day.

CHAPTER 2
THE SPENCER DAVIS GROUP

As far as I was concerned, the Spencer Davis Group I joined was the Mark 1 version, but strictly speaking, it was Mark 2. The original Spencer Davis Group had consisted of two brothers, Muff (bass guitar) and Steve Winwood (on everything!), with Spencer Davis (rhythm guitar) and Pete York (drums).

At the auditions, there were a few sets of "brother" acts hoping to replace the Winwoods, but all of them were quite awful. There was one outstanding singer, Terry Reid, who I thought would certainly get the job. Terry was a great friend of Graham Nash of the Hollies, who in turn was a great friend of Spencer's, so it all seemed rather great!

Another contender for the prime spot was Elton John, then known as Reg Dwight. His name actually fitted his appearance, since he resembled an ice cream salesman and his performance sounded like one. Reg (I prefer Reg, because it's even sillier than Elton) was determined to sing his own material, which in 1966 was not quite as you know him now. Spencer, however, was quite taken by the adolescent wailings and we went on to record two of Reg's dirges, which never appeared on vinyl, nor thankfully on any other format.

Bernie Taupin, the lyricist, was on hand to supervise the recordings and at that time he was a nice guy. I guess he was one of the first victims of luvviedom. I saw him a few years later at the Royal Festival Hall, where Reg was appearing, and he chose to ignore me totally, engrossed in his own impending fame.

Anyway, I got the job with The Spencer Davis Group! After my audition, which was held in the studio section of The Marquee Club in Wardour Street, the first thing I did was run to a phone box in Soho's Chinatown to pass on the news to my mum and dad. Then I went to Harrods, in an attempt to devise ways of spending my new-found wealth, but bought nothing. This is a fault which I have long since learnt to overcome.

Spencer had given me £100 "to be getting on with", which represented a tidy sum in those days, and I set out on a sentimental journey around my old haunts in London, which for me were never to be the same again. I was totally stunned at getting the job and old video footage from that period shows that I really was completely baffled by the whole thing. The dream had become a reality, but it all seemed completely unreal. Suddenly, I appeared to have friends I never thought I had.

The next thing to sort out was something I knew nothing whatsoever about, namely, contracts. Uncle Freddie and Auntie Maureen, impressed by what they considered to be my inevitable posting, appointed David Jacobs, the top show business lawyer of the time, to act for me. The first major undertaking with Spencer was a lengthy tour of the States, and Maureen suggested that I should make my own travel arrangements and leave the rest of the band to their own devices.

This was a tricky one. I'd started to rehearse with the band, the comradeship was starting to build and I felt that, with this thrown at them, it would instantly dissipate. I had to offend either Maureen or the band and I chose Maureen, but as things turned out, she was absolutely right. Pete York has often remarked that things would have been a lot different had Freddie Foreman stayed in the picture. For sure there would have been no rip-offs, and there were to be many.

During those early rehearsals, Freddie would arrive with an assortment of dangerous-looking minders to watch over proceedings, "just to make sure you don't get ripped off", but it was really not conducive to making music and it was also extremely embarrassing for me. My association with Maureen and Freddie was therefore discontinued, although I felt terrible to have left them, after all they had done for me. Maybe things would have been totally different had I not left them. The world had opened up for me, there was seemingly unlimited money available and Linda Eastman was appointed to take the first photographs of the new band. The session took place in Berkeley Square, but the pictures were not good.

As far as management was concerned, I was a little, if not a lot, confused. Chris Blackwell, who had managed the band prior to my joining, was our manager for a few days, and then, after some internal wrangling which I knew nothing about, a jocular alcoholic Scotsman by the name of John Martin appeared. His only credentials, as far as I could make out, were the fact that he had instigated The White Heather Club, a dreadful Scottish TV show featuring lots of kilts and the likes of Andy Stewart. On the face of it, this appeared to be a catastrophic move on Spencer's part, and I reckon it most certainly was, although, since I was a newcomer, I had no influence on any decision. Indeed, the stage name Hardin, which was to remain with me for the rest of my career, was created by a mis-spelling in the press release announcing my appointment.

In spite of this, John Martin and Spencer forged ahead to form Spencer Davis Management and set up offices in Dean Street, Soho. The idea was for Spencer to front his own management and agency company and add various artists to its roster. To Spencer's credit, he soon had a pretty impressive array of artists, among them The Nice, The Moody Blues, Billie Davis, The Flowerpot Men and Yes, plus of course The Spencer Davis Group itself, which was the only band generating any serious income. Consequently, our band was financially supporting all the rest, unbeknown, of course, to myself and the rest of the SDG.

We first bought two offshore companies to control our money, neither of which was efficient or effective in any way. All they served to do was make us lose our high investment in the purchase of them. Our accountant, to this day, brushes the affair aside, but thousands of pounds were frittered away in an afternoon. As far as the music was concerned, I was still locked into the euphoria of the moment and preparing for the very first appearance of the new line-up at the Empire Pool, Wembley (today known as Wembley Arena).

I was collected from home by a limousine, which subsequently picked up the rest of the band, and we were duly delivered to Wembley. We played two songs, one of which was "Dust My Blues" and were back in the car and home again almost before it seemed that anything had actually happened. I was stunned and sort of shell-shocked.

Pretty soon after, we had an engagement in Paris to record a TV show with Jimi Hendrix. Spencer, in his infinite wisdom, decided that we should all stay at an hotel near Heathrow, as the flight to Paris was an early one. I sat in my room alone, feeling confused and depressed, trying to watch TV, but my brain seemed frazzled and then I just collapsed.

I didn't have the nerve to telephone the others, so I called my dad, who, in turn, called the hotel doctor, who diagnosed mental and physical exhaustion and gastro-enteritis. Christ, I thought, I'm only months into this, we've only played once and here I am out of the match. I insisted that I was okay and duly flew to Paris, feeling dreadfully ill. I was being sick constantly and couldn't eat. I had no sympathy from the others and had to pretend to be on form. I linked up with Noel Redding from Hendrix's band, himself very much a newcomer to this degree of, what would you call it? Exposure, stardom, whatever. I have never felt less like a bloody pop star.

Noel sat with me on the roof of the TV station and we discussed our futures. His future we know, mine you probably don't. Noel had not yet been tipped into the abyss of self-doubt and was still acting relatively normally, which was very soon to change. I think we were both scared of what was to come and it struck me at that moment that this kind of life held no pleasure at all. We flew on to Cannes for a few days to play a couple of nights in an up-market club filled with down-market French people. The French were never a good audience for us and now I bloody well live here!

The only thing I ate in three days was a bowl of French onion soup, and I felt like shit when we flew home to England. I can remember nothing at all about the TV show and very little about Cannes, only the rantings of Hendrix because he hadn't been paid. I've lost count of the times I've witnessed similar situations since then.

After a few days in the recording studio, working on the soundtrack for the film "Here We Go Round The Mulberry Bush", as well as actually appearing in the film on location in Stevenage, and finishing our debut album, we flew off to New York. The recording of the album was completely chaotic, because it never became clear who the producer was (for a while, it was Ron Richards, who produced The Hollies) or, indeed, which record company would release it. It turned out to be United Artists, a company with no clue of the emerging power of the pop/rock market.

In New York, we had a week to get adjusted to the mayhem that would ensue. Life in the city was very, very unreal. One Fleetwood limousine after the other would take any of us anywhere we wanted to go at any time of the day or night. The trouble was that none of us had a clue where to go, only drummer Pete York, who knew of all the jazz haunts in and around the city. The hospitality astounded us all and we revelled in it. It was not until we returned to England that it became clear that all the costs were being deducted from our wages.

Our first single, "Time Seller", had reached No.1 in Holland and also charted in the States, the UK and Scandinavia. As it happened, we tended to ignore England and Europe in favour of the madness of America. In New York, we stayed at The Drake Hotel on Park Avenue, where we each had our own suite. I chose to share with guitarist Phil Sawyer, although the suite was so vast that I hardly ever saw him. Even at this early stage, Phil was already tiring of the pressure and was discussing with me ways to get out. To him, it was like a prison sentence. He had so much wanted this job but didn't have a clue about what it entailed. Neither, indeed, did I.

We had to have some new photographs done for America, so some dreadful photographer showed up and spent a day shooting pictures that all turned out blurred because he was too stoned to hold the bloody camera still. The Lovin' Spoonful called to see us a few times, and then The Troggs hit town. They hadn't changed much from the time in Kingston with A Wild Uncertainty. In fact, they were still wearing those striped suits.

We went to their reception at The Americana Hotel and their tour manager asked me if they were "OK"? I think he meant were they normal?

He said that they seemed to think that America was still populated by cowboys and that they had actually asked him where they could find some Red Indians. Eventually, they were sent to Harlem and came back quite happy.

We had American roadies, supervised by our English roadie, Alec Leslie (now promoted to Tour Manager). The roadies were staying at The Holiday Inn while Alec, of course, was at The Drake with us. I can remember two of their names, Grady Koon and Ray Reneri. Grady was from the deep south and incapable of concealing it, while Ray was like an extra from The Godfather. It was the time of the Vietnam war and I reckon they were all lost to its pointless cause, because I never saw any of them again.

I got pretty pally with Grady, who had previously worked on his grandfather's farm in the South. Grady told me some horrific stories about his past blunders, one being when he chopped all the fingers off his left hand with a chainsaw. Unperturbed, he gathered them up, put them in his pocket, hitched a ride to the hospital and had them stitched back on. The operation was not an overwhelming success, but it did provide him with a party trick: He could make the sound of a football ratchet with his mangled hand.

Grady's all-time hero was Elvis Presley, who he was convinced would drop by to see us at any moment. He mounted a vigil in the corridor outside our various suites. Of course, Presley never did arrive, but one night, I convinced Grady that he had, and that Grady must have dozed off and missed the whole thing, a piece of news which devastated him. His other passion was surfboarding and he carried the bloody board with him throughout the tour, just in case.

John Martin, with his "White Heather Club" background, was totally unprepared for the world of Rock and was the most un-hip guy you could ever wish to meet. John adopted what he considered to be trendy little sayings, which no one would actually ever dare say. On one of our first nights in New York, he left the hotel with me and asked the taxi driver to "take us where the action is!" He took us to where the action really wasn't and John slipped him a hundred dollar bill, thinking it was a ten. All the notes are the same size and it can be tricky, but I got to learn my lesson very quickly.

Phil Sawyer's wardrobe had always been a disgrace and Spencer was constantly on at him to smarten himself up. It came to the point where Spencer would open Phil's suitcase before we set off anywhere. It rarely contained more than a pair of socks, a pair of shoes and a belt, which didn't quite go round his waist! I convinced Phil to come out shopping with me in New York and get himself sorted out. He made a bit of an effort, but in the end was more attracted to the idea of buying a pair of enormous buffalo horns and, of all things, a bloody fishing rod, both of which he carried with him as hand baggage on all domestic flights within America. He did actually buy a pair of trousers, sadly slightly shy of the shoe, and another useful belt which didn't quite do up.

Aside from the music, there were other points of interest. Phil, terribly homesick and wary of groupies (he never did succumb), launched himself into an affair with the wife of a senior executive at United Artists. She was considerably older than Phil, but this didn't bother him, as he seemed to prefer the older woman. Spencer was shocked on hearing the news and did his best (unsuccessfully) to deter Phil from continuing the relationship. In the meantime, John Martin, the alcoholic Scotsman, was lurching indiscreetly around town with one of the managing directors' wives. My god, it was absolute chaos.

Sexual abandon was rife in America during the love and peace era, not that that made a blind bit of difference to any of my attempts. The executives' wives were by far the worst, all trainee Mrs. Robinsons. They were generally middle aged, manicured and very sexy women, intent on sampling the maximum number of young band members that passed through their fat, balding and generally Jewish husbands' hands. At a reception in Los Angeles, I was accosted by one of these wives. She was real Dallas material and I was terrified. She put a cigarette in her mouth provocatively and inclined her head perilously close to mine for a light. I didn't smoke then, but suddenly wished I did. I buggered up an entire book of matches trying to assist. She asked where we were staying, took the number and said she'd call later. She never did, and I wasn't sure whether to be disappointed or relieved.

Then there was the crackpot, middle aged, sensuous, sex-starved woman I actually took out for dinner. She was dressed from head to toe in a skin-tight leopardskin trouser suit - the ideal outfit for a discreet night out. When we reached the restaurant, I got out of the car and was practically seated at the table when I realised she was no longer with me. She was sitting bolt upright in the car waiting for me to open the bloody door. Eventually, she glided in and ordered various drinks and items of food I'd never even heard of and really piled on the "experienced woman" bit. She sat with her mountainous silicon breasts (I later found out they had the same feel as a remould tyre) bulging from the leopardskin ensemble as she explained that she was a clairvoyant and that she vaguely remembered me from a former life, in which I had apparently been her husband. This all seemed pretty hopeful, so I told her I had similar powers. She figured out that, as we were, in fact, married, there would be nothing at all immoral in carrying on where we'd left off in our previous life.

In 1967, America was in the grip of flower power and drugs to a far greater extent than England. They were really going for it. The most unlikely people were getting stoned. I personally always found this side of things a bit frightening, especially when kids were brought into our dressing rooms in terrible drug-induced states of confusion. It really is very disturbing to witness.

Drugs played no part in our lives whatsoever, although on one occasion, Spencer and I were appearing on the Murray the K show in New York when some asshole decided to "spike" our drinks. Spencer was the worst hit by what we could only presume must have been LSD, and spent an horrific night hallucinating and not knowing when, or even if, the effect would wear off. I just felt vaguer than usual. Spencer did eventually dabble with a drug, marijuana, under the delusion that it was, in fact, a creative drug. The only effect I could ever detect was that he would become extremely boring, after which he'd fall asleep. There would be no "Sergeant Pepper" output from him. It was a time when those who weren't actually stoned would wander around pretending to be, often with more convincing results than those who actually were. In Greenwich Village, New York, the atmosphere was so laid back that the village had virtually ground to a halt. It seemed to have been completely taken over by the drug generation.

I went there one night to see Frank Zappa, then the leader of probably the most controversial of all the contemporary bands. Zappa himself was a fine musician, though not to my taste, and when I went into the foyer to buy tickets for the show, the guy in the kiosk, who was in a virtual coma, told me that the Mothers of Invention were a crap band and that I'd be better off going to see The Yardbirds at the Fillmore, just down the road.

Pete York and I did spend some time together in the Village, listening to various black stride piano players, who were amazing. We also went to The Rainbow Room to see Duke Ellington, a beautifully melodic player, another night I'll never forget. We also saw Count Basie, which I just could not get to grips with. His economy with notes was so severe that he appeared to only play the last three chords of anything. Pete was (and is) obsessed with jazz, but I couldn't muster the enthusiasm he had. Each night, he would go to the Vanguard and other jazz haunts, where he'd sit alone, apparently quite happy with this situation. I learnt a lot under Pete's influence, but I feel it's dangerous to become obsessive about any particular form of music, as you can end up becoming blinkered about it.

Buddy Rich was Pete's hero, and he set about emulating what he considered to be Rich's perfection. This style of playing was not entirely compatible with our music, and on occasion it was very annoying and just didn't work. Spencer abhorred jazz with a vengeance and had many fiery rucks with Pete. Spencer was thus absolutely delighted when Buddy Rich was declared bankrupt. Spencer never came to a single musical outing, preferring to be the eternal PR man, attending functions and parties with celebrities.

Meanwhile, I was sharing an apartment with a girl called Denise Gross; in actual fact, it was her parents' apartment. This was a genuinely platonic relationship. I just preferred the "home" atmosphere to that of The Drake, and, as we were due to be away for so long, I reckoned this would be a better bet. Plus the little fact that her parents were away on business in Japan for three months. Denise had a friend by the name of Lorna Luft, a name which meant absolutely nothing to me. It meant even less when I eventually met her. Lorna was a "know-all" American schoolgirl.

Denise and I used to pick her up from school, following which we would drink gallons of Coca Cola, courtesy of United Artists (or so we thought). One afternoon, Lorna had to go and see her mum and asked whether Denise and I would like to accompany her. This wasn't a particularly attractive prospect, but somehow I was talked into going along. Mum lived in the crappiest part of Chinatown.

We walked into a tip of an apartment to find "Mum" hoovering and drinking gin at the same time. She did not look on top of the situation and seemed relieved to have some company. Being extremely sociable, she offered us all a drink and threw open the fridge door to reveal nothing but gin, gin and more gin. She was a tiny woman with not much hair, but was very jolly and seemed pretty clued-up on music, both past and present. She asked me what I did, to which I replied that I was in a band that she'd probably never heard of. I was wrong. She had!

She told me she knew a little about the business, but then of course everybody does. In the car on the way back to Denise's apartment, I made a few enquiries about her. It rapidly emerged that "Mum" was, in fact, Judy Garland. I was completely stunned, as I recalled the many times when I'd played "Over The Rainbow" with John and Geoff. It all seemed so very far away. So much had happened and was continuing to happen, far too quickly. I called my mum later that night and told her I'd just met Judy Garland. Mum said, "Yes, of course you have, dear. Anyway, how's the tour going?"

There were to be further social gatherings with the Garland tribe. The tip in Chinatown was replaced by two suites in the New York Plaza, which Judy Garland quickly transformed into a replica wreck of the aforementioned abode. The Garland family at that time consisted of Lorna and Joey, a baffled young boy who happily played amongst the omnipresent debris.

Judy Garland's birthday came around and I was invited to the bash, which was to be held at The Plaza. I asked Pete York to come along, because he knew precisely who she was. I thought Pete might brighten up the conversation, as he was far more familiar with the musicians of her era than I was. The party was a quiet affair. The only guests turned out to be Pete, myself, Lorna and Denise. Lorna had ordered a massive birthday cake, which I knew full well she couldn't afford, and as the evening wore on, it was evident that none of them could actually afford anything!

Pete wisely withdrew from any risk of being saddled with the bill and left, so I suggested paying for the entire thing myself; after all, I reasoned, it couldn't be *that* much. Judy could obviously sense the general unease, which became more evident when the bill was eventually produced. I never saw the amount but Judy called the *Maître D'* over and enquired whether a few songs might cover it. So sing she did, and, within moments, the ravages of booze and the strain and stress of her life fell away from her face as she became literally possessed by the music, but in a serene, not at all manic way. It was quite a lovely experience; you could actually see and feel the transformation. Most musicians are just "doing a show", but some seem, in certain circumstances, to become transported to a different plane altogether. I read that Paul McCartney, when singing his "Little Richard" orientated songs, psychs himself up into the mood and comes down again afterwards. This I can believe.

I never saw Judy Garland again and within a couple of years, she was dead. It was then that all her alleged luvvy "friends" suddenly appeared, saying what a dear and wonderful friend she'd been and how much they had respected and supported her. They had all totally ignored her at her lowest, and she had been very low. Nevertheless, they suddenly became remarkably communicative when faced with the lure of a pointed camera and a quick TV appearance. In fact, there was no money to bury the poor woman and I recall that it was months before Frank Sinatra stepped in and paid for the funeral.

Meanwhile, back at our base hotel, room service was being exploited to the extreme and it seemed that United Artists would spare no expense to keep us all happy. Our record deal was worth a substantial sum and John Martin, the inebriate Scot, advised Spencer only to take half on account, in order to save on high taxes. Needless to say, the balance was never forthcoming, supposedly eaten away with our expenses and recording costs. We always used New York as a base and made our forays from there, unless, of course, we were on the West Coast, where we stayed at the Beverley Hilton.

One night in Chicago, as we took to the stage, we were confronted by a group of women intent, it seemed, on conversation, definitely not music. Spencer, always the diplomat, walked to the front of the stage, expecting a request ... for a song, that is, The actual request, however, was rather different. The young women politely enquired whether they could make plaster casts of all our penises. These, it turned out, were the now famous Chicago Plaster Casters.

Poor Spencer was so stunned that he took three or four steps backwards, where his leg plunged through a gap in the stage boarding, resulting in him spending the entire performance in the Chicago hospital. We never did get our casts made. I'm not sure whether this is a good or a bad thing. Amazingly, these girls later mounted (so to speak) an exhibition of all the willing participants. Apparently, Jimi Hendrix was the star exhibit.

As the tour continued, we played the East Coast, the West Coast and much of the Middle and finished up in Canada. Audiences on the East and West Coasts seemed to be stoned en masse, whilst those in the middle were confused and mildly disgusted by us.

We returned to New York to recuperate for a few days before we returned to England. There was the mandatory cock-up with all our return flights and eventually I flew home with Pete York, the rest of the band following a day or so later. The in-flight movie was "2001 - A Space Odyssey", which I found very disconcerting to watch in an aeroplane. Added to my tiredness, it screwed me up even further. I just wanted to sleep, which was impossible.

On arriving home, I felt deflated and instantly bored. I had adjusted to a whole different way of life with my "new friends" in the band. While on the road, we were a very insular unit, but at home we rarely even spoke to each other. It was very strange. I was still only eighteen and pretty confused. I didn't know which life to adapt to from one moment to the next. My home life was so far removed from my working life that it was very difficult to maintain an equilibrium between the two. I don't think I ever managed it.

I literally tried to become two people. My friends John, Geoff and SPC had no interest in my travels or musical progress, they just wanted everything to stay as it was and, in a way, I wished it could too. But it was proving to be impossible.

I hope I never became big-headed. I don't think I did, because I was so wary of it happening. I couldn't go to the pub any more because, after a few Top Of The Pops appearances and similar TV shows, it really became quite unpleasant, with people trying either to ingratiate themselves or start a fight. The four of us therefore decided to spend all our time together at my home and stay out of the public eye. I enjoyed this routine, though I was never at home for long enough for anything to "settle". I began to find myself craving for the next tour, not for the money but for the experience of being in a band which, after my initial horrors, I had grown to love. Just as well, because soon after we came back from the States, there followed a series of trips of varying lengths to Europe.

In a sort of blur, we visited Holland, Belgium, France, Germany, Switzerland, Austria, Norway and Sweden, Denmark, Italy and Hungary. Work in England was far less interesting and we all definitely preferred to be away. Our management seemed to plan all these trips with no regard to distances, or even countries. In the first two years of touring, the travel bug was well and truly beaten out of my system for ever.

Another terrible error which then occurred was when Spencer was talked into doing cabaret. I think the source came from The Hollies. Graham Nash wisely quit the band before cabaret was attempted. Spencer, however, had been brainwashed into thinking that cabaret had longevity and the pop market had none. Of course, it's true that pop stars come and go every week but in Spencer's case, it was a totally different type of music and we were generally considered to be a pretty hip band.

We did one week of cabaret and that was enough for me. We all had a completely miserable time of it. We were booked to play at two clubs the same night, The Stockton Fiesta and The Top Hat Club. There was a 20 minute dash from one to the other each evening, and in both venues, we were confronted with the "scampi in a basket" brigade. The audiences were clueless about what we were doing and most of them consisted of businessmen with their dreadful brassy "bits on the side", getting very quickly and rowdily drunk each night. The waitresses at the clubs were tenth rate, no, twentieth rate bunny girls with laddered stockings and fags hanging out of their gormless mouths. Even Spencer, although he said nothing, was very depressed by the whole affair. Spencer and Pete always made the best of a bad situation, but Phil and I were really playing against our better judgement.

Our accommodation for the week was at a crappy theatrical sort of hotel-cum-bed and breakfast, a million light years away from what we were accustomed to. The other residents were jugglers, acrobats, failed comics and a smattering of doomed musicians, all of them amazed and confused to find us there. They weren't the only ones: we shared their consternation.

To make matters worse, German TV had sent a crew over to film "A Week in the Life of The Spencer Davis Group". In Germany, we had that kind of "trendy" following, the university bohemian hippy type, so what on earth they must of made of the situation, God only knows. The producer of this exciting documentary was a guy named Thomas Struck, who figured that we were as close as you could get to English "cool" and that therefore we would provide him with the perfect launch into the drug fraternity into which he was determined to break. He also thought that he would have a way into the trendy élite at the same time. Thomas would play "Sgt Pepper's Lonely Hearts Club Band" over and over again, convinced that every track was drug-related.

Well, in London we took him to the right places and I suppose he met the right faces there, but conditions up north were far from trendy and Thomas' dreams remained unfulfilled. Spencer was suffering from depression at this time and was undergoing a course of Valium and extra strong Mogadon sleeping tablets. Over dinner in our grim hotel, I convinced Thomas that Spencer was carrying some pretty heavy duty drugs. Of course, Thomas declared that he was up for taking a combination of them right there and then!

Spencer soon grasped what I was up to and joined in with enthusiasm. He offered Thomas three Mogadon and a couple of Valium, passing the Mogadon off as LSD. Some of the filming had been done in London, where buses were red, and as the Mogadon started to take effect, Thomas lurched into the streets of Stockton to be confronted by a green bus. He was convinced he was stoned and told me he felt amazing and that many things in life had become clearer to him as a result of the experience. He pressed Spencer for more pills, after which he slept soundly for two days.

Filming continued in Stockton, in and around the horrible Fiesta Club. Inevitably, a few of the replica tenth rate Bunny girls were to become the "guests" of our roadies. There was a plumbing fault in the hotel, whereby every room was audio-linked through pipe-work. The sinks all acted as kind of megaphones, with the result that all through the night you could hear wails of ecstacy resonating round the room. We naturally started to record these far from erotic events and re-played them to the embarrassed roadies over breakfast.

After a week that felt like a year, we returned with the film crew to

London in order to film a day in each of our lives. I chose Chelsea for my "day" and continued to find what an extraordinary effect cameras, especially ones which appeared to be in the hands of professionals, had on people, particulary minor and even major celebrities. Mick Jagger was around on my day out and Thomas suggested to him that we might create a segment for him in the film.

He was, as expected, boorishly rude, but luckily, Tom Keylock, his chauffeur, whom I liked a lot, was with him. We talked to him while Jagger sulked in his Mini. Jimmy Tarbuck, a sort of over the top "everybody's mate" comic, also cruised up to us, pretending to know everybody, but he was abruptly told to piss off.

The sales people in the Chelsea Antique Market suddenly turned into retired actors and actresses and came out with the most amazing bollocks you've ever heard and were overwhelmingly friendly. I returned a day or so later, minus film crew, to discover that I had long since been forgotten. So, finally, we ended up with an hour-long documentary which has only been shown in Germany. I've seen it, actually, and it makes interesting viewing today.

It was now time to get back to work again, leaving the scampi and chips people well behind. We started a University tour, which was much more like it, as the audiences were intelligent and incredibly enthusiastic. Our guitarist Phil Sawyer, however, was reaching breaking point. Phil was totally discontented and, after our burst of creativity in the studios, all he could see stretching out before him was life on the road. As his marriage was looming, he decided to call it a day. I tried my best to talk him out of it but it was a lost cause. Never mind, he still had his buffalo horns and his fishing rods, the first furnishings of his new home.

Phil played his final concert with us in Rotterdam, Holland, where the rest of the band cruelly chose not to speak to him either before or after the show. I thought, "Christ, I know they're only too pleased to see the back of him but there's no need to rub it in!'

For the following morning, Spencer had arranged a speedy audition with Ray Fenwick. This event was held, far too hastily, in the hotel reception area, with all of us about to leave for London. Spencer hired Ray there and then, in front of Phil. This was a decision which was made in too much haste. After all, we hadn't even discussed the matter as a band.

However, as things turned out, Ray was a great player, and in time I got on with him really well, but I don't like being thrown into these situations. In the event, Ray and I went on to collaborate as songwriters, writing two albums for Spencer and all the subsequent singles. Our pleasure came from writing what we considered to be memorable melodies and on a good night we would put down three songs or more on tape in demo form. Our writing was all done with Ray on acoustic and me on piano in a darkened room at my home in Champion Hill, South London.

Spencer, my initial writing partner, soon became miffed by our prolific output. He dubbed me and Ray Gilbert & Sullivan. Spencer subsequently decided to erase Phil's contributions, wherever possible, from the recordings we had made prior to Ray's joining. This, we felt, was plain sad.

After a few rehearsals, we set off on another round of endless tours. Europe, America and the UK went round and round and round.

There were many disastrous incidents during the course of the various SDG line-ups, and I will endeavour to recount a few that spring to mind. In Sweden, the entire band was arrested for non-payment of some minor bill and were subjected to much of the day in a Swedish nick. During the Swedish tour we all (except Pete) bought guns (which only fired blanks, but very loud blanks). These weapons were to become crucial on our days off. We devised all kinds of entertainment, one of the best being to "plant" a roadie at a bus stop and then drive past and shoot him. Of course, he'd fall to the floor and play dead, while the other passengers would run in all directions. Before the police had time to arrive, we'd pick him up and disappear.

The climax of the gun affair was the day we decided to go to the cinema. We all went to see "The Alamo", which none of us actually wanted to see, but it was the only thing on. The film was in Swedish with sub-titles. We all knew what a battle scene was, so, at the climax of the film, we naturally joined in, guns blazing from the back rows. Pete York was disgusted.

On another memorable occasion, Ray Fenwick stuffed the exhaust of our tour bus full of glue and feathers, which he'd taken from pillows he'd dismantled in the hotel. When it came time to fill up, he crammed the exhaust full of these feathers and a guy pulled up behind us. When the driver got back in and started the engine, a massive wad of feathers exploded from the exhaust pipe and stuck all over the car. Well, you had to be there.

At the end of the American tour, I wanted to go home but in lots of ways, I didn't want to leave. I had rapidly developed a passion for America, although under the circumstances in which we experienced it, the illusion was probably mis-judged. I had become a bit, if not a lot, tired of the musical restrictions within the band. One afternoon in America, totally out of the blue, as we were doing a soundcheck and were working on the organ sound, I started to mess around with the Beatles' song "Norwegian Wood". As I improvised, Pete York just kind of crept in and started to play along. It was like a breath of fresh air and it also sounded great.

There had been unrest within the band for some time, because Pete's drumming had become too jazzy and we were definitely not a jazz band. Spencer had begun "discreet" rehearsals with other drummers. It was all beginning to get too secretive and childish for my taste, so on my return to England, I started rehearsals with Gordon Barton from A Wild Uncertainty. I'd written piles of songs and had knocked them into good shape with Gordon, but I still lacked the balls to quit The Spencer Davis Group.

On Ray Fenwick's instigation, I think, they found a new manager by the name of Peter Walsh, who also managed The Tremeloes, The Move and Fleetwood Mac. Walsh was doing pretty nicely, but I took an instant dislike to him. He was another Northerner (after my experiences at the Stockton Fiesta I was still a bit shell-shocked) but his background, far from being musical, was in fruit and vegetables. I have nothing against Northerners, by the way, it's just that this particular one should have stuck to fruit and veg!

A summit meeting was called and it was announced that Pete was out. In contrast to what had gone before, this was not secretive and childish at all, it was laid on the table there and then. It seemed that Ray had assumed control of the group. Spencer said little and I'd had enough as well, so I announced, "Well, actually, I'd like to leave as well". Spencer was completely shattered and tried to talk me out of it, but Ray merely said, "No, Spencer, let him go". There was bad blood between Ray and me for some considerable time after that.

So there we were: I'd finally done it, maybe in haste, as ever, but I felt free and now I really had the opportunity to get motoring musically. After my departure, Spencer pulled in Nigel Olssen on drums and Dee Murray on bass, both of whom were later to work with Elton John. They did a few tours of America, released a duff single and soon fell into disarray. Spencer hit the bottle and later teamed up with Peter Jameson as an acoustic act.

Meanwhile, I rehearsed with Gordon Barton! Gordon was a great drummer, very much in the style of Ringo Starr's son Zak Starkey, but we found it was a hard act to sell. Pete York was at a loose end and totally depressed after his unceremonious sacking. We kept in touch and he eventually talked me into letting him replace Gordon, which I was loathe to do, and becoming Hardin & York. The rest, as they say, is history.

Royalties, indeed all aspects of a group's earnings, were, and I'm sure still are, an enormous problem for any band. Spencer, twenty-five years on, is still fighting for his money. There was certainly a great deal of money around during our working period but the problem was that much of it appeared to have been eaten up in hidden costs. Enormous amounts of cash would vanish on equipment hire, maintenance, air fares and general transportation costs. In those days, the scale of a concert was nothing in comparison to nowadays, and I would imagine that most of today's concerts produce no profit whatsoever, indeed, more like further debt. They are totally dependent on outside sponsors, TV rights and live recording rights. At least, that has certainly been my experience.

We were each drawing about £200 per week in my time with Spencer, which for 1967, and being only 17/18 years old, was okay, I suppose. The advantage was that we were never in any one place long enough to spend it and, secondly, all travel and other expenses came off the top. Management was the major expense, being 25% and in some instances even 30%. That was before expenses and also included 30% of all record royalties. Spencer and I had the benefit of songwriting royalties, which made an enormous difference. Try as they might, I managed to keep 100% and give the management nothing of this, but they did have a good attempt at depriving me of some of it.

To sell Spencer was a breeze for these managers and agents. Spencer was, after all, a world-wide name, so all they had to do was pick up a phone and send him off on tour, normally with no regard to logistics. That effectively was the sum total of their costs, a bloody phone call. If any problems cropped up, we were on our own; we were always the ones who paid. The group's finances ended up in total turmoil and were "locked" for about a year after I'd left the band.

Spencer gathered a strange bunch of "friends" around himself. Some were American and others were just general no-hopers, but they told Spencer everything he wanted to hear and, as he was paying, it suited all of them excellently. He dabbled in the film business, again dealing with a notorious rip-off artist who sold him film scripts. The same person later tried to sell me the same scripts! In America, the guy who started out driving us and collecting the money, had moved into Park Avenue and was now managing and ripping off some major acts.

I was really quite relieved to be out of all that and at last in control of my own destiny.

CHAPTER 3
HARDIN & YORK

A disgruntled Gordon Barton went off to work on his own and Pete York and I set about learning and adding to all the songs I'd written. Pete was a drummer of great virtuosity, but he wasn't exactly what I had had in mind for my new project. Gordon had incredible power so I had to re-work all the songs to suit Pete's style. We actually rehearsed day in and day out for a solid year. We were soon to realise that we had to start right from the bottom all over again. Sure, the Spencer Davis tag was a bonus, but we'd left the band a year before and a duo was unheard of in the rock world. We went from stadiums right back to playing the Marquee for £15!

Management posed a previously unknown problem. Everything had always been arranged for us, but now we had to do it all ourselves. Even John Martin at this stage had no time for us. Publishing was my only real credibility and as a writer I was offered deals of varying degrees of insanity. I accepted an advance of £50 (!) for my first batch of ten songs. Next, we had to have some kind of a record deal and under the dubious guidance of a very temporary manager by the name of Mel Collins, we signed to Bell Records ... for nothing. Well, Mel Collins told us it was for nothing, but it transpired later that Bell had paid him a considerable advance.

After we'd paid Collins off (yes, he made us pay to be released from his clutches) we came across our new manager, Ian Smithers, a man who was to become a constant source of amusement and amazement for years to come. He had clearly decided to devote his entire life to fun, but he had absolute confidence and faith in our work and really loved us as a band.

Ian re-negotiated the contract with Bell, so that we actually did get paid, and he also set about arranging some pretty duff venues around London for him to show us off and launch us onto greater things. Our first appearances at The Marquee were pretty uneventful, with a few paying customers and hundreds of Ian's friends. In this way, it actually looked like we were doing great business. Slowly but surely, the audiences grew and Ian's face would glow with pride as he encouraged us from the wings.

One Saturday, Ian telephoned me to ask if we'd be prepared to play an audition at my home in Champion Hill for a German promoter by the name of Frank Dostel. At this stage in our careers, we were loathe to be humiliated further, but, under protest, we reluctantly played.

Frank was suitably stunned. He was overwhelmed by the originality and power of the duo and was fascinated by my use of the bass pedals. Ian glowed in triumph and pride, and we were immediately booked to appear at a huge festival in Essen, in Germany. Following this, we were to play two nights at the legendary Star Club in Hamburg.

The Essen concert had a fantastic line-up including The Nice, Fleetwood Mac, Jethro Tull, Deep Purple and even Spencer Davis with his new acoustic show. There was a crowd of around 18,000 people, and on this night, fate dealt a blow that would establish us in Germany overnight. We took the stage with great apprehension, not surprising considering that there were two of us and eighteen thousand of them. It does sound a little unlikely, does it not?

Anyway, the reception we got on our opening song was staggering; there was a roar from the crowd that I hadn't heard even during the Spencer days. Our confidence considerably bolstered, we soldiered on through a blistering show, following which a riot broke out. There was total mayhem. Around the auditorium were dotted various film crews. They were initially there just to film clips for archive footage, but they soon picked up on the developing chaos and that night and all the following day, Hardin & York were on German national TV, accused of inciting a riot.

It was ridiculous, but we had "cracked it" over-bloody-night. Flushed with success and excitement, I went backstage, where Ian Smithers and I found ourselves quite overcome. After a while, I noticed, hovering in the background, a tall lady who appeared to be a hippyish-looking type but with obvious tinges of sophistication. She introduced herself as Florentine Pabst, a writer from a well known German publication, so she said. Being still on a high from the performance, I at first dismissed her and was, in fact, rather rude to her, but she politely persevered. It was just the way she stared at me that I found disconcerting.

It turned out that she was, indeed, a sophisticated lady and was actually of some importance at "Stern" magazine, which was Germany's biggest-selling weekly colour news magazine. We subsequently became very good friends, and our relationship very nearly turned into an affair. She asked where she could come and see us again, so I explained that we would be playing at the Star Club in Hamburg for the two following nights. She cancelled all other arrangements she had and was at the Star Club for both performances.

Florentine arrived at the club with a crowd of friends who clearly did not at all fit into the surroundings of the Star Club, and I was beginning to sense that there was a seed of infatuation in her eyes. It was then that I noticed that she was in fact quite lovely. She was baffled as to why we were not playing at a larger venue. The Star Club was a very basic club but I personally loved it there and again, we received a rapturous reception.

On the second night, Florentine told me that she wanted to use me and Pete for the front cover of Stern magazine and would come to London the following week to carry out interviews with us.

Back in London, I got a call from Florentine, who was staying at the Cadogan Hotel in Sloane Street. She invited me for lunch at Alvaro's, a very trendy restaurant in the Kings Road. Of course, I went, and was again disconcerted by her mystic gazes, but we began to get on really well and she suggested I should bring Pete along the next day.

We completed the interviews, Pete went back home to the country, and I was left to entertain the lovely Florentine. She seemed quite scared of me in a way. It certainly was not a casual affair situation and she handled matters with extreme caution. I, of course, had reached the stage where I'd have blundered straight into a romance, but Florentine maintained her sophisticated composure totally. She was, as it turned out, in a very high-powered position at the magazine and had appointments all over the world, interviewing the biggest names in all walks of life. She was definitely not a pop journalist.

Our "front page" was reserved for two weeks' time and "Stern" sent photographers over to London for more pictures. Everything was set for the next issue, and then disaster struck (in more ways than one). The actress Sharon Tate was murdered in Los Angeles and Charles Manson got "our" front page.

Undeterred, Florentine maintained our friendship, which was now becoming quite involved. She'd call me from all over the world for a chat, which was fine, but I began to feel slightly intimidated by a woman in such a powerful position. I was beginning to feel comparatively insignificant, and I told her so. I hated going to expensive restaurants with her picking up the bills, which she always insisted on doing, and I could not surmount this strange feeling which was developing. She had a way of making me feel like a little boy, which I hated because it made me feel very awkward. I didn't like being stared at adoringly all the time.

One time, Florentine came over to London to cover the new Bond film "On Her Majesty's Secret Service", for which she had interviews and meetings set up with John Barry, the composer, George Lazenby, the new Bond, and Cubby Broccoli, the producer. As far as I was concerned, this was very high-powered stuff and I couldn't stop wondering what on earth was she doing pissing about with a guy from Hardin & York?

On this visit, our relationship was very nearly consummated at The Cadogan. I'd gone round for breakfast and, as things took their course I suddenly just couldn't come up with the goods. Why, I don't know. I guess

I was simply intimidated and out of my depth. We did, however, maintain our relationship until, a couple of years later, she married a doctor in Hamburg.

Hardin and York returned to the Star Club, which was now our real launch pad, as it had indeed been for The Beatles. We were now regulars there, although the club was getting so packed that it soon became impossible for us to play there any more, and we had to start using much larger venues.

Whenever we were in Hamburg, we stayed at a grotty little hotel called The Imperial, which was on the The Reeperbahn. (I still make a point of visiting the Imperial every time I go to Hamburg!) In the evenings, we'd always walk to the club, cutting through The Eros Centre, a legalised brothel, en route. The coat lady at the Star Club had a daughter who was on the game and she loved talking about the Beatle days. In fact, there were always quite a number of hookers in our audience!

I loved Hamburg, and every time we went there, the atmosphere was electric and we made some good friends in that period. After the shows, we'd go to discreet bars in the "Grosse Freiheit" and sit and talk till daylight. Those were great days, but after a couple of years, the news came that The Star Club was to close down for good and become yet another strip club. The final night was on New Year's Eve 1969, and Hardin & York were booked to play the closing show. The club had become a legendary landmark in musical history and we were honoured to play the last show at the venue which had given birth to The Beatles and countless other successful musicians.

That night was absolutely stunning. The audience were literally hanging from the walls and rafters. The heat was so intense that the walls genuinely ran with humidity. Pete and I ended up so exhausted after the show that we just lay on the floor! Pete was absolutely pouring with sweat. After the show, Frank Dostel took about twenty of us out for a Chinese meal, but it turned out to be a bit of a solemn occasion for all of us.

After the demise of the Star Club, we went on to play much bigger halls. Now, when we came to Hamburg, we played at The Musikhalle, more the home of classical music rather than rock. These places were okay, but the crowds must have felt intimidated by the surroundings and didn't feel inclined to go as wild as they had. But playing in such surroundings was a necessary evil, because they were just the only places large enough.

At our base camp at The Imperial Hotel, the staff were finally becoming pleasant to us. When we had first arrived there, months earlier, at around six o'clock one morning, we were told that our rooms were not ready and that we would have to wait outside until noon. It was a freezing December morning and we froze in our Transit van for six hours.

The hotel porter was soon christened "Wimpey", à la Popeye, and behind the reception desk sat a frightening chap who reminded me of Joseph Mengele. They never quite got to grips with our names and, as our success escalated, their attempt at friendliness extended to calling us each by our surnames. To be fair, most people in Germany always did this. I was never addressed as Eddie, always as Hardin, which I found quite strange.

We eventually graduated to the Atlantic Hotel or the Hamburg Plaza, and it always felt strange to me to leave the luxurious surroundings of the hotel to play in some fleapit, however crowded and busy it may have been. Our loyal followers didn't take to our new, opulent lifestyle. We had started as a "people's band', but found ourselves drifting into respectability, which was not expected of us. On the other hand, mayors and dignitaries welcomed us into their company, which they would certainly never have done on our initial visits. It was all bullshit, really.

Now we were beginning to be offered a lot of TV appearances. We appeared on "Beat Club", something like an early German version of "The Old Grey Whistle Test", on several occasions. As one of our singles was entitled "Candlelight", the producer decided to abandon studio lighting and just have masses and masses of candles burning. It actually looked pretty good and there was no problem with the candles burning away, as we played live and were so well rehearsed that everything was done in one take.

On one occasion we had to fly in and out of Hamburg in a day with our equipment. It transpired that the only plane with a big enough hold for a Hammond C3 was a 747. When everything arrived in Hamburg, all our gear appeared in the Arrivals Hall via the carousel transporting all the others passengers' luggage. The sight of an enormous (and very heavy) Hammond organ, complete with its huge Leslie speaker cabinets, rather shocked the assembled travellers, who were concerned about their luggage getting squashed. Our manager, Ian Smithers, had obviously not got to grips with the concept of freight!

The president of our then record company, Bell Records (Larry Uttal) finally decided to fly over from the States to see what all the fuss was about. After all, we were making him a lot of money (not a single penny of which was ever passed on to us as artists). Larry arrived in some obscure town in the middle of Germany dressed in executive attire, cashmere overcoat, the biggest cigar available and, of course, chewing gum.

The queue outside the venue stretched way down the street. but the self-important Uttal ignored this, marched straight to the front of the queue and presented himself to The Pike, our roadie, who was standing at the front door. The Pike had no regard at all for authority and told him to "Fuck off to the back of the queue like the fucking rest".

Despite selling tens of thousands of albums in Europe, we never received any royalties whatsoever from Bell Records. I even made a futile trip to New York in a vain attempt to salvage something from the situation, but to no avail. Fortunately, I made substantial sums from the writing element. Poor Pete, on the other hand, was stuffed rotten. While in New York, I tried to set up a new publishing deal, but the nasty little publishers cared only for sales figures and had no regard whatsoever for the music (very much like the industry remains today!).

One guy listened to two bars of a song and said, "How much do you want?" In those days, I actually had musical integrity and was very offended at this treatment of my work. As it happened, Johnny Mercer was in the room and, after listening to maybe twenty seconds of a song I had written called "Deep In My Despair", pronounced that he reckoned it had something ... on twenty seconds! No, no, this was definitely not for me.

For our early shows in Germany, our fee had been £75, but after the Essen triumph, Ian Smithers re-negotiated this and then, after the Star Club, he re-negotiated again. I was all for investing more and more money in equipment to make our show bigger and better. Pete, on the other hand, was content to stay as we were. His attitude was that it worked OK as it was, so we should just take all the money available. I increased the organ power to deafening levels and added massive bass cabinets to drive the bass pedals, which, while increasing the power of the music, made playing smaller venues totally impractical. We tried it once and all the glasses and bottles of booze were literally shaken from the shelves by the bass. Pete unsurprisingly developed tinnitus, from which he suffers to this day. He constantly reminds me that it was all my fault.

Very soon, our nightly fee was becoming substantial, and it was now time for us to indulge in the odd luxury item. Pete wisely chose property. I, on the other hand, unwisely ploughed through an array of Rolls Royces. We toured constantly in Germany and effectively abandoned England altogether, even though Smithers was determined to crack the English market. Having finally extricated ourselves from Bell, we signed a lucrative deal with Decca records, which enabled us to also make solo albums.

Being now financially secure, we decided to take it at our own pace to "crack" England. Smithers booked us into The Reading Festival and all of a sudden, it was like Germany all over again. We found ourselves on the front pages of most of the UK music press and at last it looked as if we would be able to work in our homeland.

Following the Reading show, work offers came flooding in. On Smithers' advice, we turned everything down. He had a cunning plan. What we'll do is this, he said, we won't work for three months, and then we'll come back bigger than ever.

Fine. But as it happened, we didn't work for three months and then we didn't come back big. In fact we didn't come back at all! The momentum of Reading had been lost and besides, we were becoming lazy. The reason was that we could do a ten day tour of Germany and live comfortably for months, so why bother with England at all? We started to work whenever I wanted a new car or Pete needed to re-decorate his house.

Deep Purple, with whom we had formed a pretty close relationship, were forging ahead in leaps and bounds and invited us to support them on their British tour. This turned out to be great fun and we covered most of the UK in three weeks or so. Deep Purple's drummer, Ian Paice, travelled with me on most journeys, but only for the comfort of the Rolls Royce. When, on occasion, I used another car, he was most put out.

Decca records, the company which had rejected The Beatles, confirmed their powers of perception by signing Hardin & York around two years too late, by which time our enthusiasm had waned. Ian Smithers, however, negotiated a three album deal, a solo album from both Pete and myself, plus a Hardin & York album, for which reason the next year was largely spent in the studios, leaving no time to tour.

The Spencer Davis Group had by now ground to a hopeless halt and Spencer retreated to California on a permanent basis. It was now that Ray Fenwick suddenly re-appeared. His career was re-started largely due to the intervention of Pete and myself.

Ray began writing with me again and we co-wrote my first solo album for Decca, which was entitled "Home Is Where You Find It". Mike Hurst, ex of The Springfields, was "producing" the new Hardin & York album, which had the title "For The World". Hurst is still around, producing albums for the likes of Belle and Sebastian, but his production technique, at least when he was working with us, pretty much involved him not actually being there for much of the time!

I managed to talk Pete into using Ray on a couple of tracks, which was not an easy task, considering that it had been Ray who had largely instigated Pete's dismissal from the SDG. It was as a direct result of these sessions that Ray was launched into the world of the session player and, unsurprisingly, he soon afterwards disappeared from our lives yet again.

The publicity "machine" surrounding Hardin and York had always been haphazard, if not non-existent! Our career had largely been self-promoted and built on good reviews of our live shows, so Smithers felt we had reached the point where we needed a full-time publicist working for us and on our payroll.

The first guy we engaged was by far the worst and it will be hard to describe him in a way that will do justice to his eccentricity; however, I shall endeavour to do so. We had a show to do at Southampton University. I remember that Renaissance, at that time with Keith Relf singing, were the support band. Smithers rang to say that our new "publicist" would be there, that his enthusiasm knew no boundaries and that the even better news was that he only wanted £20 per week. We later found out that this was to supplement his income from his day job, working on the petrol pumps at a garage in Clapham!

Pete and I drove separately to Southampton, where, on arrival, our first joint vision was of an extremely odd-looking guy dressed in top hat and tails with dyed, blonde shoulder-length hair, distributing piles of embarrassing-looking leaflets which were primitive daubs of me and Pete waving from a very childishly drawn aeroplane. The text of the flyer went on to catalogue our forthcoming trips around Europe. This, it turned out, was our new publicist, who went by the name of "'Flag".

Personally, I was both very annoyed but at the same time amused, so, to save face in front of the already bemused students, we (Pete and I) chose not to introduce ourselves until after the show. Flag told us that business had not been too hot of late and that he was "between offices". Nevertheless, should any hot news item crop up, we could always call him at the petrol station. That night, he had hitched from London to Southampton and was now bereft of any transport home. The situation had deteriorated and we were sort of lumbered with him, having to arrange a lift home for him with one of our roadies.

Flag had obviously been impressed by our performance that night and by the following week, London was literally littered with his dreadful infantile leaflets, so much so that it became necessary to restrain him. Indeed, the GLC took out legal proceedings against us for littering the capital. Despite this, his enthusiasm continued apace. He had yet another sideline, in the form of his own band, called The Balloon And Banana Band, which featured a quite unbelievable bunch of characters, the drummer being Del Boy, (long before "Only Fools and Horses"), another fantastic character with a mop of red hair.

The B & B band, as I shall abbreviate them, had a vast repertoire, most of it being unwitting comedy. Another band member was "Blind Geoff", a seriously visually handicapped lad who was always being advised to stand well clear of theatre curtains for fear of setting them ablaze with the monstrous lenses in his glasses. The B & B band carried on for some time with their chaotic show, culminating in an appearance on "Opportunity Knocks". God alone knows how they got through the initial auditions, but somehow or other they made it onto the TV screens of Great Britain.

They attempted to condense their three hour act into three minutes. This was quite a challenge, because the full act apparently involved strangling chickens (again, long before the antics of Alice Cooper, though I doubt that his influence came from The Balloon and Banana Band, but then again who knows?), numerous explosions and as much "music" as possible going on in the background. The result of this appearance was pretty well self-explanatory. Yes, it was a fucking mess, topped by the fact that Flag was trying to sing a song that the rest of the band weren't actually playing.

This is honestly a factual account and if there should be anyone out there who watched it ... well, I envy you. Or maybe I don't. As a result of their one and only TV appearance, the B & B band disintegrated and finally disbanded, with Flag returning in dubious triumph to his post on the pumps at Clapham. Del Boy and Blind Geoff set themselves up as elite roadies and worked for the Keef Hartley Band.

Blind Geoff didn't work out for Hartley, so he set himself up as an independent roadie. Lacking in any funds, he could only afford a very suspect van, which he hired out with himself at the wheel. His first booking was his last. He drove a band from London to Luton (which he surprisingly found), but after the show, disaster struck. The gearbox blew up, resulting in Geoff having to drive all the way back to London in reverse gear, that being the only gear that functioned.

Meanwhile, Hardin and York were still "Decca Recording Artistes". The headquarters of Decca Records was a dreary old World War 2 building on the Embankment in London. Ian Smithers had done the deal, whereupon I was invited for a celebratory lunch in the Decca boardroom. The French pianist Jacques Louissier was also there on a visit. Smithers, as was customary, got pissed, as did Hugh Mendl, Decca's Managing Director.

After the largely liquid lunch, Hugh fell from top to bottom of a vast flight of stairs, breaking his leg and thus being hospitalised throughout the making of our new album. The inebriated Smithers pointed out to

Hugh the appropriateness of the showbiz expression "Break a leg", but Hugh's response was not recorded. As it happened, Hugh had a stunning secretary, who we were all instructed not to mess with, as it was "company policy not to fuck the staff"! Not particularly feeling part of the company, or any company come to that, I ignored the warning.

There was another famous guy at Decca, in the shape of Dick Rowe. Dick was actually famous only for one thing, which was being the man who turned down The Beatles. After this disastrous error, he decided that he should, on behalf of Decca, buy everything that was presented to him. This was convenient for Ray and myself. We had a backing track, with which we made three separate recordings with three different singers. Dick bought all three, plus he had already paid for the backing track in the first place. His policy was to leave absolutely nothing to chance, but I reckon he just didn't know what he was doing, having quite obviously no ear for music, an ideal qualification for working in A & R for a major record company.

The Decca building resembled a hospital and had that same antiseptic smell about it. There was a commissionaire on the door, whose policy was to let no one in, whoever or whatever he or she was, without a silly badge that he was adamant should be affixed to one's jacket. He probably couldn't read, but so long as you wore the bloody badge, you were allowed in. In my opinion, The Beatles had a very lucky escape. Hugh would sit behind a large G-Plan desk (this company had style), his little legs dangling from his chair but not quite reaching the floor, as he gave his verdict on various tracks that were played to him. It was plain that this man did not have a clue.

Ray Fenwick was the next artist to "raid" Decca, climbing in on the shirt tails of Hardin & York. He went on to record an incredibly expensive album featuring seemingly hundreds of guitarists. Although it was very good, it has only just seen the light of day, but not on Decca, who had paid for the whole bloody thing! Another thing that particularly annoyed me at the time was that Hardin & York were considering recording "Pomp And Circumstance", the Elgar piece, and I had discussed this concept with Ray, who thought it was a great idea. So great, in fact, that he crept off and recorded it with his fucking guitar orchestra.

Royalty statements were (and still are) a problem. With Decca, for example, we got reams and reams of paperwork which meant nothing either to us or to our accountants. There was always a deficit, even though the album had reached Number 1 in Germany!

Ray Fenwick was still being managed by Peter Walsh. Walsh was totally the wrong man for the job. He was a Northerner with a lusty appetite for what he called Bugs Bunny (money) and none of his dealings were as they appeared. Peter aimed to convince Decca to record absolutely anything and of course, with the weight of all his hit bands behind him, they did.

As a band, Hardin & York were financially sound, well, reasonably so. In order to be in a position to have total control over our recordings, I decided rather pretentiously to become incredibly over the top and boringly artistic. I suggested to Smithers that I should go to Paris to write songs for the new album. I would thus be un-disturbed and could create in peace (ho ho!). Smithers naturally jumped at the idea, having visions of the odd riotous weekend in Paris.

We decided on the Georges V, which I believe was the hotel where some of "A Hard Day's Night" was written. I noticed from photographs that the Beatles had an upright piano in their suite. As Smithers and I were not into the concept of economy, he went to great lengths to have a grand piano installed in my suite. The suite was vast but the entrance to the hotel was not vast enough to get the enormous instrument through the door, so a crane had to be hired to do the job. The hotel was happy to go to great lengths to accommodate us, as I was intending to be there for a month.

So, off I set for Paris and on arrival, went to my maze of a suite, at which point I realised I had no idea what to do. As a first step, I drank the contents of the minibar (or in the case of the Georges V, the megabar) and then proceeded to ring all my friends in England. The piano, meanwhile, sat silently in the corner.

The first night's sleep came earlier than planned, as I did have a few contacts in Paris! So, after an interesting bout of 4-poster activity, I did get round to writing a few lyrics. In fact, I completely wrote the words to a track called "Some Places Are Better To Be" which appears on the "For The World" album. I'm ashamed to admit that I added the melody in England.

Morning arrived and, being alone again, I wondered how to spend the day. The piano did not feature highly in my ponderings, so I went to Montmartre for a solo lunch, after which I was propositioned by a number of hookers. Surprisingly, I resisted and returned to the austere surroundings of the Georges V, which really was a bit like staying at Madame Tussauds, by which I mean populated by lots of very, very old people, some of them probably either dead or perilously close to it.

By now rigid with boredom, I telephoned my girlfriend and got her over from London on the first available plane. She was used to these odd phone calls and often ended up on random visits all over the place. Upon her arrival, she wasn't much fun either, complaining of air sickness and throwing up in the taxi from the airport. So she just went to bed, straight to sleep, so that once again I had no conversation (or anything else, come to that) until the morning.

After breakfast (cold, of course, food in the room was always cold), we decided that we'd had enough and went back to London, leaving the hotel with not only the dilemma of what to do with the piano but also what to do with the suite, which I had booked for a month. We did, of course, get the bill, but Smithers managed to do a deal. Denny Laine later told me that he stayed there when he was with Wings and that all he wanted was egg and chips, which of course they gave him, along with a bill for £60 a time.

I really should have learnt my lesson, but I did return to the Georges V some years later with a guy I knew as Mark from Sark who had taken the job as my driver. This time, we had two adjoining suites at an even more ridiculous cost, but I actually did have the plan to carry on to Midem, the music festival in Cannes. In Paris at the same time were the piano player from Renaissance, Peter Gosling, and the dreadful Christine McVie from Fleetwood Mac who, flushed with their astounding success at the time, insisted on paying for everything with her Kryptonite Amex card.

Prior to their arrival at the Georges V, Mark and I were in the bar. Mark insisted on buying the first round, which was a white wine and a gin and tonic, a snip at £35. Mark, in a state of near collapse, whispered to me that there was no danger of getting pissed in there. However, the Fleetwood Mac cavalry arrived in the nick of time and ordered Dom Perignon, the first bottle of which Christine knocked off the table, making it necessary to hastily order a second one. It was not completely clear who was paying and at £90 odd a bottle, I was a little concerned, but the Kryptonite card came out, as did numerous more bottles of champagne. It was not, however, a jolly time, as Christine was just being fucking flash, so I was pissed off rather than pissed up.

Christine then suggested dinner. We were given no choice of restaurant, instead having to go where SHE wanted to go. We were cabbed to another grossly over-priced place, where all the customary moaning and groaning in ecstasy over the French food started. Mark ordered a starter which was little more than a raw egg and the following courses were little short of disaster, but the enormity of the bill convinced Christine that it must have been wonderful. Bollocks, it was crap.

But there was more to come, as we all then went on to some dimly lit pop stars' palace of a hotel where more buckets of champagne were ordered in the obligatory pop star fashion. By this time, I was dreadfully pissed and had been joined by an old French flame who was equally out of it. I think we got back to our hotel at around 5 a.m.

I woke up at around 11a.m, alone, and feeling like there were major roadworks going on in my head. I almost immediately got a call from the Gosling/Fleetwood brigade who were STILL at it. I declined to join them and pressed on to Cannes.

CHAPTER 4
ROADIES

I reckon that, as far as characters go, there are far more of them behind the scenes in the form of the roadies, who are often more interesting than the so-called "stars" they work for. With this in mind, I shall now endeavour to catalogue some of ours.

Del Boy and Blind Geoff I have already described, so let's return to the beginnings of Hardin & York. Having quit the Spencer Davis Group, life was not the easy ride we anticipated. Being just a two-piece was the first obstacle to overcome, largely because most promoters thought the concept was ridiculous and, more to the point, that it would be impossible for two people to entertain a crowd for two hours or so. Despite our pedigrees, we found obtaining any kind of work impossible, so instead we just rehearsed ... for a year!

After a few months, we took on a roadie, really just so that it seemed like we were a band. It did in fact give us some kind of mental stimulus, even though the guy was completely useless. All the professional roadies we knew didn't want to know about us, even if they were to be paid the normal rate. There is a great deal of snobbery amongst roadies. They can be very dedicated to the point of obsession, and if you get a good one he'll be your greatest fan and will do anything for you.

Thus we ended up with Victor Brophy, an unemployed bricklayer recommended to us by Alec Leslie, our roadie from SDG days, who of course saw no future himself in working for Hardin and York. Next, Pete bought a van which didn't actually go anywhere for a year. Victor just sat and listened to us rehearse for that year and as nothing had to be moved anywhere at all, he had a pretty good job. The joke was that when work did start, he left us!

So, as there were no gigs, Victor was given odd jobs around the house. My dad had him build a wall and my mum had him doing all kinds of daft things, just to occupy him. He had not the slightest clue what we were trying to achieve musically and I think he was just generally baffled by the whole situation. We started recording a few demos at home and would send Victor out on futile missions to arouse interest with the very rough tapes. This was quite a challenge. I mean, how can a guy sell an idea which even he doesn't understand?

Occasionally, we'd get him to make phone calls on our behalf while we stood beside him, cringing at the blunders he was making. He once called the BBC and was so shocked that he had actually got through that he double-checked, asking if this was indeed the British Broadcasting Co-operation he was talking to. Things seemed hopeless, but suddenly, to Victor's credit, he accidentally came across the young DJ Johnnie Walker. Walker was impressed by our tapes and decided to devote his next three shows to the development of Hardin and York. This was a breakthrough, firstly because Victor now had something to do and secondly, so did we. Our first live show was in Bristol, where we played to a bemused college crowd who just didn't know what to make of it. After a few Marquee dates and an appearance at The Plumpton Festival, we were sort of on the way again.

Our next roadie was Denny Brown, a guy who had jumped up on the stage in Paris during an SDG show and asked for a job ... which he got. Denny was a street-wise guy from Clapham, totally out to look out for himself and himself alone. During his SDG days, he had become besotted by the American way of life and married an American girl, largely because of her voice. The two of them proceeded to have a kid who grew up with a sort of Los Clapham accent.

Denny soon got his mates in to work for us, and so we found ourselves with three roadies, although their true identities were never quite clear to us. One was called the "Ginger fella", for obvious reasons, and the other was called "Robbo", simply because he had the habit of nicking anything and everything that he could lift, regardless of whether he actually wanted it or not.

Our roadies were viewed with great distaste by the professional crews that were around at the time. Despite this, Pete and I enjoyed their company, even though they had little to no actual ability. They would present us with regular bills for servicing the van (which of course never was serviced) and gigantic petrol bills. They just got books of receipts from their mate in the garage and filled them in themselves.

The next on the crew was certainly the most famous, as far as we were concerned. He was known as the Pike. Again, we never knew and to this day still don't know what his real name was. The Pike came highly recommended by Robbo, and was launched into an immediate German tour. Although he loved the music and became a good friend to us, he was completely useless. He even fucked up my wedding night many years later.

Night after night in Germany, there would be power failures, broken organs and sometimes broken audience heads, caused by the fact that the Pike could not communicate too well in foreign languages and, if in doubt, preferred to use blunt instruments rather than his tongue. By now, we had a huge following in Germany and one night, as we prepared to go onstage in a packed hall, the Pike proudly pointed to all the illuminated amplification lights which, for once, appeared to be working. He took up his post behind the array of Leslie speakers and we took to the stage. I played the opening chord and was greeted by blissful silence. The entire lot had fused, apart from the P.A. which, unfortunately, was not affected. I was furious, so, making sure my microphone was switched off, I launched into a torrent of abuse at the Pike, reducing the poor man to tears.

As he sat crouched beside the Leslies, which were all miked up, the Pike pointed out to me that it wasn't that bad as the crowd were only a "bunch of fucking Nazis". There was a momentary stunned silence before, as the crowd consisted mainly of very left-wing motivated students, the venue erupted into a scene of flying bottles, chairs and all kind of projectiles. There was nothing we could do but leave, leaving the Pike to battle it out with an irate crowd of "fucking Nazis".

We continued our German tour, the Pike with his tool kit (which consisted of a pair of pliers), until the night which was my 21st birthday and we had a pretty big show in Hamburg to play. This was the 19th February and snow had fallen quite heavily overnight. The Pike went to the hall early to ensure there would be no problems; as it turned out, he was just ensuring that there were.

He enlisted help from the usual "liggers", who just wanted to earn a free ticket, to unload the van. Needless to say, all the gear was dropped from the van into the thick snow. Now Leslie speakers are open at the rear and I had eight of them. The Pike carefully dragged each one through the snow, backwards, so the snow neatly compressed into each of them. He set up the mountain of igloos (which by now they were) in a mound around the concert grand piano.

Pete and I set off for the hall at our usual 8 o'clock. As we hadn't played in Hamburg for a while, we were really looking forward to the show, as Hamburg had been, in effect, our birthplace as a band. The atmosphere was perfect and there was a huge roar from the crowd as we took to the stage, but when the Pike flicked the main power on, the whole lot burst into a massive inferno, temporarily blacking out the entire hall and probably numerous suburbs of Hamburg as well. The Pike just sat under the grand piano and cried ... again! Yes, once more he had failed.

After this, I returned to England for a day to have a proper birthday do. The following day, I stupidly flew back to Hamburg. Considering that we were to play in Munich for three nights, I've no idea why I didn't fly straight to Munich. Anyway, we drove through the day and most of the night and arrived in Munich to find we were booked into the Residenz Hotel. It just sounded naff to us, so we caused a ruckus with the promoter. In fact, it turned out to be one of the nicest hotels in Munich. The Pike surveyed his suite, pronouncing that he felt like James Bond.

The next night we played at the Blow Up Club, a vast place in the centre of Munich, set on three levels. We climbed down onto the stage, making our grand entrance, only to be upstaged by three German women making an even grander entrance to their front row seats. It seemed that they were far better known than we were and, as a bonus, they all looked stunning in various bits of "spray-on" clothing. We didn't think for a second they would have any designs on us; well, you don't, do you? It transpired that they were at all the major events and obviously had their pick of all the major musicians, working as a kind of elite musicians' union.

That night, we actually played on equipment which worked, and the Pike's tears were, for once, tears of joy. After the show, the three ladies appeared in the dressing room. Well, it would have been impolite not to grant them admission. After a certain amount of banter, they agreed to come back to the hotel "for a drink", which unfortunately was all it bloody well turned out to be. Pete, I think sensing this would not be a pushover, went to bed, leaving me and the Pike to entertain these wondrous beauties. The Pike was not a musician, so it soon became clear his presence was not required. Two of the guests left and I was now alone with Munich Nora and the Pike.

Nora became quite terrifyingly seductive and said that hotels were cold and why didn't I go back to her place? Being even more stupid than normal, I asked the Pike to come along. Anyway, she led me a right dance until the early hours, when I decided that enough was enough and we left. The Pike, sharing my frustration, jumped through the roof of Nora's Mercedes. Interestingly, Nora eventually became Mrs Johnny Rotten.

Trudging back to our hotel through the snow, I noticed that the Pike was limping. When I enquired what the problem was, he explained that he was wearing his treasured snakeskin boots and that, as it was so cold in the van, he'd filled his boots up with anti-freeze at the same time as he filled the van. His logic was, and still is, pretty astounding.

Our next journey was to Denmark, and a few die-hard fans decided to trail the Pike on this very long trek. The Pike had picked up some useful items on his travels, bearing in mind it was mid winter. Yes, he had bought some swimming trunks. His other useless item was a huge knife, which swung casually from his belt. He arrived at the border crossing, where the van broke down in No Man's Land and officials on neither side were prepared to help. Luckily, the die-hards were behind and they pushed him into Denmark.

Denmark proved to be even more desperate for the poor Pike. Pete and I had flown home to England, as we had three or four days off. On my first night at home, I received a call from the Pike, who was complaining about being stuck in a Danish hotel where no-one spoke a word of English and that he was desperate to order some proper food. Not being particularly eloquent even in English, the Pike had seemingly endured bacon and eggs for every meal, presumably on the proprietors' assumption that all English people like bacon and eggs and, as they couldn't understand him, they were on a pretty safe bet. Unfortunately, not being able to speak Danish either, there was little I could do other than leave him in danger of becoming egg bound. Overcome with boredom, the Pike began throwing his trusty knife into the wooden floor but, as his aim grew lax, he impaled his foot into the floorboards. This necessitated another phone call to us, this time from the hospital.

Eventually, Pete and I returned to Denmark and found ourselves staying at The Oesterport Hotel, which was all on one level, like a massive bungalow. Staying there at the same time were Rod Stewart and The Faces, so we arranged to go and see them play at a club around the corner. Ian Smithers had arrived in town and the three of us set off, Smithers, as ever, bent on self-destruction.

Rod Stewart was not a huge name at that time and their show was "loose", to say the least. In fact, Rod spent much of his time on stage wandering about drinking endless glasses of port and brandy. Stewart, however, paled into second division when compared to Smithers, who was drinking red wine as if he feared they would make no more. While we were "jollying up" in the club, heavy snow had fallen and was still falling very heavily when we set off back to the hotel.

Smithers by now was in a terrible condition, unable to stand, let alone walk. This was a situation Pete and myself had become accustomed to and it became our job to manoeuvre him back to the hotel. We propped him up between us and dragged him through the snow.

Pete was always, and still is, of the opinion that an Englishman abroad is his country's representative and should at all times put on a civil front, so we leant Smithers up against the reception desk, hoping he wouldn't try to speak, while we asked for our keys. Smithers gradually started to slide, ending up with just his head perched on the counter. In a desperate attempt to regain some form of dignity, and very much aware of Pete's annoyance, Smithers summoned up enough energy to break free from us.

As I said, the hotel was all on one level and sadly, Smithers' room was at the very end. There were three steps down from reception that led you to the seemingly mile-long corridor. Smithers, having taken the steps at a lurch, broke into a run, thus giving himself tremendous impetus. We watched helplessly as his pace got faster and faster. Eventually he just slammed straight into the door at the end of the corridor and slumped uselessly to the ground, a bit like you see in cartoons.

The days of the Pike were now numbered and, at the suggestion of Mike Hurst, we moved into the uncharted waters of the "Professional Roadie". Mike knew a guy by the name of John Jacobs, a Henleyite who was working for some piano player whose name escapes me. Our first meeting with John was at our offices in Wardour Street. It was more a case of him interviewing us and at the end of the meeting he pointed out, in an incredibly cultivated English Gentleman's accent, that he would give the matter some consideration over the weekend.

By Saturday lunchtime, John was on "the firm". We had several dates around England lined up and John brought along a Scottish assistant by the name of Dougal. Dougal's accent was so fierce that you needed subtitles. At the first venue, we were surprised that John required his own dressing room. On further enquiry, he told us that it was his custom "to change for the performance". And so it transpired. During the show, John sat mid-hall behind the mixing desk dressed in a bow tie (honestly) and a dreadful gold lamé jacket which Pete christened the "Terry's All Gold Coat".

When we started playing, John's enthusiasm was extreme, verging on embarrassing. The audience appeared to get as much from his performance as they did from ours. He would spur the audience into more applause, in fact he was probably an asset in some sticky musical moments. Whenever or wherever there was a problem, John seemed capable of fixing it. He boasted that, if there was ever a dodgy piano at a venue, he could, with the aid of a couple of tin cans and a soldering iron, turn the wreck into a perfectly acceptable musical instrument.

John was forever complaining about our van. He wanted some particular vehicle, can't remember what it was, which we proceeded to buy him. On his days off, he would spend the time customising the van into what he considered "adequate transportation both for the equipment and for himself and Dougal".

He presented us with bills for aircraft seats, I mean genuine aircraft seats, taken from the First Class section of planes, obviously no Economy Class for John. In the end, we bought so many bloody seats that he even had some installed at home in front of the fire. It was an unusual sight, John and his wife settling down for an evening in front of the TV in two First Class aircraft seats. John had an unusual relationship with his wife. He never told her where he was going or how long he would be away, but, fortunately for him, she was very quiet and accepted anything he said, which was very little (to her, anyway).

John was soon christened "The Wing Commander", and became a popular character with all the touring bands. He was the ultimate eccentric. He would never eat with us on the road, preferring to march off alone into the night in order to sample the genuine fare of whatever country or major town we were in.

On one occasion, in Germany, I was having problems with the Hammond, but John was convinced he could fix it. We were staying in a lovely hotel in Southern Germany where John, determined to get to work on the Hammond, commandeered the entire reception area, where he set the Hammond up, along with ALL the gigantic Leslie speakers. The hotel manager was so overwhelmed with John's presence and immaculate voice that he even dashed off to get his own tool kit and set to work to assist in every way possible. Within hours, to his credit, John had solved what I thought was a terminal problem, and proceeded to demonstrate his triumph by playing the thing at maximum volume, after which the management and staff gave him a round of applause and congratulated him on his skill. Then, with their assistance, he loaded everything back onto the van.

He had some great "chat-up" lines. He seemed to come from an era that I certainly never knew. He'd stop Fräuleins in the street and say, "My dear, you look as though you've lost a Mark and found a Pfennig!"

A classic tale which springs to mind concerns one of our German roadies. He was one Henning Finda, an enthusiastic chap, and we were his first charges on a major tour. Henning arrived at the airport looking efficient and immaculate and we had the feeling that, for once, everything would go okay (a rare occurrence on the road). He loaded our bags into his Opel Kapitän, "one of only twelve ever made", as he pointed out, and off we went. We drove for two hours with Henning making polite conversation, until Pete and I realised we could still see low-flying aircraft remarkably close to us. It turned out that we had been circling the airport's perimeter road for two hours!

Pete is not a patient man on such occasions and on this occasion something had to be said, otherwise we'd have still been circling the airport to this day! So the first row erupted and poor Henning was devastated; he had ballsed things up before we'd even left the airport. The next morning, after a frightening journey the night before (Henning was by no means a great driver), he appeared for breakfast dressed in the same suit, same tie, same shoes, as he was to do for the next six weeks. The smart executive deteriorated into a virtual tramp by the end of the tour. The Opel Kapitän didn't fare much better either. On a daily basis, bits of this rare car would fall off, Henning oblivious as parts flew in different directions. About mid-tour, the Opel was in a desperate state, as it never entered Henning's head to consider checking oil or water levels.

One day the water temperature gauge soared to an all-time high, to the extent that it looked dangerous, and Pete and I were just waiting for the bang. As Henning turned round to assure us it was OK, he narrowly missed a passing cyclist.

"That's bloody dangerous," pointed out Pete.

"Only for the cyclist," Henning reasoned.

Minutes later, and for no apparent reason, Henning mounted the pavement and we all smashed into a low wall. A few more bits fell off and we continued on our way. By now, Henning's employers had come to realise that he was as useless as we already knew, and he was sacked. Henning, however, was determined to see the tour right through to the bitter end. We started to feel sorry for the poor guy and began paying him ourselves. At the end of the trip, according to Henning's calculations, we still owed him £30. We felt that we'd actually done enough and at the airport, we boarded the plane and left him standing at the Departure gate. Amazingly, two months later, Henning turned up to a show in Bradford to ask once more for the £30!

The Wing Commander, meanwhile, toured on with military precision, accompanied by the ever-faithful Dougal. But his days were also coming to an end, due to his constant demand for wage increases and more aircraft seats. We fully expected one day to get the bill for the fucking plane itself.

Hardin & York undertook a tour of France, which was by far the most doomed we ever attempted. We found ourselves playing largely to moronic farmers, the majority of whom were seemingly paralytic for most of the day. Pastis is the local brew, a horrible Pernod-style aniseed drink which has drastic effects.

Having an in-built fear of hospitals and everything connected with them, I was horrified, on our arrival in Paris, to find that our tour bus was in fact to be a converted ambulance. Pete was, as usual, prepared to accept pretty well anything that's thrown at him, but I dreaded the prospect of three weeks in a blacked-out bus, complete with two stretchers!

Our first show was in a dire club in the centre of Paris, where we didn't get onstage until 3 a.m. Drugs were very high on the agenda that night, though I much preferred a stoned audience to a pissed one. Dougal the roadie managed to find himself a one-breasted (it was central) girlfriend. As it happened, most of Dougal's girlfriends had some kind of affliction. One had a plastic leg.

I think we were in Paris for three or four shows and, in comparison to the provinces, it was actually quite civilised. We also had the bonus of staying at a nice hotel, the Lutetia, which we both enjoyed. Pete and I were an odd pair. During the day we'd act the part of affluence and love it. In the evening we'd totally change image into what seemed to be expected of us. This often entailed changing out of smart clothes and into scruffy ones for the show. We were chameleons.

After leaving Paris, we found that provincial audiences enjoyed punching each other during songs, and in the gaps they'd go to the bar for more booze. The entire tour was absolute hell, just as it had been with Spencer Davis when I toured France with him. The promoter in our case was a brainless man with absolutely no idea whatsoever of the logistics of keeping a band on the road. After the ambulance packed up, we got through a seemingly endless stream of old bangers, all of which broke down, resulting in the promoter having to provide us with taxis for enormously long journeys at ridiculous expense to him.

He eventually provided us with a fairly intact Mercedes and suggested that we should all go out for a fantastic meal together and forget about the traumas. It was true that the meal was pretty good but, just as the promoter felt he'd done his bit and that we'd all now be content, the *Maître d'* arrived at the table with much wringing of the hands and sweating visibly. It transpired that an entire wall of the restaurant had collapsed. This didn't seem to be a great problem to us, until we realised that the wall had collapsed on top of the Mercedes, totally engulfing it. Yet another taxi was called.

This French tour was our first and our last and, thinking about it, it's quite amazing that I'm now living in a country in which I have had so many terrible experiences. By now, I was sick to death of touring and just wanted to record. I remember that Pete and I set up what was to be a pretty final rehearsal in Henley. We were both drained, and you can see it in the photographs that were taken that day. I'd driven a journalist down for the day, I think he was from Beat Instrumental or something, and he did a three-page spread which merely slagged us off. And I was driving the prick around!

So that appeared to be the end of Hardin and York. I can't recall doing anything after that day. I went straight into recording and party mode and Pete went into "sitting in" mode with all his jazz mates.

CHAPTER 5
LOVE IS ALL

It was around this time that I was to meet the first real love of my life. Whilst out clubbing one night in London, I saw the most stunning blonde girl I'd ever seen. As I was pretty forward in those days, I went over to her and introduced myself.

I was amazed that I got a response and I immediately sensed that this would be no ordinary situation. It was certainly one I personally had never experienced before. It transpired that she was on a week's visit from Los Angeles (oh God, I thought, not the obligatory American girlfriend) with her boyfriend Todd Rundgren, whom I didn't know from Charlie Chaplin. Anyway, he was in London producing Badfinger.

In spite of this unfortunate bit of news, I was undeterred and suggested we go somewhere a bit quieter on our own. Surprisingly, she agreed. By now it was 4 a.m. and London's night was drawing to a close. I was desperate that it didn't close for me, so we went to the only all-night coffee shop I knew, which was just next to the Hilton on Park Lane, and there we sat until daylight, completely besotted with each other.

We left the coffee shop and walked through Hyde Park for a while. It was freezing cold and people were starting to set off for work but I still didn't want it to end. Then I suppose it must have occurred to me that her boyfriend was probably getting a bit concerned, so I drove her back to Shawfield street, just off the Kings Road. We sat in the car for a while and there was all this great chemistry going on. There was absolutely nothing physical, it was all mental stuff. It must have been nearly 9 o'clock in the morning by now and I suggested a lunchtime drink ... in 4 hours' time!

I had my doubts about whether she would be there but, having found it impossible to sleep, I set off again at lunchtime for the Chelsea Drugstore, where we'd arranged to meet. She'd arrived before me, and there she was, even lovelier than I'd remembered. Marlene Pinckard's week in London turned into two and a half years.

After the Drugstore, we returned to Hyde Park again. It was one of the happiest days I'd ever had and I felt I had everything anyone could ever possibly want. That night she moved into my house in Dulwich. We were still not physical in any way, but I just had to have her around. Ray Fenwick came round that night and was amazed at the speed of things. He could sense that this was not an ordinary fling.

Marlene pleaded for an early night, which was fine, as Ray and I were writing some new material. In the early hours we were disturbed by someone walking around the house and were surprised to find Marlene sleepwalking. I'd never seen this before. It's a very weird experience and you don't know what to do about it. Well, we didn't, anyway. In fact, it all became so strange that it was frightening, like watching a ghost glide about the house, with me and Ray following in her wake. Eventually, she tucked herself back into bed, oblivious of anything untoward.

Our days back then consisted of deciding where to go, what to do and how much to spend, and then going out and doing it. I quite miss that aspect of life now!

Ray had a bit of work in Holland, so I thought we might as well go with him for a few days. Off we trooped to Amsterdam, where Marlene and I stayed at the Hilton and Ray stayed with his mates in town. It was here that our relationship was finally consummated. It was a blindingly happy time and all I can remember is fun. We were in Amsterdam for four days or so and I did a vocal for Ray. I can't remember what it was, since other things were on my mind.

One morning, I got a call from Pete saying that we'd been offered a three-week tour of Switzerland and did I fancy it? We (Marlene and I) thought, why not? We flew into Zurich, where we were booked into The Atlantis Hotel, which was total decadent luxury, set amidst snow-capped mountains. Nothing could have been planned better. The great thing was that, as Switzerland is so small, we stayed at the same hotel for the duration of the tour. Pete and I had never got on so well and we played better than ever to places that were crammed to the rafters. Our attitude was: Fuck the guy from Beat Instrumental!

I was on a serious high and just felt like travelling a bit with Marlene, so we then accepted a brief tour of Germany which turned into six weeks! We flew to Munich to be met by Carlo Enchelmaier, a very dear friend, sadly now dead. Carlo was the biggest (fat) man in Germany, and the fun we had in that period is unrepeatable. Carlo was so huge that he barely fitted in the car. Marlene found him a bowler hat, which he proudly wore, making him look exactly like Oliver Hardy. The only trouble was that he had to have the sunroof open at all times, as part of his head needed the extra space, especially with the bowler now a permanent fixture. Pete and I got into a mode where we could have just gone on and on, it was fantastic.

Eventually, we got back to London, where Marlene wanted to start doing something for herself. She very quickly got work as a model and I hated it. She suddenly got so busy and in the first few weeks she went to Greece, Italy and, the final blow, back to bloody Los Angeles. While she was in California, I set about re-decorating the house I'd bought for us to live in. Every night, Marlene would ring for a progress report. By now, I'd enlisted Ray Fenwick to help out and, frankly, we were making a total hash of it. In fact, we only painted the front door and half the hall. In the end, I went to Sandersons and they did it all for me. I then saw a sign in Knightsbridge in a carpet showroom, saying "Laid In A Day". That kind of thing appealed to me, so I went in to get laid! The trouble was that I had eighteen rooms to get laid in a day. As it turned out, it took them three days, but eventually it was all done and we finally had a home.

Marlene flew back from L.A. and we settled into life together. Below the house there was a huge cellar, so I put all the Hardin & York gear down there and Ray and I began to write songs in earnest. Marlene had this habit of saying "Catch You On The Rebop" at the end of all her telephone conversations. This became the title of one of the first songs to emerge from the cellar and would later be a Spencer Davis Group single. Cooking, however, was not one of Marlene's fortes and I don't think we ever ate at home. She did make one disastrous attempt at cooking breakfast, but I was so horrified at the result that I remember taking off my jacket and grinding it into the horrible burnt mess of eggs and bacon. Very rock and roll behaviour!

My brother John shared the house with us, though he pretty much lived in Japan, so was very rarely there. Once, he came over for a visit with his Japanese girlfriend Miki, who struck up an instant friendship with Marlene. John was quite horrified at Miki's eagerness to adapt to the western world. Marlene suggested that they should have a shopping trip together, so John and I gave them £100 each. That afternoon, when they returned, any Japanese culture had been erased from Miki's outward persona. Between the two of them, they'd spent all the money on make-up and she returned looking like an extra from "Madame Butterfly". John went completely mad at all of us, although personally, I thought that Marlene had done a pretty good makeover.

My mum and dad were totally opposed to my relationship with Marlene and made life very difficult for me, in fact impossible is more the word. In the end, they, especially my mother, were the cause of our eventual break-up and this is something for which I never forgave her until her dying day. One Sunday, they relented and invited us for Sunday lunch *en famille*. This was a total, total disaster. Miki, as her culture determined, had to have raw fish, whilst the rest of us wanted roast beef and all the other "'bits". My mum, of course, had not the slightest clue about Japanese cuisine, raw fish etc., and so presented Miki with a complete uncooked plaice with a tomato to add a bit of interest. Well, it was a raw fish, after all.

Miki smiled but ate nothing, while Marlene ate everything and anything that was to hand. After lunch, there was the washing up to do, so, as all good Japanese women do, Miki got up and began the task. Marlene, on the other hand, began to polish her nails and you could have cut the atmosphere with a chain saw. Then a tumultuous row erupted, in which I chased Marlene round the garden with every intention of killing her. There was an old fridge outside in the garden. An enormous surge of energy came over me and for some reason I picked the fridge up and ran after her with it. While all this chaos was going on, Miki, who thought the entire family had gone mad, hid behind a sofa. John just left, which was probably the best thing he could have done. Meanwhile, my mum, in total despair, took off her glasses and for some reason jumped up and down on them. It was an incredible scene and obviously our last invitation to Sunday lunch.

Back at home that night, relations were a little strained, to say the least. John was in his room playing Japanese music at ear splitting levels and I was in my room matching the level with European music. It was some days before anyone spoke.

I finally began recording my solo album for Decca, and Pete started his too. Ray and I had amassed a fair selection of songs and I had the intention of using different musicians. This was an entirely new concept for me and meant that I had to be disciplined, to which I was unaccustomed. With Pete, I could write a song and just play it in whatever way I wanted, but now I had total freedom, which was in theory a wonderful concept, but, to maintain our interest in the project, we constantly had to come up with interesting bits of "new" arrangement. For a while, we managed this, but we were starting to become a little complacent.

The first "Home Is Where You Find It" session was, as usual, at Olympic studios in Barnes, which was where I felt most comfortable and got on well with all the engineers. It's very important for me to be on good terms with the engineer, otherwise I tend to get self-conscious and even embarrassed when recording new songs.

So, for the first track, which was the title track, I used Miller Anderson on guitar with Gary Thain on bass and, I think, Pete on drums. It was a total disaster and none of the work was used. I then re-recorded it with Ray Fenwick and Tony Newman and the difference speaks for itself, well it speaks to me anyway, as I'm the only one who heard the first disastrous attempt at what I thought was a good song.

For most of the remaining tracks, I used Tony on drums and Dee Murray on bass. In fact, I recorded the entire album without bass and Dee came in for one night and overdubbed the whole thing in one bloody take. This was because I was, as usual, way over budget. Decca had allowed £5,000 and I went up to £15,000!

Ray and I wrote a couple of tracks for Pete's album, but they were never used. Pete had the problem of not being a writer and therefore of being at the mercy of people offering him stuff that wasn't necessarily very good.

We actually planned a British tour featuring Hardin & York, plus our separate bands. I personally couldn't be bothered to spend the time it required to rehearse a new band, so I decided to do it with just piano and Ray on acoustic guitar. This was, in fact, quite nice, as it was such a contrast to the power of eight Leslies and Pete's frantic drumming. Pete's "own band" never quite got organised and it only appeared on a few dates, during which Ian Paice played alongside Pete.

The tour culminated in a show at a venue called Bumpers, on the site of the old Lyons Corner House in Piccadilly. For this show, I had a full band of my own which consisted of Tony Newman, Dee Murray, Ray Fenwick and myself. We STILL hadn't rehearsed enough, but it was just about acceptable, although I would have preferred it to be note-perfect which, given time, it would have been.

The finale of the evening was to be a "jam" with Pete's band and mine, but we were joined by an uninvited guest in the shape of Keith Moon, who reduced our afternoon rehearsals to utter chaos. He had no intention of listening to what was going on, he just wanted to bash anything and everything as hard as he could to the detriment of all others. This all started off quite funny and jolly, as in "good old Keith, he's a lad!", but it very soon became extremely irritating. To this day, Pete speaks with annoyance about Keith's unwanted intrusion.

So, for the time being, we scrapped the three band idea and went back to the trusted H & Y formula. We recorded a live album at the Marquee in Soho, which is one of my favourites, as it features the best Hammond sound I personally ever got on record. It was monstrous. I've heard Traffic live albums which are basically just a "dither", and even The Nice live recordings were duff as far as the Hammond was concerned, although of course Keith Emerson's playing was always magnificent.

Anyway, it was at the Marquee that my "film career" was almost launched. After the show, there were two American guys wanting to get into the dressing room, which, as anyone who played the Marquee will know, was not much more than an elongated toilet! They were introduced to us, but I hadn't a clue who they were and was a bit offhand. Pete, however, obviously did know who they were, because he suddenly launched himself into bits of very strange, very phoney and very embarrassing "acting", which took me more than a little by surprise. One of the guys, it turned out, was Joseph Losey and the other was John Mackenzie, who went on to direct "The Long Good Friday" with Bob Hoskins, so they were both in fact pretty heavyweight characters. They disregarded Pete, who was left doing his King Lear bit in the corner, and asked me to come to a meeting at their offices in Bruton Street the following day. As ever, Smithers was on hand and mentally had planned all kinds of fantastic things for my future.

I duly arrived with Smithers at their office the following morning and they presented us with the plot. They wanted me to co-star with Carol White in a film entitled "Made". Amazingly, I had heard of Carol White, so it all seemed a pretty reasonable plan! They also wanted me to write music for the film. I was far more interested in this aspect, but Smithers by now was bedazzled by the Silver Screen and saw his own career launching itself into the world of starlets and all kinds of new sexual adventures, of which he was a keen enthusiast.

John Mackenzie gave me the script, which was actually pretty naff. It was about a pop star who had made it, thus the title. How very original! Smithers immediately negotiated a ridiculous fee just for the time I would be spending on the project, as he said it would conflict with my other vast money-making ventures. It went on for weeks. I learned bits of the script and rehearsed with Mackenzie. The whole concept of filming was a complete bore and it brought back memories of having being bored stiff doing a fragmentary appearance in "Here We Go Round The Mulberry Bush" some years earlier, along with the SDG.

This film, Mackenzie explained, would probably take up to six months, and possibly even a year, to complete. Pete was pretty devastated, not only by not being the "chosen one", but also by the fact that we wouldn't be able to operate as a band for a very long time and, since he had no income from writing, he would be pretty well buggered. Firstly, I went into IBC studios in Portland Place to record the title track and a couple of other songs. I think they were amazed at the speed with which the songs were created. I'd love to hear a tape of those sessions, but it was one of the few times I didn't take a rough mix home with me.

The film-makers loved the songs and soon we were rolling along, drawing a very nice salary each week while they groomed me for what Smithers was convinced would be eventual stardom. As for acting, I personally thought I was great! I think, well, I now know, that Mackenzie had reservations, but he did persevere. They filmed bits of me and Carol, and the first criticism levelled at me was that I was too pretty. In an attempt to solve this problem, Mackenzie instructed me to grow a beard. So we had now reached the point where I was being paid to sit at home growing a fucking beard! The beard took around three weeks before it began to look healthy, so once again I set off with Smithers to the production office. Mackenzie took one look and said that I now looked too much like Jesus Christ!

To be honest, during my beard growing period, I didn't only sit around. Instead, I rehearsed with my band at Joe Brown's house in Essex, where Tony, Dee and Ray showed great interest in my transition to the screen. I have to say that I was actually very confused, as I wasn't sure at this point what I wanted to be or even who I was any more. The acting bit held no interest but I fancied getting to grips with all that went with it. These guys wasted money like I'd never seen. I'd by now recorded virtually an album's worth of titles for the film and they'd paid for everything. And they weren't little demos, they were proper orchestral jobs and I'd even brought in the arranger I'd used on "Home Is Where You Find It", Phil Denys, to do the arrangements.

It had to end. Smithers got the call from Mackenzie, saying they had found a guy who looked far more rugged than me and that they were going to plump for Roy Harper. It was true that Harper looked more rugged, but to me he looked more like a tramp! I would never have been prepared to change my appearance that drastically.

I later saw the film (which bombed, by the way) and it was so bad that I was relieved that I hadn't done it. It would have dashed any future hopes of a film career, just as it did for Harper. (Harper did a soundtrack too, but I personally thought it was awful and very cheap-sounding). Mackenzie remained intent on using me for some other production or other and a series of lunch meetings continued for months. He eventually suggested that I should go to Drama School, which I refused to do, and so the relationship gradually dwindled. There would be more later. But if things had turned out differently at that stage, who knows what might have happened?

Meanwhile, rehearsals continued with my band, though they had really now deteriorated into just having fun. Tony Newman, the drummer, was by far the worst culprit in our escapades. Tony had played with Sounds Incorporated and had toured with The Beatles on their Shea Stadium trip, and had some pretty astounding tales from that time, which I definitely can't go into.

Tony was married to a girl called Margo, who together with Vicki Brown (Joe Brown's wife), formed a vocal backing duo. Tony led Margo an awful time of it and she eventually had a nervous breakdown, which I assumed was a direct result of his lunatic behaviour. I understand that Tony is "straight" now, but I can remember feeling that he was actually dangerously eccentric. On occasion, he would become sort of possessed. His eyes would glass over and you never knew quite what would happen next. In an echo of the Johnny Cash song, he had a son, now also a drummer, whom he constantly introduced as Susan. To this day, I still don't know the boy's actual name, but I do know that he dated Jon Lord's daughter, so I guess the "Susan" tag didn't derange him too badly.

Tony would teach the poor child the wrong words for everything. For example, the Cat was the Door and the Door was the Cat, and so forth. On one occasion Tony was called into his son's school, as the boy had been acting strangely. After a weekend at home, he'd returned to school and, on being asked how he'd spent the weekend, he told his teacher that he'd been to Africa. In actual fact, Tony had taken him to Richmond Park and told him that it was Africa.

Tony was also proud of his record collection, but treated it with contempt. He would play tracks to me and Ray and, if we didn't look impressed, he would take the arm of the record player and scratch it all over the album, before hurling it across the room like a frisbee.

Another of his passions was DIY, but of course he was completely inept, causing Margo total despair. They had wanted to utilise the space under the stairs, so Tony set to with his hammer. The entire staircase collapsed and had to be shored up with a fridge. I don't think any of his DIY attempts were ever repaired, and it's certain that none of them were ever a success.

Golf was an interest of of his, but it wasn't long before he was banned from his local golf course. In order to take revenge, he planted bombs in several of the holes that were in plain view from his bedroom. He had an impressive array of pyrotechnics left over from his days with Jeff Beck, which he let off by remote control as golfers neared the final putt.

Tony's other habit was shouting. He had a convertible Jaguar, in which would just drive round central London at night ... shouting!

Probably the summit of his madness came when he was the drummer in the orchestra for the Eurovision Song Contest. That particular year it was held in Ireland, to where Tony travelled with Margo and Vicki, who were a part of the backing singers. There was a huge dinner organised for all contestants, hosted by the Mayor and various other dignitaries. During the course of the dinner, Tony, who for some reason had brought along fishing lines and lots of hooks, decided to "hook" the entire restaurant together. He simply flitted from table to table, patting people on the back and planting the hooks in their clothing. By mid-lunch, the whole restaurant was "linked", so that the first person to go to the loo set the whole place into total chaos.

Then there was a trip to Cannes for the Film Festival, where he once again was the drummer at a gala do, with Margo and Vicki as backing singers. Tony employed the garb of an Elvis impersonator from beginning to end of the trip. Present at this gala was Dustin Hoffman, who for some reason took a liking to Tony and decided that they would be mates for the whole event. When Hoffman had to make a speech prior to receiving some award, he insisted that Tony be on the podium with him, Tony still dressed in what remained of his Elvis kit. They both got as drunk as sacks and were, from what I've heard, a disgrace throughout.

On arriving back in the UK, Vicki and Margo were waiting in the baggage hall at Heathrow, having lost Tony. The carousel started to turn and the first bags slipped out, followed by Tony, sitting naked on the conveyor belt. No wonder Margo reacted badly.

Surprisingly, Tony went on to play in David Bowie's band, along with Herbie Flowers, another maniac. Tony was by now so uncontrollable that screens had to be put up around him, because his comic actions were taking the limelight away from his boss.

After one particularly lively band rehearsal, we adjourned to a nearby pub, which happened to be Joe Brown's local. It was Christmas time, so we were all feeling a little festive, though not quite as festive as Tony. First, he bought dozens of bags of crisps, set light to them one by one and hurled them round the bar. Having been told to behave, Tony decided to set light to himself. He was wearing one of those old blue reefer jackets and he lit it. The barman thought, as we all did, okay, that's funny, but he'll put it out in a minute. But he didn't. Soon, there were flames lapping up his arms, while he stood there sipping his pint regardless. The flames were now getting out of hand and even if Tony didn't care, the barman did, leaping out with a soda syphon to "put him out". We were all given life-long bans from Joe's favourite pub, and Joe was not at all impressed.

My father had a key to our house. He said that this was because we were away so much that he needed to keep an eye on things, but he had an annoying habit of coming in every morning and calling out, "Are you all up yet?". He would never acknowledge the fact that I was actually living with Marlene and this was his undiplomatic way of noting that there were actually two people in the house. He'd developed an extreme hatred for Marlene by now and chose to pretend that she wasn't there, although she quite clearly was.

On one occasion, we were having new phones installed and Marlene, prone to over-sleeping, was not up when the engineers arrived. Unfortunately, they called at my father's house first, so he naturally marched round with them to supervise the fitting of OUR phones. Hearing the "Are you all up?" signal from below, I hurriedly bundled Marlene into the wardrobe, stupidly keeping up the pretence that she wasn't there. The engineers and my father entered the bedroom, condemning Marlene to spend some considerable time hiding in the wardrobe. The wardrobe frontage consisted of louvre doors and one of the engineers said they could do a much neater job if they put the cabling inside the wardrobe. Marlene must have been busting for a cigarette, as I noticed smoke starting to waft through the doors. Not surprisingly, I replied that I wasn't bothered about the wires showing.

Finally, with the house virtually finished, there was little to do each day but play music and watch T.V. We were not, at that time, "pub people", so socially, our evenings were restricted to the company of John Fisher and N. Twai. Twai would show up without fail every day we were in England. These were pre-video days, so I bought a 16mm projector and a huge screen and we rented films most nights. If we did go out, it was never until around midnight or later, by which time we were finally alone together, as Twai and Fisher had gone home. Mostly, we went to Tramps. This club had a neat system whereby you could pay the account with a cheque but you didn't actually need to have your cheque book with you, simply wrote out your own cheque on a piece of paper. I've never encountered that system before or since, but it seemed to work.

One day, we decided to undertake a trip to Cannes. The departure was pretty depressing stuff, because, as Marlene was not deemed to exist, there were no goodbyes from anyone to anyone. We took the Rolls and managed to get lost before reaching Lewisham. However, we finally made it to Dover (of course missing the ferry we had intended to take), and successfully crossed the channel.

Being a romantic couple, we decided to stop in Paris for the night. I couldn't find the hotel we planned to stay in but we accidentally stumbled across the Inter-Continental, where I was most flattered when the manager said, "Bonsoir Monsieur Hardin, welcome back to Paris, and may I say how much I enjoyed your last concert here". Blimey! He even sent some champagne up to the suite, but, as I had other things on my mind, it remained unopened. I was in one of my happiest moods.

The following lunchtime, as we set off on the long journey South, it was an idyllic day. Most days did seem idyllic then. Paris to Cannes is a fair old trot, but it seemed to pass in no time and we immediately installed ourselves in The Martinez. We had wanted to stay at The Carlton but decided against it when we noted that was full of "dead people".

Each morning, we drove to various spots like Monte Carlo or Antibes and had very long lunches together, completely oblivious to the presence of anyone else. "How or why should this ever end?" I thought, and with this in mind, I suggested to Marlene that we should get married, to which she replied yes.

We stayed in France for about ten days, at which point we were rudely interrupted by a concert for me and Pete in England. We delayed our departure until the very last minute, and as a result, we had to make the journey non-stop. Just outside Cannes, a massive lorry crashed into the back of us and the boot of the Rolls was much reduced in size. Marlene had a very impressive ruck with the lorry driver and a small crowd gathered to witness her rantings, which resulted in the guy admitting liability (very rare in France), allowing us to continue our journey in a slightly less impressive vehicle. The drive took eighteen hours, during which we only managed to keep each other awake by chewing gum and smoking fags! When we arrived home, Marlene went straight to bed, while I went off to the concert in a rather fragile state.

The main thing on my mind was marriage, but then Marlene did a really dumb thing. One morning, I got a call from my very annoyed accountant, asking me if I'd read the Daily Express that morning. I attempted to purchase one from the local newsstand but Marlene, totally uncharacteristically, had got up early and bought every copy of the Express, so I wouldn't get to read it.

It turned out that she'd done an interview for the William Hickey column which, accompanied by a large and pretty sexy photograph of her, went on to say how rich and happy we both were and that I was buying her a Rolls Royce at the same time as renovating a Victorian mansion prior to our forthcoming marriage.

Thanks, Marlene. A tax inquiry was immediately launched and I was presented with all kinds of problems. Then, out of the blue, I got a call from John Mackenzie. He claimed to have more film ideas, so I went with Marlene to have another "filmy" lunch at Overtons in St. James's. Marlene took on a different identity that day, much like Pete had in the dressing room of the Marquee, and I think John was pretty captivated by her. She wore the most outrageous outfit (what there was of it). Considering that it was a restaurant favoured by MPs and Sotheby's directors, I was amazed they even let us in. I think the *Maître D'* was so overwhelmed that he just didn't know how to handle the situation.

I was dressed in a sober suit but Marlene had jeans shorts that were so short that most of her arse was in full view. As for the top bit ... well, all you could really make out was boobs. Looking back, I'm surprised I was willing to go with her like that in the first place, but she did look good and we did, against all odds, get in. Later that night, we went to the Playboy Club, where we got badly treated by the bunny girls because they were very much "out-bunnied" by the fearless Marlene, who loved the competition (or lack of it).

Strangely enough, the next drama was when Playboy magazine contacted us (I wondered whether Mackenzie might have had a hand in this) to invite her to be a centrefold. I didn't see those pictures until some time later when I was in Hamburg. Suddenly, there she was, staring at me from a huge poster in a window on the Reeperbahn. I was horrified and very upset. It all then got even more out of hand when Hugh Hefner invited her to stay at the Playboy mansion in California. It all went to her head, culminating in her mother doing a centrefold as well!

Unsurprisingly, I was pissed off at getting calls detailing the fucking splendours of the Hefner Mansion in Hollywood. All I wanted was for our domestic bliss to continue, but it had been rudely interrupted. So, temporarily, Marlene was in L.A, where she even bought her own apartment. I thought "fuck this" and flew to L.A in order to sort matters out. Unfortunately, on arriving in L.A., I discovered that Marlene had had the same idea and flown to London. In L.A., I had dinner with Marlene's mother (clothed). We talked about the proposed marriage and she was all for it, so at least I'd cleared one hurdle.

A month later, I went back to California. This time, we had arranged things properly and Marlene was actually there. Her apartment was in the Hollywood Hills and I think she thought that she was now bigger than Jean Shrimpton, or whoever was big at the time. I felt myself starting to hate ALL models, who you'd see prancing round London with their fucking portfolios.

Marlene now wanted to make things work between us and had the first week in L.A. planned out. She'd decided to learn to cook ... a little. Me, I was a trifle pissed off to see fucking bunnies adorning everything, the duvet covers, the pillows and even the coffee cups. So I went all out to be a prat. I phoned all my musician mates and went out on a drunken rampage.

After the third night, I got home and she wouldn't let me in, saying that she'd taken all my things round to Spencer's house. Getting a taxi in Los Angeles is not easy at the best of times, let alone at 2 a.m. After an hour, I gave in and pressed Marlene's entryphone and asked her at least to call Spencer and get him to come and collect me, which he eventually did. I didn't want to stay at his house, so I ended up in the Chateau Marmont Hotel, where I stayed for the rest of the week, hardly seeing a soul, except for one visit to Santa Monica beach with a still irate Marlene.

I was at an all time low when I finally flew back to London, reluctantly coming to terms with the fact that I had messed everything up, based on pure jealousy. Weeks went past and I got more and more morose, until, one morning, my mum got a letter from Marlene. It was not a nice letter. It explained that she blamed them (my parents) for everything that had gone wrong. It was a very well constructed letter which hit the nail right on the head. I could only agree that it was my parents who had ruined my happiness.

There were two more attempts at reconciliation, once when Marlene flew to London to come and see me. She was very tearful and wanted the marriage to go ahead. As we sat in what was to be our home, my mother arrived, giving me very negative looks and creating a horrible atmosphere all over again. Marlene wanted me to go and set up home in L.A with her, but, like a complete fool, I declined. I made one last futile trip to California, but couldn't feel comfortable because of my parents' attitude back home. It was a horrible, horrible time and was to be one of the last times I ever saw her.

We were driving around aimlessly and Marlene's car overheated. We pulled into a garage and, while the guy was fixing it, I called a taxi for her. I kissed her goodbye and she was gone, taking a fair chunk of me with her. I probably haven't really done this episode justice, but if it is possible to be broken-hearted, then I was. In condensing such a vital part of my life into a few lines, I have to wonder in what ways things would have been different if I had had more strength of character. There were to follow a stream of relationships, some nice, some not so nice, but by comparison they were all only filling in time.

I now had the house I had bought with my brother. In an attempt at helping me, he suggested that I should go into the antiques business with him. He could see the mental depths to which I had sunk after the break-up with Marlene, and he had tried very hard to talk my parents round, but to no avail. This was a challenge, in that I had no interest in antiques whatsoever, the only knowledge I had being the fact that I had been brought up amongst my father's antiques.

Our first business trip was to New York. It was horrible being there and not playing. We stayed at plush places, of course, but for me there was no appeal without the anticipation of a show. We attended boring auctions and bought various things and sold various things, but I didn't really care what happened. John could see that I was bored out of my mind and so he "set me up" with the daughter of one of his Sotheby's associates. This turned out to be a farcical move, as I actually vaguely knew her via the infamous Bebe Buell, friend of Marlene and in fact friend of most everyone who was involved in Rock and Roll. Still, she was a nice girl, in fact she was a very nice girl, and we went to dinner. Of course the conversation was totally non antique-related and immediately turned to music. She asked me why I didn't play any more, which at that point was what I'd decided.

By the end of the evening, I was convinced that my only future was in fact that of a musician, so thank you, Clare from Connecticut! During the evening, I'd thought how nice she was and what a cut above the women one tends to meet on the road. Unfortunately, when we returned to my hotel for the inevitable night time "closer", she informed me that she had the clap! Bugger. Of course, it was very decent of her to have told me, but you just can't win, can you?

My brother John spent much of his time in Japan and, during the period when I was helping him out, we dealt mostly in Japanese art, screens, paintings and Chinese Ming and Tang stuff, very expensive but in general, as far as I was concerned, horrible. John freighted paintings to the UK and they were stored at our house, where we had set up a gallery. Sometimes, we freighted the most incredible things from Japan. On one occasion, we even shipped over the wooden remains of a junk, with a view to using the wood as the basis for a pagoda in the garden. Of course, this never came to fruition and the wood just rotted into an even worse state than it had been in when it was delivered. In the end, we just buried it. So, if you now live at 52, Champion Hill, London, S.E.5., you have a junk in your garden! Go and have a look.

We also shipped over huge chairs carved from tree trunks and, as they came air freight, the cost was horrendous. Most of these now lie rotting in our various houses and I've even got a few remnants here in France. Yes, I shipped a rotting lump of wood to France!

Somehow or other, we were making vast amounts of money, which was stored in cash in a walk-in safe in the house. There were dollars, yen, francs, marks and sterling, literally in piles. We never had an accurate idea of exactly how much was there and any time either of us went out, we would simply take a handful and stuff it in our pockets.

This must all sound horribly decadent. Well, all right, it was horribly decadent, but we had some great times. I bought a Bentley Continental "from the safe" and, thinking that John might like one as well, I rang the garage and ordered a second one. John didn't like the colour, so he bought another, with the result that at one point we had three Bentley Continentals, plus my trusty white Rolls in the drive.

I then bought a huge bronze "actual size" figure of a horse's head, which we sold at a vast profit to a guy in New York on one of our visits. The art world was even crazier than the music world. Various deals would come up and I would speculate in John's absence. On one occasion, I was offered a Lowry painting for £20,000 , which may sound like a lot, but it was kind of insignificant at the time. I went to see the guy, Martin Summers of the Lefevre Gallery in Bruton Street London, who had this particular Lowry in the window. I actually liked the Lowry style and was tempted, until Martin showed me piles and piles of further Lowrys in his basement. He explained that it wouldn't be prudent to release them all at once, as the price would plummet. I discussed the purchase with my father, who strongly advised me against it. A couple of days after I had declined the purchase, Lowry died and the price soared into the six figure bracket! Yes, more sound financial advice from home.

I did a few more tours with Pete but my heart was no longer in it, or anything come to that. I deteriorated in many ways. For a start, I made stupid decisions about everything. I sold my share in the house to my brother and bought a bloody big boat and an Aston Martin, thinking they would cheer me up. They didn't. Again, this was down to my parents. I'd found a lovely house near Tunbridge Wells but they didn't want me living so far away, for goodness sake! I mean, L.A. I could sort of understand, but Tunbridge Wells!

Despite being a fully grown adult, I swayed to their way once again. The joke about the boat was that I hardly ever got to go on the thing, as my father was constantly at St. Catherine's Docks fiddling about with the engines and my visits were "inconvenient". My various decisions were definitely not financially sound, but they all suited their ends in maintaining "happy families"'. I started to drink far too much and only managed to maintain a reasonably safe level due to with my involvement with Roger Glover with work on "The Butterfly Ball".

Roger and I became very close during the making of that album, which came about after I was offered the job to write the music for a Lee Marvin western film. I'd known Roger for some time and, as he'd recently been unceremoniously dumped from Deep Purple and was suddenly at a loss as to what to do, we just seemed to hang around a lot together. Roger and I used to have "spending contests". We vied with each other as to who could spend the most on whatever. It was a close run race until he went out and bought a huge house in Farnham Royal, which gave him a temporary lead.

As to my western film music, basically it just fell apart and I didn't do it! Roger, however, had his side of the deal arranged and "Butterfly Ball", financed by the Purple office, went ahead. It was Roger who came up with the idea of using other artists to sing the songs. which is a concept that I went on to use for three "Wizards Convention" albums.

Roger is not what I'd call a "writer" in the true sense of the word, but he is certainly a very creative guy, especially when it comes to production. He is absolutely tireless, almost to the point of tedium. He'll spend hours and hours on a mix, only to scrap it the following day. I used to like to be at the studio as much as possible during the recording of "Butterfly Ball", as my input creatively was substantial.

There was one huge hit song to emerge from the album. Its title is "Love Is All", and over the years I've sometimes been saddened to hear Roger speaking on the radio about "his song". Some 27 years later, when I joined Deep Purple for their now legendary concerts at the Albert Hall with The Royal Philharmonic, Roger did thank me for "Love Is All"! It would be nice, however, if he shared his appreciation with the rest of the world, because immediately after the Albert Hall shows, when Purple embarked on a world tour performing the same show, including "Love Is All", it reverted back to being "his song". Still, that's life and I bear Roger no grudge.

Roger and I were both at peak creativity during "Butterfly Ball" and we decided to form a band together with Henry Spinnetti, the drummer. We got as far as contracts being drawn up and a three album deal with Purple records was sort of agreed. We'd recorded the Beatles' "Strawberry Fields Forever", with Roger on drums, and it nearly made the charts, having received great reviews and massive airplay. We spent weeks recording that song and it turned into one of the most expensive singles ever made. Roger was never happy with the mix, but that wasn't unusual, because he's never completely satisfied. If I hadn't exerted discipline, we'd still be mixing the "Butterfly Ball" album today.

Poor Roger was beset by marriage problems and was by now starting to go on bad bouts of heavy drinking. Sometimes, he'd drive into London and check into a hotel for a few days, where he'd just drink himself into oblivion on gin, of all drinks. In between, the recording continued on "Butterfly Ball" and, as I was no angel as far as alcohol was concerned, the production seemed to go on for ages and ages. We recorded all of it at Ian Gillan's studio, Kingsway Recorders, and only left there to do orchestral overdubs at Air Studios. The problem was that Kingsway was in the basement of a building which held the Civil Aviation Office above, and we could only record from 6 pm onwards because our noise factor was disrupting the everyday business above. As a result, our days disappeared, we worked all night and slept all day and for about a year I didn't see daylight. Roger said to me recently that he could only remember the sunrise during all of that production because that was all we saw prior to getting to bed.

It was a great time, however, and we had good fun with all the guest musicians and their various tales. Musicians are a breed apart and I still find it very hard, if not impossible, to fit into normal society. I am only completely relaxed when I'm around musicians or people who can at least relate to music.

The engineer on "Butterfly Ball" was Louie Austin, a keen advocate of dope. Every evening, he'd roll the hugest joint, which he and Roger would smoke at the end of the session. There were, of course, also lots of little ones throughout the session. The size of these joints became ludicrous, reaching the height of silliness when Louie joined three empty toilet roll holders together, Blue Peter-style, and stuffed them with dope and a bit of cigarette tobacco. I always thought that Louie needed heavy shoes to keep him on the floor. Some nights, he used to virtually go into orbit.

When faced with a project such as the initial stages of "Butterfly Ball", the first hurdle to overcome is, who will you be writing this stuff with? In this case, it was Roger Glover, so there was no problem. But to co-write anything with anyone, you have to overcome your embarrassment, particularly in the lyric department. Every song has a different meaning to each writer. For example, I assume, in fact I'm sure that Roger doesn't have the same feelings about "Love Is All" as I do.

When I write with Ray Fenwick, we kind of bare our souls so that each of us knows exactly what the other is trying to say, both melodically and lyrically. The same kind of situation arose with Roger, in that we just sort of "clicked". In fact, it's a bloody shame we never went on to write more songs.

When we recorded "Love Is All", we had a key element in the diminutive shape of Ronnie James Dio, whose work I was familiar with from his recordings with a band called ELF. They were thus known because they were all very small. Ronnie was the nicest of guys and was blessed with a voice to die for.

We recorded the song initially with Ronnie taking a verse, then me and finally Roger. The rhythm section was just me and Roger, with Roger on drums. I thought it sounded great and would have been happy to have just tidied it up and put it out. However, Roger "multi-mix" Glover was convinced that we could do better, and indeed he was right.

Ronnie Dio came into the studio one morning, after we'd completely re-done the backing track, using Mike Giles, Mo Foster and Ray Fenwick. Ronnie sang it once ... great, then he sang it again ... greater.......... then he sang it again ... unbeatable! But no, to my amazement Roger said, "He can do it better!" Well blow me, he did, and what you now hear is what he did that morning, one straight take with no drop-ins. At the end, he ad-libbed a line which went, "When your back's to the wall and you're starting to fall ..." (tearful stuff), which just exactly fitted in with my life at the time, and from that moment on Ronnie was my hero.

We had another nice melodic song called "Homeward", which was completely different from the "rocky" vocal style of "Love Is All", but Ronnie sang it like an angel. It was beautiful (more tears). My only disappointment came when Roger and I had written a song entitled "Little Chalk Blue" and Ronnie, who would have been ideal to sing it, was suddenly no longer available. There were internal boring Purple politics, of which I then knew nothing, but do now.

Ronnie had been rehearsing with Ritchie Blackmore's Rainbow and was forbidden to work elsewhere. This ridiculous farce continued right up until we did the Albert Hall show, and all Roger would tell me was that Ronnie couldn't do it. I couldn't believe it, and I'm sure Roger must have had the deepest of frustration in not telling me exactly what was going on.

So Ronnie was replaced by John Lawton, who had originated from the Les Humphries Singers in Germany and went on to be the singer with Uriah Heep. Roger flew to Hamburg to audition him. John had a great voice, but, having not been involved with the concept, had no option than to sing the songs as ... well, just songs. John added his vocal to "Little Chalk Blue", but, as he did so, there were some awful interruptions from what I can only assume was his then wife (I hope it's not still his wife ... whoops).

Roger and I obviously played tracks very loud in the control room, but even at these levels you could still hear this fucking "twitter" going on. It became very annoying. Anyone who is familiar with a studio playback will know that the level has a tendency to "creep up", and people intent on talking begin to talk louder and louder.

Roger and I were become more and more irate, but were too courteous (if can you believe that!) to say anything. Nonetheless, furious glances were being exchanged. Finally, Roger snapped and, with one quick flick of the wrist, pulled the master volume fader down to zero, leaving the manic Ms. Lawton shouting at the top of her voice like a rampant banshee amidst a silent room. Problem solved!

So we did the Royal Albert Hall without Ronnie. "Homeward" was sung by, of all people, Twiggy. Now I have nothing against Twiggy, in fact she was a very nice person. She was managed by a streetwise guy called Justin de Villeneuve (real name Frank!), who was fine as well. Twiggy could probably wear clothes to sell or whatever, but a singer she most certainly was not. Anyone who has a bootleg copy of the concert will notice that we had to play the intro twice just for her to get her bearings, which she never quite got anyway. Still, women seem to think that she had a nice dress on.

Some thirty years later, Ronnie Dio did finally get to sing "Love Is All" at the RAH. This was on the occasion of the anniversary of Deep Purple's Music for Group and Orchestra concert with the LSO, during which each member of Purple did their own little section. When it came to Roger's spot, he naturally picked "Love Is All". Ronnie said to me, "Sorry I'm so late!"

One amazing thing about "Butterfly Ball" was the amount of parties that seemed to be arranged. There was even a party before we started recording it. This event was held at Biba's, the trendy shop on Kensington High Street, where Purple had taken over the rooftop restaurant for the day. This was the first time I'd met Alan Aldridge, who was the guy who did all the illustrations for the book and had had a massive spread in the Sunday Times Colour Supplement, featuring every drawing from every chapter. He was a very fine artist, and also very unassuming.

Roger, Alan and I sat drinking tea in this most pretentious of settings. I've never seen Roger looking more awkward. It was just hysterical. Everyone sort of took on a "creative genius" air. We really should have all had enormous cigarette holders and paisley dressing gowns to complete the farce of it all.

But at this stage, the only creative genius amongst us was Alan Aldridge, because all that existed were his drawings and the prospect of a musical concept album. Alan told me a very funny story relating to "Butterfly Ball". He'd been invited to Kensington Palace by Princess Margaret, for dinner, no less. He assumed, of course, that it would be a standard "royalty" do, with cold food and canapes. However, he arrived to find that he was the only guest. Apparently they sat at a vast banqueting table, with Princess Margaret at one end and Alan at the other, sort of a quarter of a mile apart.

I can only assume that they must have shouted at each other during the numerous courses, after which the staff were dismissed and Princess Margaret asked Alan if he'd like to dance! Can you just imagine it, a dining room the size of Wembley Stadium and the two of them waltzing around it. Alan said to me, "The only thing I could think of in this situation of total lunacy was ... If only my mum could see me now!"

During the making of the album, there were interim parties and "finish of album" parties. I went to one end of album party at Roger's house in Farnham. He'd stocked up with a gargantuan amount of booze, the intention being that, as the guests arrived, there would be the finished product playing in the background. However, the more booze that was drunk, the more to the foreground it came. Roger, being more than a little inebriated, took to his bed, leaving everyone downstairs. Judy, his then wife, came over to me and said, "I think you'd better go and see Rog, he's not at all happy with the album".

So off I went upstairs to the "master bedroom", which in itself was a bit of a shock. There lay Roger, tears flooding down his cheeks, with his head buried deep in the biggest array of pillows and cushions I have ever seen in my life. Judy had taken a liking to Liberty's in Regent Street and had clearly bought up their entire stock of lavish bedding. There was no consoling Roger, but then there never is when one is in that state. The next day, he seemed to have got over it and made no mention of it. The party raged on, as parties do when the booze is free and the host is absent, while I went home, completely happy with the album.

Doing "Butterfly Ball" was a bit like going back to school, which I loved. Eventually, when it was finished, we had a massive hit on the continent. I remember when I took the first rough mix of "Love Is All" in to John Craig, the publisher, he said to me, "That song will never leave you alone", and I'm happy to say that he was absolutely right ... it didn't. It was a hit again in France some 25 years later, reaching No. 2 in the national charts and at the same time being used for a huge television advertising campaign. Sacha Distel had a Number One with it in France and, shortly afterwards, so did we. There have since been many cover versions, some good, some not so good and one fucking awful. Oh yeah, and Cliff Richard did it, although his version was a bit, if not a lot ... no, it was totally "muzak".

When Cliff's version was launched, I was despatched to the Shepherds

Bush Empire as the writer representative and was supposed to be nice to Cliff. I found this very hard, as he didn't smoke or drink and seemingly had no sense of humour. When I got to Shepherds Bush, I remember being disappointed on hearing his limp version. Cliff asked me who the singer on our version was and how we had managed to get the sound we got on our recording. Really, the only answer was that we played with a great deal of bollocks and Ronnie Dio, the singer, was basically just fucking great. But you just couldn't convey this to a God Botherer, well at least I couldn't, so our brief encounter was not a success. I didn't particularly care, though, as I was not a Cliff Richard fan and never had been.

John Craig then sent me on another strange mission, to meet with Tony Hatch and Jackie Trent, who were about to record the song and were considering recording some others of mine. I thought, "What a fucking compliment, my songs may be recorded by the guy who wrote the theme music for "Crossroads". Still, I duly went to meet them and found them to be very strange "old showbizzy" people. They were on another planet, yet thought they were so creative and clever. The guy may well have made a great deal of money but you've only got to listen to his recordings to realise that creative he ain't ... well, not to me anyway. Jackie Trent sang with enormous false gusto and it just made me cringe. I was not the best person to send to any of these meetings and I didn't go to any more.

It was now decided that we should perform a "Butterfly Ball" concert at The Royal Albert Hall with the entire cast, which was a pretty formidable task even by today's standards. First, there had been a three-minute cartoon made to complement the song, which I personally wasn't too sure about. I suppose that it's stood the test of time, but I'd have still preferred a clip of us doing it as a band.

Then again, I have to say that it's been the cartoon, certainly in France, that's given the music its longevity. Anyway, the clip, which was eventually to have been continued into an entire feature film, had proved so expensive that the cheapest solution was to film the concert and put the clip at the end! The cast for the concert included Vincent Price, Twiggy, Ian Gillan, Roger Glover, David Coverdale, Glenn Hughes, John Gustavson, Al Green, Ray Fenwick, Mo Foster, Les Binks, Lisa Strike, Barry St. John, Tony Ashton, Jon Lord, Eddie Jobson, Mickey Lee Soule, plus a few more I can't even remember (oh, and me).

We rehearsed solidly for three weeks and eventually, when we played the concert, it was a complete sell-out. Roger went through terrible anguish over this show, fearing that it would be half empty. The concert was filmed and Roger and I went along to a viewing. It was great, so we spent some time mixing the soundtrack before the film went away for editing. It's a shame it ever came back. The producer had cut whole chunks out of the footage and replaced us all with people dressed up in the most crappy animal costumes you could imagine. Tony Klinger was the name of the man responsible for this catastrophe. I would imagine he's now a wedding photographer or something.

We went to the première at the Odeon in Chelsea, unaware of the celluloid horror that was about to offend our eyes. Then the lights dimmed and the film started. The first half of the first song was fine, but then the first prat in a cheap mouse uniform jumped into view and from then on it became a complete embarrassment. Klinger was not around at the end, and the party afterwards was a fairly quiet affair which must have attracted only the most desperate of liggers, hanging on for the free drinks and shitty bits of "little food" piled in mountainous heaps on their plates as they fought for a corner of the room to devour it.

For me, a serious amount of "clubbing" now began, as, for the time being, there was little going on musically. Still, there was an awful lot of fun to be had. The Speakeasy was by far the most popular haunt amongst musicians, with Keith Moon being the star of many a night there. He used to come to the club with a theme in mind. One night, he'd be an American policeman and on other occasions, he'd be Adolf Hitler. He even developed a liking for the Noel Coward way of life and, in fact, his speaking voice altered noticeably and stayed strange until his demise.

Keith lived in Chertsey and sometimes travelled into central London in a milk float, the back of which he'd had converted into a sort of front room. He'd sit in the back with his hair slicked back, bearing a huge cigarette holder and dressed in a paisley dressing gown. Most nights, however, he came down in a horrible Pink Rolls Royce with a TV aerial on the roof. I have to confess that I had a TV put in the back of mine as well, but it was hopeless, the reception was awful.

I remember one night when Keith and Tony Ashton were standing at the Speakeasy bar and it was decided they would have a pint of brandy ... each! The idea was that they had to drink it down in one, which indeed they both did. After the deed was done, Tony remained much the same, but Keith sort of folded up onto the floor. Tony, meanwhile, ordered a lager and continued as per normal (well, his normal!)

Keith's Hitler ventures were pretty amusing. He was generally accompanied by Viv Stanshall, also dressed as a Nazi general. Taking tactlessness to previously unscaled heights, they used to go on a quest for bagels in Golders Green! And this was during the day. By night, they reached such enormous levels of alcohol consumption that anything was possible, and I was always amazed at their staying power. Tony Newman was another frequent visitor to the Speakeasy, and one evening he and Pete York (a rare visitor to the club) were standing at the bar talking drums, Pete enthusiastically, Newman drunk.

Suddenly, Newman's trousers were round his ankles and, while looking intently at Pete, he set light to his balls. There were actually flames, and it must have caused him some considerable pain, but his facial expression didn't flinch and he was eventually "put out" by a friendly soul with a soda syphon. Pete didn't quite know how to handle the situation and pretended that it wasn't actually happening, which I suppose was a pretty cool response.

Obviously, this sort of madness could not continue indefinitely, and it was my brother John who suggested that we should re-form the Spencer Davis Group, partly, I think, because he fancied a trip to California. I wasn't too sure how things would be with Spencer, as the split had been a little fraught, but he was fine and seemed to welcome the idea of a "hello again" tour. We hatched the plot at Spencer's house in Laurel Canyon, but there was still a lot of bitterness between Spencer and Ray, especially on Spencer's side. Spencer felt that he had been completely manipulated by Ray, which was in a way true, although, to this day, Ray fails to understand why there was/is a problem.

After Pete and I had left, it had really become Ray's band and Spencer's name had become merely the vehicle for Ray's projects. But I finally talked Spencer into having Ray back in the band. I couldn't have faced looking for another guitarist. I found them difficult to play with anyway, especially after all the freedom I had had with Pete. Ray and I complemented each other perfectly, plus he knew all the material and he and I could, and did, write an awful lot more songs.

CHAPTER 6
A NIGHT AT THE WALDORF

I had a lot of freedom in the Mark III version of the Spencer Davis Group. It was I, not Ian Smithers, who negotiated our first deal with Phonogram via Mike Hurst, who thought he would be the producer. Charlie McCracken was recruited on bass and his audition, for want of a better word, took place at The Speakeasy. I was there with Roger Glover and we began a conversation with Charlie, who was seriously drunk. Eventually, he slid to the floor, so Roger and I decided there and then that he was our man. Each member of the band received a pretty healthy advance which was not subject to any deductions for recording costs, so we were all in pretty good financial shape before we even started.

Ian Smithers, who had managed Hardin and York, was appointed as our manager. Rightly or wrongly, I've always liked Ian (who turned up in my life out of the blue many years later) and I'm sure he did what he thought was best for us. Spencer and Pete still complain about his cock-ups but he had a pretty monumental task getting us co-ordinated. Spencer and Pete were, I suppose, far more organised than Charlie McCracken, while Ray and I were off doing our own writing and stuff and had no time for the everyday running of things. We just let him get on with it, so I don't feel we can knock the guy that much.

Smithers resided in a flat in Clare Court, just off Russell Square in London. This flat rarely, if ever, saw the light of day, as the curtains were permanently drawn and the lighting was so dim you could hardly manoeuvre yourself round the furniture. It was, in fact, an extension to his "clubbing" activities. He would leave the London hotspots at dawn and continue his debauchery throughout the day, with a constant flow of women popping in and out and Smithers himself fuelled by an uninterrupted supply of Amyl Nitrate, champagne, wine and cognac. He never operated within normal business hours and had his own personal time system, which didn't seem to fit in with any other in the entire working world.

On occasion, he would withdraw to his apartment for three to four-day sexual and alcoholic binges and no-one would be able to make contact with him. This was not the most satisfactory of positions for us, as a band, to be in (though doubtless Smithers was in a number of satisfactory positions). Because his face never actually came into direct contact with daylight, his eyes were reduced to slits and he covered them up as best he could with heavily tinted glasses. He was also as blind as a bat. Smithers indeed lived in some style. His first apartment was in Belgravia, but how he afforded it was quite beyond us. He would always be dressed from head to toe in Gucci, at a time when that was an eminently fashionable thing to do. He would always drink the best champagne, the best brandy and, when he did eat, which was rare, he'd eat at the finest restaurants.

There was an older guy of Russian origin occasionally in tow, who Smithers always introduced as "my farver". This was a very odd situation indeed. Farver lived in Belgrave Square at a prime address and out-drank and out-womanised even Smithers. At weekends, the pair of them would retreat to the country near Henley, where Farver had a lovely home, which was eventually bought by Jon Lord.

I suppose I was the closest to Smithers, as together we'd go on frequent forays into London's clubland any time we weren't working. We had some memorable nights out. We'd start off at The Speakeasy, which I suspect was owned by the Kray Twins, as the guy on the door was Laurie O'Leary, who worked full time for the twins. I'd met Laurie way before my SDG days, as he was good friends with Freddie Foreman and had major connections within the music biz. He sort of ran a studio off the Tottenham Court Road, which went under the facade of The Clarke Brothers, an old time American dance duo. I suspect that, behind the front, this was another Kray venture. Jimi Hendrix recorded "Hey Joe" there and the SDG recorded segments of "Here We Go Round The Mulberry Bush" there also.

After The Speakeasy, we'd adjourn to Tramp, the new ultra trendy and hard-to-get-into club of the moment. Anyone who was familiar with Tramp will know that, after you'd negotiated yourself past the main desk, there was a fair old length of staircase (much like the Speakeasy), leading into the bowels of the earth. Smithers, by now well-lubricated after his time at the Speakeasy, often lost his footing and simply fell down the entire flight of stairs, landing at the bottom, which was a sort of lounge area. As this was as dark as his own apartment, it felt a bit like home from home for him. Without fail, he'd always say "Good evening, everyone!" as he lay on the floor.

The cast list at Tramp was always impressive. It was run by a guy called Johnny Gold, whose guests were the likes of Michael Caine, Laurence Harvey, Joan Collins, George Best, and of course Keith Moon, who, having also done the same rounds as ourselves, would change his persona yet again for the up-market surroundings of Tramp. Mind you, it was so dark in there it was probably a craphouse in the morning.

Apart from Keith Moon, Smithers knew none of these people, but got around that by saying things like "Hi, Michael" (Caine), "catch you later!" and "Oh, hi Laurence, must get together soon", after which he'd breeze past them, leaving them bemused and baffled. Invariably, though, he would then send them over a drink, which confused them even further, as they raised their glasses to a total stranger.

In the restaurant area of Tramp, they had novel ways of serving the simplest of food and charging the most outrageous prices for it. They did Bangers and Mash, probably for about thirty quid a time, and the presentation was just a huge sausage with two balls of mashed potato at the end, giving the dish the appearance of a set of male genitals. But this was okay because, as I mentioned before, they'd let you write a cheque on a scrap of paper, had you forgotten your cheque book, and it always seemed to be honoured by the bank.

It was soon to be Smithers' birthday and I felt that, as a band (SDG), we should present him with a gift that was totally obscure. I toyed with the idea of a huge stuffed gorilla which was outside a shop on Tottenham Court Road, but sadly it was always chained up at night, with a metal grille pulled across the entrance.

Then the ideal gift presented itself. When doing "Top Of The Pops", we found in the props room a number of Daleks, and even the telephone box which was used for the Dr. Who series. Half in jest, I told the roadies to nick a Dalek and, if possible, the phone box also. They did! Everything went according to plan and we were now the proud owners of one Dalek and one Dr. Who telephone box.

The following morning, the daily papers had banner headlines proclaiming the loss of said items. I gave it a few days for things to settle down. but they didn't. Eventually, it was clear that a Dalek and a phone box were too hot a property to hold onto. Nonetheless, we (Geoff and John Fisher) were daily driving the Dalek up and down a public road without a problem. It was a pretty basic affair, just a seat inside and pedals, so you drove it like a push bike.

The other problem that presented itself was that the Dalek, and certainly the phone box, didn't fit into the lift leading to Smithers' flat. There were emergency staircases, but we couldn't get them up there either. Eventually, I asked the roadies to dump the phone box on Wimbledon Common and to hold on to the Dalek for a while. The following day, the headlines read: "DR. WHO'S PHONE BOX FOUND ON WIMBLEDON COMMON".

By this time, my dad was becoming worried, fearing I'd committed a serious crime (although I was a non-starter compared to Freddie Foreman). It was agreed that my brother would confess that he had found the Dalek in the front garden of the home I owned with him. Obviously I had to keep out of the way, having appeared on TOTP literally days before. The unfortunate side was that my dad actually resembled Dr. Who and brother John was not far short of the same appearance either. Anyway, the Dalek was surrendered to the nearest police station and the "Blue Peter" team was sent to film the handing-over ceremony. Smithers never did get his birthday gift, although my intentions had been good, but my father and brother both got to appear on "Blue Peter".

The re-formed SDG started recording straight away at Advision Studios in Gosfield Street, London and after the first night we found we had our first single completed. It was "Catch You On The Rebop". Having something of the feel of the old Winwood-era hits, it was certainly an "airplay hit", which was well-promoted and brought the band back into focus. We found it very easy to set up tours, but we made the mistake once more of doing an American tour first and not maximizing on any impact the single had generated in the UK.

Ian Smithers gave us no concrete details of the American tour, other than where it started and where it finished. It would have been nice, for example, to know what fees we would be getting! So we all arrived in Toronto to rehearse for a few days and it was then that he announced that the money was in fact pretty crap and that we'd be touring with Focus. Aside from the fact that we had a problem with the money, we didn't really want to be on a bill with a band which, with respect, was stylistically poles apart from our music.

This became a problem as the tour went along, because there were some states which loved Focus and others which loved us, so we kept having to switch round the billing. I personally never cared who went on first or last and I don't think the other band members did either, so we were pretty easy-going in that direction and were quite happy to let the prima donnas (Focus were nice guys and we had no problem with them, but there were others!) get themselves worked up into a frenzy about fuck all.

Meanwhile, I'd made another dreadful error by importing a girlfriend from Sydney to Toronto for what I thought was a few days. Unfortunately, she thought it was for a few months! I hadn't seen her for a year and when she arrived at my hotel room door she was nothing at all like I'd remembered her. Her weight had ballooned and she was kind of busting out of an outfit which obviously dated from the last time I'd seen her. It was a horribly embarrassing moment and I confess that I immediately arranged for her to fly on to London the next morning. She was far from impressed, but I had learnt a lesson: never look back!

After a night off, the tour finally began. The first night was pretty fraught, with each band trying to outdo the other, though after the show we soon found common ground with the Dutchmen, who took their drinking just as seriously as we did. A routine was soon established whereby the bass player with Focus, whose name, I think, was Bert, would set up a bar in his hotel room every evening, where he would act as "mine host".

New York was to become a highlight of the tour, certainly socially! I have noticed during the writing of this book that there has been strangely little mention of musical content, more of the general madness of the time. Well, that's the way it was. The second he arrived, Charlie disappeared straight off to the Irish sector for darts and vast amounts of Guinness. Ian Smithers took control of social activities and, within an hour or so, had located one of the biggest and (as it turned out) best, parties in New York, namely the "Decadence Ball", which was to be held at The Waldorf Astoria, the biggest and probably the best hotel in the city.

The Waldorf party was, without doubt, a serious highlight in anyone's social calendar. The music came courtesy of The New York Dolls, a band which, despite its huge influence on future musical generations, was frighteningly awful but mercifully un-noticed, certainly by us.

Getting into the party involved a fair degree of strategy as it was, although we didn't know at the time, the ultimate "do" and a very trendy New York event, for which we might have been considered a bit too old-fashioned. Spencer, the only "name" amongst us, was ejected from every possible entrance to the Waldorf whilst Charlie, by this time extremely merry, seemed to breeze in and out of everywhere completely unchallenged. It was therefore a good decision that I chose to accompany Charlie the entire evening.

The whole ballroom area, and indeed most of the reception and ground floor, was littered with the most outrageous selection of people I have ever seen, before or since. There were men and women, some part naked, some totally naked apart from various colours of paint spray, and people in states of fancy dress reaching the most incredible extremes, far beyond the fantasies of even my most decadent imagination. Smithers, always one to milk any situation, had gone to every effort to become an extrovert New York partygoer. He had rented a Mad Hatter's outfit (tame stuff for Smithers, a pretty decadent character in his own right, though even he was not prepared for this onslaught of debauchery) for the evening. The rest of us didn't bother, other than Charlie, who wore his Tam O'Shanter, but then again he wore this for most of his more liquid excursions.

Unsure as to precisely where the hub of the party was, Charlie and I got into a lift. I'm still not quite sure why we did this, but the result was that we arrived at an upper floor, to be greeted by the startled-looking bride and groom at a massive wedding reception in a palatial suite. By this time, Charlie was having the greatest of difficulty in walking, let alone communicating with the happy couple's family, who were totally baffled as to who and what we were but felt obliged to offer us every hospitality and therefore ushered us to the buffet and then, foolishly, to the bar. Charlie downed several impressive measures of Jack Daniels, toasting everyone and anyone in a confusing mixture of Irish and gibberish. Not wishing to appear excessively greedy, he pocketed what remained of the bottle and, leaving the wedding party totally confused, we set off towards the lift again, but not before Charlie had offered the bride what he considered to be some sympathetic and practical advice on how she should handle her "nuptials".

Our departure proved to be even more embarrassing. Charlie was by now completely legless, and with me acting as his sole means of support, we burst into the lift to be confronted by a group of elderly women with blue hair and varying coloured poodles. Upon seeing us, they scattered to the extremities of the lift, hiding their poodles' eyes and leaving Charlie centre stage.

Charlie's legs were like rubber (he literally used to become "rubberised" when pissed) and I struggled to hold him upright as he blew the most amazing raspberries in a circular motion, while the women attempted to shield their multi-coloured pets, and themselves, from the alcoholic spray.

Eventually, we arrived at the lower level, where the party seemed to be in full swing. Charlie burst from the lift to be confronted by a very gay Julius Caesar and some even gayer looking centurions. The main centurion, clearly sensing trouble, drew his rubber sword and dangled it threateningly at Charlie and myself. He was also wearing an impressive false nose which Charlie made an immediate grab for. Unfortunately he made contact successfully and drew the nose back some two or three feet. The gay centurion feared the worst. Pete York had appeared and he and I clung onto the nose in the vain hope that what was about to happen wouldn't - but it did! The huge rubber nose smacked the centurion squarely between the eyes, which then began to water profusely.

Charlie was quite beside himself with joy, unaware of the other centurions clutching their rubber swords and ready to spring to their friend's defence. Charlie immediately adopted, or tried to adopt, a boxing stance and, as he flailed about in completely the wrong defensive directions, several huge security guys came from nowhere to defuse the affray and we were off yet again down the corridors of chaos.

Manoeuvring through the maze of the Waldorf, we came across Smithers, who already had half his Mad Hatter's outfit missing or lost, complaining about the possibility of losing his deposit in the morning. More raspberries were blown, and off we went in search of the next encounter.

Pete York approached from yet another direction. He had, since our last sighting of him, struck up what appeared to be a bit of a relationship with a girl he introduced as Victoria Viper, who was lit up from head to toe in Christmas tree lights, at the same time as which, dry ice billowed from the heels of her shoes. This was no normal party.

By now it must have been around 3 a.m. and, as we re-assembled (still without Spencer) in the main ballroom, Todd Rundgren was about to perform. He was introduced by a the DJ Howard Stern, who informed us that we were to hear a performance by a Mr Ted Rutkin. Ted played solo piano and looked as if he wished he wasn't there. By now, I was starting to wish I wasn't.

Smithers now burst into the ballroom, wearing all that remained of his Mad Hatter's outfit: a cane and his underpants. He was still unattached and, like all of us, totally confused as to the likely gender of anyone at the "do", so he began to conduct some fairly detailed anatomical research into identifying male from female. Finally, he asked what he thought was a woman to dance with him and they then proceeded to flail about on the heaving dance floor. At the end of the dance, the floor cleared to reveal a solitary Smithers, cane still in hand and underpants almost intact, lying prostrate on the floor.

By now, even the hardcore New York party set were beginning to wilt a little, but not Charlie, who seemed to be constantly getting second winds. Waiters were still ferrying drinks by the trayful, many destined for Charlie, who playfully decided to trip one of them up. The guy balanced and twirled around with the stacked tray for what seemed like a quite some time until, defeated, he threw the lot to the floor and walked off.

At this point, I spotted a stunning-looking woman wearing a spray-on leopardskin outfit. She was chained to another girl. Her ensemble was so fantastic that she deserved another look, and I was amazed to recognise her as the daughter of the Sotheby's director, whom I'd met earlier, on the visit to New York with my brother. You may remember that she was the one who had an unmentionable sexually-transmitted disease. Anyway, she looked so frighteningly good that at first I didn't even dare to speak to her. Eventually, though, I did, and our friendship was re-kindled.

I can't really say what time it was at this point, only that Charlie was intent on carrying on the madness at whatever cost. As the Waldorf affair was starting to wane in Charlie's opinion, he suggested we (he and I) go on to a club called "Your Grandfather's Moustache" in Greenwich Village. We found our way out of the Waldorf and, while hailing a cab, spotted a forlorn Spencer, who was still trying to get in!

A very brave cab driver finally picked us up, but Charlie thought he knew the best route to the club and decided it would be best if he were to sit up front with the driver. Now NY taxis in the 70's had very small partitions and Charlie was very large, so, needless to say, he got stuck halfway, with the driver and me undecided as to whether to pull him backwards or forwards. Eventually, we got him through one way or the other. I can't remember if he ended up in the front or the back, but the guy eventually dropped us off, me standing and Charlie lying on the pavement.

Actually getting into the club was a pretty tricky business. I was the only relatively sober one and, as the metal grill of the club door slid open, the door man was faced with me looking in and Charlie on the pavement looking up at him. He was confronted with a bit of a dilemma but, as it was so late, he decided to let us in. There was a Dixieland jazz band playing and Charlie insisted on a front row seat, which we got, I assume because, as we'd be so close to the band, any noise we'd make would be drowned by the brass section.

There were huge bowls of peanuts on every table and Charlie began taking peanuts from our bowl and throwing them into the bowl of the trombone. He started off with maybe one or two nuts but eventually there were handfuls flying into the poor guy's instrument, which by now had pretty well seized up. This caused great hilarity for Charlie, but considerable embarrassment for me. A few handfuls of peanuts later, we were thrown out. But still Charlie was not done, suggesting we go back to the Waldorf, which of course we did. By now, it was pretty well daylight and the foyer was littered with bodies in all kinds of states. And still the New York Dolls played on.

We met up with Spencer, who by this time had finally gained admission. He'd missed all the chaos and was eating breakfast in the coffee shop. Charlie was in breakfast mood, so ordered a very large Tequila sunrise which temporarily saw him off. Pete had slipped back to our hotel with Victoria Viper, all lit up and smoke still billowing from her shoes.

When Ray Fenwick turned up, he and I were left with the job of manouevring Charlie through the early morning NY traffic. What a bloody night it had been, and, to make matters worse, we were playing that night at Madison Square Gardens with Genesis. This was not an ideal situation.

We ordered another taxi from the Waldorf, only for the cab driver to point at our hotel, which was in fact directly opposite. So we carried Charlie through the traffic into the relative safety of our own hotel. We were on the 25th or something floor, and carrying a dead weight, still managing to blow raspberries, across a lobby, past reception and into a lift, was no mean feat. We got him in, after a fashion, but when we arrived at our level, couldn't get him out.

The lift doors had opened and his torso was outside the lift, while his legs remained in. So the doors opened, then closed, stopped at Charlie's legs and opened again. This went on for some time, until finally bells started to ring and lights were flashing and a guy was shouting through the intercom. Next thing, the hotel bloody security team were upon us. They actually found our predicament amusing and were pretty decent about the whole thing, proceeding to help me and Ray carry Charlie to his room where, after one final raspberry, he collapsed.

The tour continued for weeks, with Charlie maintaining a steady liquid consumption across America, and Smithers becoming engaged to a total stranger. Of course nothing was ever to become of this liason, other than that she travelled with Smithers the length and breadth of America, all expenses down to the band.

While I was in New York, John phoned me to say that my father had had a slight stroke. I wanted to fly home immediately, but John instead flew to New York . He assured me that our father was okay and suggested that we have a night out on the town. Together with Pete York, we went to see a show called "Good Evening", starring Peter Cook and Dudley Moore. I spoke to John in the afternoon to ask how many seats to book, to which he responded "fifty-six". I really should have known better. Anyway, we had plenty of room that night.

After that, I developed the same daft habit as John of ordering silly amounts of anything. I was in a hamburger place in London one night and there was a quiet couple making real pigs of themselves on chocolate milk shakes. For some reason, I sent them over a further 98! The waiter never got to deliver the full 98 and the couple were not at all impressed by my humour. When the waiter asked me why I'd ordered 98, I pointed out that it was funnier than 100.

There was another time in Amsterdam, again on an SDG jaunt, when we visited a bar at god knows what time in the morning, accompanied by our roadie/minder Bazz, or Barrington Marsh-Ward as he preferred to be called. Now at this stage of the evening, he couldn't look after himself, let alone us, but he had a reputation to maintain as an Olympic Liverpudlian drinker. I decided to put him to the test, firstly by saying, "I bet you couldn't drink one of those huge beers down in one". Of course, he did! But I couldn't let it rest at that, saying "I bet that's all you can drink though." He boasted that he could drink for as long as I would pay. This was a fatal challenge for me to accept.

I ordered a dozen more beers and a stunned barman watched in awe as Baz worked his way along the line. About midway through, he hesitated and looked at the barman, who had worked his way along with Bazz from behind the bar, looking on in amazement. There was a bit of rumbling from within Bazz, followed by a few belches, before he threw the whole lot up all over the barman. Liverpool 0, Hardin 1.

On one of our German tours, we decided to charter a plane, as it seemed an economical idea, ho ho! I think we were flying to Stuttgart, to where the normal flight time is around one hour or so. In fact, it took us five. The pilot was clueless and got lost on the return flight.

We'd flown in for a festival and took a Canadian DJ with us, whose first name, I think, was Mike. We set off from Biggin Hill, which was quite an inspiration with its wartime connections. Earlier in the morning, our roadie Bazz had loaded the plane with booze, but when we assembled at Biggin Hill, the light aircraft turned out to be an awful lot lighter than we had envisaged. The worst thing was that the pilot had a business just down the road from where I lived ... a junk shop! I even remember his name, which was Bobby Denwood. Never fly Denwood Airlines!

So off we set. At first, it seemed okay, as the first of a few bottles were opened, but it soon became so turbulent that any movement within the plane was impossible. The DJ sat behind me, rigid with fear, Bazz spent much of the time throwing up and the rest of us just waited for the bang.

We did arrive in Stuttgart and we did do the show, by which time, of course, it was dark. As we assembled on the tarmac, there was lots of very heated shouting from airport staff and it transpired that we hadn't paid for landing permission, though by now we had boarded our "private jet" and intended to set off for home. An official stood in front of the plane waving his arms, to which Ian Smithers suggested we should take off anyway and just run him over. Even the pilot/junk dealer drew the line at this, and eventually Smithers alighted and gave the guy the cash, after which we were finally cleared for take-off. Then the same horrors started as during the first flight. We crossed the Channel, or at least some stretch of water, and the "pilot" announced that he was lost.

Smithers, by now pissed, joined him in the cockpit and relayed progress back to us. Having taken off from Biggin Hill, where all our cars were, we assumed we would return to Biggin Hill, but this was not to be the case. The DJ by now was beside himself with both fear and nausea and sadly also beside me as he turned a deep shade of green. Bazz continued to chuck up vast amounts of German beer in the back. Communications were apparently going on with air traffic control, although for all we knew it could have been Denwood's mum.

Our "pilot" decided that it would be best if he lowered height and looked for recognisable landmarks. He started off with pubs, but when he couldn't recognise any of those, we ended up looking at fucking road signs. This was not by now a pleasant experience. Finally, he got through to what must have been air traffic control and was told that he was so far off course there was no other option but to land at Gatwick. Unfortunately, he had even less of a clue about getting to Gatwick than getting to Biggin Hill, plus it was a busy airport. At Biggin Hill there's not that much you can hit, but at Gatwick ...

We did finally arrive and our chartering days were over. But first, we had to hire yet more transport to get us back to Biggin Hill. I think I got home at around 5 a.m. Had I taken a regular and cheaper flight, I would have been home around 10 pm.

Eventually, our enthusiasm began to wane yet again. The band had not turned out to be the huge money-making machine we'd anticipated, largely due to, I can only presume, bad management. Smithers had been having too much fun and not spending nearly enough time at his desk. We were all to blame, because we had allowed fun to take precedence over everything. The band now once again split into two definite camps, myself and Pete and Spencer and Ray, Ray being still determined to continue undeterred with some form of Spencer Davis Group no matter what. Poor Charlie sat baffled in the middle, unclear as to which camp would offer him the best deal.

One morning, I was at home in the house I had bought with my brother John when the phone rang. The caller wanted to speak to Spencer Davis, who was staying with us at the time. My brother had absolutely no time for any of my musical friends or aquaintances, so passed the phone straight to me. The voice at the other end said, "Is Spencer there?" As he wasn't, I offered to take a message. The caller said, "Sorry I missed him, but could you ask him to come to Abbey Road this evening?"

It was only then that it occurred to me that I was talking to the man himself, Paul McCartney. Spencer and I set off for Abbey Road that evening, where McCartney was putting the finishing touches to his album "Red Rose Speedway". As we arrived, he was finishing the vocal on "My Love". The ending he sang when I was there was very like Little Richard and sounded absolutely great. For some reason, he plumped for a mellower version in the end.

There was a fair old crew assembled in the control room for the playback, including Denny Laine, who was later to become a very good friend, Noel Redding, whom I'd met on various occasions through the years, and Wings guitarist Henry McCulloch, who was to become our host for the rest of the evening. Henry was a "down to earth" guy, to say the least, and was already tired of the endless "takes" needed to attain perfection, so suggested that we should we go for a quiet drink round the corner. I personally would have preferred to have listened to the album over and over again and I could also see the delight in Spencer's face as every track began. But instead, we went to the bloody pub.

Henry was under the influence of whatever he had managed to take that evening and lunged to the bar, where he searched his pockets for money. As he did so, he came across a huge bag of grass, which he plonked on the bar while continuing his search for some cash. The pub was full of extremely sensible St. John's Woodites, out for a civilised drink. Spencer and I found ourselves what we thought was a discreet and reasonably private table, only to be joined by a horrible little poodle belonging to one of the customers. Henry kicked the poor dog up the arse and sent it flying several feet into the air, following which we were asked to leave.

Next stop was the Speakeasy, by which time even I'd had enough and left Henry and Spencer to carry on on their own, as they were quite clearly bent on self-destruction. Indeed, Henry went on to break his leg that same night.

Another meeting was arranged at the McCartney household in Cavendish Avenue, the idea being that we would get Paul to produce the forthcoming Spencer Davis Group album. Paul had a studio set up in Scotland but seemed apprehensive about us lot arriving and generally disrupting his family life.

Paul's house in London, although crammed with every imaginable trapping of success, was also, to say the least, a bit untidy. It was a friendly enough place, if you managed to avoid the huge piles of shit dropped by his sheepdog Martha. The household seemed to be run by a Scottish housekeeper whose name, I think, was Mary. The drinking at Paul's house was very modest in comparison to our normal nights out. All that was

With my father's Buick. Could this be the source of my life-long interest in big cars?

My parents' wedding

The Hardings

June, 1960: And so it was to be ...

A Wild Uncertainty

*L - R: My mother and Maureen Foreman, with my grandmother
and Freddie Foreman.*

SDG Mark 2

*The première of "Here We Go Round
The Mulberry Bush"*

Eddie in action.

Supported by Black Sabbath!

Cars

Marlene

SDG Mark 3

One of our Daleks is missing!

Herne Place: My home ... then

... and some well-known characters

Zak: Future star session drummer in "formative years".

Wedding bells

Wedding band:
Me, Keith Emerson and Rick Wakeman

Liz: My inspiration

Emma: Music is in her blood
(and she is in my heart)

Tony Ashton: What was that again?   *Good grief! The chief Griswold.*

Back at the Star Club

York, Pike, Hardin

SDG 2004

Eddie and Spencer, Germany, 2003

Aaaaaah!

available was a couple of bottles of light ale and a bottle of whiskey. I had both light ales and Spencer and Paul drank straight from the whiskey bottle.

Paul had just recorded the music for "Live And Let Die", and I asked if I could hear it. He obviously didn't want to share his music, because he implausibly claimed not to own a record player. During our discussions, Paul McCartney was pretty non-committal as to whether he'd be willing to produce us or not, so we departed none the wiser. When we didn't hear back from him, we gave up hope, which was a mistake, because some months later, he rang me up and said, "I'll do it". By then, it was sadly too late.

Pete and I once again began touring spasmodically and with no real purpose, this time with Charlie McCracken on bass guitar. To be fair, it was a very tight band, but as far as I was concerned, any sense of ambition had waned. We did the obligatory tours of Germany and even recorded another album for RCA, which was given the inspired title "Hardin & York with Charlie McCracken", but there was no direction. We would literally just play anywhere we were asked to, as long as the price was right and it suited our routing. I remember playing in one ludicrously small club for three consecutive days for no apparent reason, other than that it was fun.

I can't remember where in Germany it was, but it was a nice little town and the club was owned by a raving lunatic, who was bent not only on self- destruction but also the destruction of all those around him. Night after night, he would ply us with champagne on and off the stage. He spent considerable time building pyramids of champagne, whereby he poured the liquid into the top glass and it flowed into however many he had been foolish enough to assemble beneath it. This guy created massive pyramids, most of which he dropped on the way to either the stage or our table, but, undaunted, he would immediately start the process all over again, until eventually a gallon or two arrived intact. At the end of each night, he would lead a huge sing-song of some awful tune and we would all join in! This was, of course, all totally pointless and in no way any kind of career move, but nevertheless great fun.

CHAPTER 7
WIZARD'S CONVENTION

In many ways, the "Wizard's Convention" album marked a dramatic change in my life, not only musically but in every imaginable way.

I had arranged to go to Midem with John Craig, with whom I'd had a close working relationship during Butterfly Ball and we'd become firm friends. The original plan was to try to "place" a solo album I'd completed, called "You Can't Teach An Old Dog New Tricks", and at the same time try to set up a deal to record a new Hardin & York album with various guests.

We set off for Cannes at around 7.30 in the morning, assembling at Dover for breakfast. I chose to drive with Merv, my chauffeur and general "do it all" in his Jaguar XJ6. We stopped overnight in Dijon, where we met up with Tony Edwards and other members of the Deep Purple management team. A friend of a friend of a friend, by the name of "Amorous Irma", cadged a lift with us. That night, in Dijon, she lived up to her reputation and I was to be "accompanied" by her for the rest of my stay in Cannes.

The Purple Records team had chartered a yacht, the Conquest, owned by the comedian Norman Wisdom. Yachts may well sound grand, but unless they are hundreds of feet long, they are never comfortable. After the first night, most of the cabins were empty and everyone had moved ashore into the comforts of a hotel, using the yacht purely for daily meetings to impress whoever they wanted to impress.

I stayed with Merv at a hotel just outside Cannes, the Mas D'Artigny in St Paul de Vence. I still stay there today and it's great. Once settled, we just set about attending as many parties as we could manage. At one of these fateful parties, aboard yet another chartered yacht, I met a woman who was to lead to my eventual near financial, emotional, and every other kind of ruin.

I ploughed headlong into an affair with her, for all the wrong reasons, and it staggered on for eight years or so. Most of this I would prefer to forget, apart from the fact that it produced my dear daughter Emma, with whom my wife and I still have the closest of bonds. Other than that, I prefer to erase this entire period from my memory. Nevertheless, in the coming pages, suffice it to say that, like a ghost, she will be there in the background.

John Craig and I set about trying to arrange a deal for my completed solo album. We had a meeting with Jonathan King, who pronounced that it was too good and therefore stood no chance. He told us that people wanted crap, like the stuff he recorded. Well, he said it! Eventually, my album was placed with a Canadian company called Attic, which was pretty aptly named, because that's exactly where they put it!

It was during a meeting with Ariola that I, much to John's surprise, announced that I was planning to record some songs featuring various guest singers, Steve Winwood being one of them. Steve, of course, had no idea of this, and neither did anyone else. John immediately joined in with enthusiasm for this non-existent project and a sort of deal was established there and then.

Purple Records funded the recordings, during which I recorded songs as and when they were written and arranged for the vocals to be added at a later date. Steve Winwood, no one will be surprised to hear, never did appear, but the whole concept nevertheless snowballed so that, with every name I managed to get, I had the ammunition to inspire others to appear.

Kingsway Recorders, where we did the recordings, was a studio owned by Ian Gillan, otherwise known as Garth Rockett. I really liked Ian, though always found it hard to ascertain whether he actually liked me in return. He has one of the greatest Rock voices of all time and, outside of Purple, he can certainly give Little Richard a good run for his money.

One night, when he had recorded a track of which he was justifiably proud, there were little bits of vocals which he played me over and over again. I can relate to this, because when you get a rock vocal just right (I'm talking about rock in the sense of Little Richard or the good days of Elvis Presley) you want to hear it over and over. In my case, you feel it isn't really you, that you're getting close to the guys who did it in the first place. It's a great feeling.

Ian had a fantastic outlook on life. Like me, he felt that life was for exploiting to the full. I always saw the music business as a stepping stone to greater things, as I'm sure Ian did. Ian left Deep Purple with what I assume must have been a considerable fortune and set about, not spending it, but making it work. His first venture was to buy a monstrous sized house near Henley, which he converted into a hotel and called "The Springs". It's still there to this day, though sadly under new management.

It was a magnificent building, with panelled rooms and vast open fireplaces in which you could stand! Ian immediately installed a guitar shaped swimming pool, which is probably not the kind of thing I'd have gone for personally, and fax and telex facilities in each and every room, despite the fact that no one knew what a fax was. There was also a helipad, which was supposed to have been for the use of flash newlyweds. During the conversion of the house to a hotel, there would be many excursions from Kingsway Recorders down to Henley for a night of mayhem.

The Springs was finally opened for business and I heard that indeed one guest arrived to check in. There were no staff around to take the booking, so the guy helped himself to a key and went to bed for the night. In the morning, there were still no staff around for him to settle his bill, so he left.

One of Ian's other bizarre inventions, detailed in his own book, was a motorised garden fork, which was designed to take the strain out of gardening. The only design fault was that no one, apart from perhaps Geoff Capes, could actually lift the thing.

Ian was obsessed with inventions, as can be seen in his own book. He started a motorbike factory, a venture which he saw as knocking Yamaha and any other major motorbike company, even Harley Davidson, right out of the game. The motorbike factory began to function in Bristol, where a showroom was also added, but to my knowledge only one bike was ever completed.

One of Ian's finest inventions was a car that ran on nothing, i.e no petrol, oil or any other form of propulsion. He once showed me the vehicle, which was parked in the car park in the bowels of Kingsway Recorders. I was intrigued to see what was beneath the bonnet, but Ian explained that it was in fact a sealed unit and far too secret to be revealed. I have to say I admire Ian for his spirit and endurance and he remains today one of the finest rock singers around, with Purple still going from strength to strength. I'd just bought a new Aston Martin, and Ian, upon seeing it, said, "Amazing, what you can get from the Matchbox series these days."

I even had a pre-conceived idea for the cover of "Wizard's Convention", something along the lines of "A Hard Day's Night", with rolls of informal shots of all the musicians and singers involved. With this in mind, I employed an up-and-coming socialite photographer called Corinthia West, (I'm starting to sound like Pete York now), who subsequently filmed the goings-on from beginning to end for a fee of £250.

Corinthia was an Amazonian woman who favoured the most outrageous clothes (what little there was of them). She naturally proved to be a major distraction on many occasions, as she contorted herself into the most unusual positions to get the shots she was after. She was so sensual and frighteningly striking in appearance that not even the die-hard lecherous musicians working on the project dared make an approach.

I started work with an engineer called Louie Austin, with whom I'd worked on The Butterfly Ball. The first track I recorded was "Swanks And

Swells", for which I used the entire Chris Barber Jazz and Blues Band, with Tony Ashton on vocals and Pete York on drums. Things had become more than a little tetchy between Pete and myself. He'd joined The Chris Barber Band full time. As I'd used the band on the album, I naturally wanted a picture of Pete on the cover. John Craig, as a matter of courtesy, rang him for clearance and Pete asked him for £1000 for permission to use the photo! This was totally out of the question. No one else had asked for a penny for the use of their photograph ... They didn't dare, with Corinthia behind the lens. Fuck me, it was an honour for her to look at you at all, even if only from behind a camera!

Anyway, I was, as ever, way over budget and being constantly helped out by Jimi Boyks at RCA in Germany. The upshot of the episode was that Pete's picture never appeared on the cover. The Barber Band was not Louie's cup of tea at all and, fearing that this would be the direction the album would take, he opted to go off and engineer for The Sweet instead. I felt badly let down and hated the idea of working on such an intimate project with a total stranger. However, Louie suggested that I should try out John Acock. After a subdued start, each of us testing each other and me trying to record things I thought he'd like, we began to find common ground and this turned out to be the beginning of a thirty year working relationship!

"Swanks And Swells" was a twenties style song which, after frightening the life out of Louie Austin, turned out to be a popular track. I co-wrote the lyrics, under duress, with a guy called Selwyn Roberts, who was a close friend of Robin Nedwell, one of the actors from the then popular "Doctor" series on TV. To be fair, Selwyn came up with the title but I'd have preferred it if he'd left it at that and, in the end, I don't think we actually did use many of his lyrics. When I first played the backing track to Tony Ashton, he was even more confused than usual, but after a bottle of whiskey, he threw himself into the song and came up with a unique performance. So, having completed the first track, a drunk Ashton and I embarked on a night at The Zanzibar club to celebrate.

The Zanzibar was situated just around the corner from Kingsway Recorders studio which was, as the name suggests, in Kingsway. Tony Ashton was by now far from well and spent the evening in deep conversation with a complete stranger, who eventually fell asleep. I decided that the nightclub scene was not going to contribute to a fruitful working situation, so after that night, John and I spent most of our break times in the Newton Arms, a pub right next door to the studio.

The next singer to be utilised was Glenn Hughes, one of the two new singers with Deep Purple, and blessed with an amazing voice. Glenn was undergoing treatment in Birmingham for cocaine, alcohol and just about every other addiction one could imagine. As far as I could make out, the cure consisted of simply keeping him asleep and constantly supervised during his few waking hours.

The Purple office was terrified of letting him loose on a session outside of his isolated world, especially with me! I was given a really hard time by the office and it was suggested that I really ought to find someone else to sing the tracks. However, I had my mind set on Glenn and got into a rage because of the interference of his "minders". Arriving home that night, I slammed my hand in the door of my car. I slammed it so hard that the driver's window completely shattered and the door shut completely, crushing my fingers. This was not a good move for a person whose livelihood depended on manual dexterity, and the pain was excruciating. I opened the door and staggered inside the house, where I was violently sick and then fainted. Still, the damage was not as bad as feared and the album got some publicity from a news item about the accident in Melody Maker.

Soon afterwards, I heard from the office and they had agreed to "release" Glenn for the day, on condition that he didn't stray from the studio and was driven home immediately after the session. My attitude was that here was a man being totally manipulated. Why couldn't he make a decision for himself? Well, the fact was, I suppose, that he couldn't. The irony of the situation was, I understand from a reliable source, that he was allowed drugs if it meant him getting through a show.

Anyway, Glenn arrived on a Saturday morning with his minder and girlfriend and he seemed fine, a little overweight but otherwise okay. On a Saturday lunchtime, we all normally went to the pub, which of course on this occasion we couldn't, so I sent out for ample supplies. Glenn wanted whiskey, which he drank straight from the bottle (you can see photographic evidence on the album sleeve). Next, he asked for fish and chips, a strange mix with whiskey, one would have thought, but it was duly sent for.

I played Glenn the track "Until Tomorrow" a couple of times and went through the melody line with him, then off he went and we had it finished in two takes. He was sounding so good that I decided to use him on "Light Of My Life" as well. This was a fairly straightforward affair, as I'd already recorded all the harmonies and just wanted him to "scat" around them. John and I sat in amazement as his voice soared all over the place.

Glenn was, I think, really pleased with his performances on both tracks and decided that some extra harmonies might sound good. The whiskey, however had taken a bit of a hold and he was starting to ramble quite a lot. We had reached that point when you just know it's not going to work, so I left it to John, the eternal diplomat, to tell Glenn that it was fine as it was. At that point, the poor sod was taken back to isolation.

Ray Fenwick and I had written a song called "Money To Burn", which at that point had a nice melody. I sent David Coverdale (who was now living in Munich) a demo and he agreed to come over to London and sing it. Unfortunately, he re-wrote bits of it on the plane over and what started out as a melodic piece turned into a Barry White kind of thing. Still, it has proven to be one of the most popular songs on the album, so what do I know?

David had joined Purple at the same time as Glenn, having been discovered in a menswear shop in Middlesbrough or somewhere like that. He was reputedly cross-eyed and quite a bit overweight, but with modern technology and Purple's money, he was transformed. Since then he's been transformed a good deal more and looks nothing like the guy who originally joined Purple.

David soon adapted to the star role of being a member of Deep Purple and became brash and loud overnight. On arriving at the studio, he demanded "mood" lighting and preferred to hold the microphone, rather than just sing into it. Unfortunately, the mood lighting was so moody that he couldn't see across the room (his eyes not having been been fixed at that stage). He careered round the studio while he sang and landed in a pile of mike and music stands during the course of the performance. In case anyone doubts this, I have it on tape! Nevertheless, David had a fine voice and the results speak for themselves.

Kingsway Recorders had no outboard equipment at all, apart from echo. Anything extra had to be hired in. However, Louie Austin devised a cunning way of enticing clients in. He invented ingenious bits of crap, mounted on blank rack plates. He glued grommets and rubber things onto the plates in an intricate design and then threaded recording tape around them. He then gave these useless bits of "equipment" impressive names, which he printed freehand onto the metal. They did, in fact, look as if they did something and the names he gave them further bewildered clients.

One was a "Hyperbolic Thrumplethrottler Vocal Transducer". Obviously, it did nothing at all, but on one occasion, David Coverdale was unhappy with his vocal sound, so Louie suggested he bring the transducer into play ... at a cost of £200 per three minutes! David was now happy with his vocal sound.

The tax situation at the time was such that it was beneficial for big name bands to record outside the UK, thus avoiding English tax. There was an awful lot of discreet recording going on in England, where the time was not logged. Ian Gillan and his new band "Gillan" migrated to Paris, the plan being to take up residence. I recall Ray Fenwick, who had joined Gillan, ringing me up and gloating a bit about his new-found tax exile and what he thought was eventual fame. Unfortunately, neither the exile nor the fame lasted long, as Ray turned the Gillan Band into a virtual jazz affair, complete with long boring guitar solos, whereas Gillan just wanted a bloody rock band.

Their brief stay in Paris was punctuated by numerous rock star-style atrocities, for example, an entire apartment being emptied into the street from a height of several floors. The French police made Gillan clear up the mess himself. Hire cars would be taken back by the poor roadie with no doors, no windows and very little of the interior left. The tour manager eventually suffered a nervous breakdown after some even more disgraceful goings-on in America. On the flight over, one of the band crapped in his briefcase and shortly after leaving the airport in the US, they were stopped by the Highway Patrol for a routine check. The tour manager opened his briefcase on the bonnet of the car to get all the passports and documentation, to be confronted by ... well, it's obvious. The policeman was, of course, unimpressed, and they spent their first day in America in the nick.

At this stage, a Purple offshoot band was was about to be launched. The band consisted of Ian Paice, Tony Ashton and Jon Lord, and thus was christened PAL. Naming your band after a brand of dog food was a doubtful strategy, and it turned out that the dog food was a better long-term bet!

I went along to the official launch, which was, as far as I can remember, at the Rainbow, where there was much merriment going on in a not entirely full theatre. This was not what Purple people were accustomed to at all. The whole event was to be recorded and filmed and the compère was the actor Ronald Frazer, whose favourite tipple was what he called "Frazerwater", a pseudonym for a monstrous Gin and Tonic. Frazer had clearly overdone it on the "Frazerwater" way before the show was even near to starting, with the result that he never got as far as compèring at all.

Poor old Tony Ashton had finally reached a stage in his career where it seemed that everything was finally starting to go well for him, as long as he behaved himself at this crucial moment. Sadly, he seriously over-celebrated prior to the performance so that, on his grand entrance onto the stage, he toppled over the edge and landed in the orchestra pit, breaking his arm. Despite this, some sort of a show ensued and was filmed live, as was the recording of their first album in Munich. The film reels were never numbered and the entire thing got lost anyway, as did all the footage for Butterfly Ball. No one has a clue where it is, nor the live recording.

Anyway, the PAL recording sessions in Munich were apparently a tricky business, because the band could only work during Tony's sober moments, which were few and far between. It's amazing to think that they managed to record a couple of albums, my favourite track being Tony's "I'm Gonna Stop Drinking", which of course was an over-optimistic title.

Another frequent but sadly unwanted visitor to our sessions was Danny Kirwan, the young guitarist who had been plucked from obscurity to become a member of Fleetwood Mac. He was seriously mentally ill and I understand he's now in a mental home in or near Brighton. He would turn up at all kinds of strange and inconvenient moments, convinced that he had a session booked, which of course he hadn't.

Due to his "fame" with Fleetwood Mac, Dick James offered Danny a publishing deal and took him out to a posh Italian lunch. During the main course, something triggered Danny into tipping his entire dinner over Dick's head. Dick seemed to accept this strange behaviour from band mem bers, especially if they were from an important band, because he believed that every bit of publicity would help.

Peter Green, the leading light of the original version of Fleetwood Mac, was another casualty of success. He famously decided to give all his money away, and I saw him do it! We, that is Hardin & York, had done a four day stint in Germany with the Fleetwoods, for which we were all paid in cash. Back at Heathrow, we all joined the queue to cash in our Marks. Peter Green merely handed his wad of notes to a young cashier and told her to keep it. Peter became a virtual recluse and for many years refused to accept any royalties, although in recent years he has made something of a comeback. The rest of Fleetwood Mac now live in America, still enjoying success, although it's well known that a lot of their assets went up various noses.

Jimmy Helms, who had sung a track on "Butterfly Ball", came down to record a couple of titles for the album. One was "She's A Woman", which was a monstrously complicated song to record, as there were so many "edits" which had to be pieced together at the end. I think John Acock thought I'd gone mad when he heard all these sections being recorded individually. Jimmy sang bits which were also spliced together at the end. There were three separate piano solos, all recorded on different sessions. Jon Lord did one, aided by a bottle of Bells whisky, and Tony

Ashton did another, aided by two bottles of Bells plus a few lagers. In fact, we didn't use this one, as Tony had become a little too abstract. Instead, I brought Rick Van Der Linden (of Focus) in from Holland and he and I shared a solo. He flew into London with piles of keyboards (which were not very transportable in those days), seemingly oblivious of the fact that I only wanted a sixty second solo! Still, he had some interesting effects on his other keyboards and they crop up throughout the track.

Roger Glover came to a session and I roped him into playing bass on "Loose Ends". Roger was extremely put out by the presence of Corinthia West, the Amazonian photographer, who was by now literally hanging from the ceiling in her quest for an interesting and unusual angle. I felt like saying, "For Christ's sake, Rog, it's only a fucking picture!"

Mike D'Abo was next, and he arrived with Mike Smith, the former singer with The Dave Clark Five. Now Mike Smith has a great voice, especially on rock songs, and I wished I'd used him on a track of his own. D'Abo, as ever, took over the entire production. John Acock usually had the desk set up so that we could do a mix as soon as the vocal was down. D'Abo knelt before the desk and thrust all the faders in all kinds of directions to achieve what he thought was a better sound. As a result, a whole day's work was lost.

The rest of the album progressed without incident. All the vocals were done with just a few overdubs needed here and there, and even Corinthia managed to untangle herself from her contortions, leaving me and John to spend the next two weeks piecing it all together. Chas Watkins, our tape op, was temporarily replaced by "George", an Arthur Daley type who would bring suspect goods into the studio every night for a quick sale. George seemed to know people from all walks of life, mostly the wrong walks, though I knew better walks than him. I never did find out his other name and he disappeared, never to be seen again.

Henry Spinnetti was the drummer throughout. Henry was in great demand around this time and started to adjust his price accordingly, eventually pricing himself out of work! I recently heard a story about Henry, which may be apocryphal. It was while Henry was working with Tina Turner, in the 90's, I guess. By then, his demands had apparently become even grander than in my days with him and on one occasion, he demanded a limousine. The limousine did arrive, but all it did was take him straight to the airport and put him on a plane home!

Session players can, in general, be a mean lot. Mo Foster, a great bass player whom I like a lot, would arrive for sessions with a calculator and charge for everything he possibly could: VAT, petrol, porterage (he had to carry his bass at least fifteen yards!) shoe leather, etc, etc. For most session players, there was no such thing as a good turn, every note had a value. Some of them had a superior attitude and a lot of resentment, because they well knew that, whatever happened to the track, they would still only get their session fee. Back in the Sixties, many musicians had been severely exploited in this way.

Herbie Flowers, a bass player who worked with Blue Mink and David Bowie, played on quite a lot of Hardin & York's first album "Tomorrow Today", simply because he liked it. He was straggling behind after a session he'd done at Olympic and when he heard H & Y start the session, he just joined in, as did Vic Flick (the James Bond Theme guitar man). Neither of them wanted payment.

String players are the most dogmatic clock watchers of all and will not have it if you say they're a little out of tune. I once had an eighteen-piece orchestra which played the wrong fucking chord. It wasn't exactly their fault, as they were merely playing what the arranger had written, rather than go out of their way to rectify a glaring error. In the end, I re-wrote the song round the wrong chord! More recently, when I worked with Deep Purple and the RSO, the orchestra stopped playing halfway through a piece because it was their union break time!

Roger Glover and I both invested in pretty well the first good synth to come on to the market. It was an ARP 2600, which was, and still is, very good for strings. The drawback was that it was monophonic, meaning that. for a full string sound, you had to play each note individually, then bounce them together over and over again until you achieved the orchestral effect. It literally took hours and hours to get the finished result. Stevie Wonder used it to the best effect I've heard on "Songs In The Key Of Life", on which some people are convinced it's an orchestra.

Roger and I had a gadget race, buying everything new that came onto the market, without having any idea how it worked. I've still got a whole room full of obsolete crap. Roger was another "oddie", much like myself. He was living with an American girl, as most of us did at that time! She, realising she had struck the proverbial oil field in Roger, was constantly badgering him into marriage. Roger, on the other hand, was clearly undecided and would check into an hotel on occasion for a serious re-think. Having re-thought, he did in fact get married, only to get divorced a few years later.

Roger tried to create a Paul and Linda situation with Judy Kuhl, only Judy couldn't sing as well as Linda, and was thus a non-starter. One of their Christmas cards, which I still have, featured him and Judy Kuhl in the stables of their home in a Joseph and Mary pose, surrounded by donkeys and various farm animals. Maybe Roger was becoming convinced that he was in fact "Him".

The divorce rate within the Purple empire (which is what it had become) was enormously high. The only non-divorcee was Ian Paice, for the simple reason that he was not married! People sometimes say that money would never change them but I have to say that the changes within Deep Purple were quite frightening. The management was falling apart and every member was going off in different directions, each time giving the lawyers a good income. In fact, Purple had their own in-house lawyer!

I was loosely involved with the hierarchy of the management and was at one point used diabolically by someone called Andrew Tribe. He was little more than a "gofer", but he treated me like a complete idiot and I fell right into the trap. The managers of Purple were Tony Edwards and John Colleta. Tribe had moved to the Colleta camp during a disagreement and used me as a source of information, at the same time as making ridiculous promises and ideas for my own future career. I neither know nor care what the outcome of the dispute was but I have always resented being used in such an underhand way. Andrew still arrives at "important" events but neither he nor I ever speak.

Back to the trip to Cannes for Midem, which was eventful from the start. I was at the time living with Maureen Thain, the ex-wife of Gary Thain, the bass player with Uriah Heep. I'd met them both when Gary was playing with the Keef Hartley Band. Maureen was a nice girl and we had some happy "bits" together, although I of course would never commit to taking the relationship any further.

One night, another ex-girlfriend of mine, Christine Faulks, invited me to a party on her new boyfriend's yacht. He was John Brewer, who had started an ill-fated record label called Avatar. He was a very flash guy and had the biggest available yacht in Cannes, which he kept floodlit day and night! I don't think it had a working engine, as it didn't move an inch. Luckily, the on-board chef was quite fantastic. Brewer and Christine would cruise up and down the Croisette in an open top Corniche, whatever the weather. I don't think they ever stopped to attend a meeting, but people did wonder who the fuck they were, with the big yacht and the flash Rolls but seemingly no music to make, sell, buy or offer.

On the eve of the big "do", I went to see John Craig on the Conquest to see if he fancied coming to the party with me. John didn't want to come but the person who turned out to be my "ex" seemed very enthusiastic about going. I didn't think this was a particularly good idea, as she was at the time trying for a reconciliation with her husband, who was none other than my publisher Tony Edwards.

She was very insistent that she came with me, and eventually Tony said it would be a good idea. He wanted to stay on the boat, negotiating more multi-million dollar deals, and didn't seem to give a monkey's where his estranged wife went. At the end of the evening, she asked where I was staying and suggested she come back to my hotel. I was more than a little surprised and thought this was an even worse idea than taking her to the party in the first place. I refused, but we met several times thereafter at various dinners, and that's where it all began.

One thing led to another and we got more and more involved, but there were a few shocks to follow. She had three children, of whom I was of course aware, though during my visits to her house in Richmond (following our return from Cannes), I hardly ever saw them, as they had a permanent nannie.

This was now becoming a pretty grim period for me, no longer being part of a touring band and reliant upon production and writer's royalties for my income. There were endless rounds of meetings with people I'd rather not have even met, and during the long hot summer of 1976, I contracted pneumonia. I was on my boat, sweating profusely, and felt as if Goliath was sitting on my chest.

I thought, "My God, I'm an alcoholic" and tried to solve the problem with a few drinks, which only made me feel even worse. I struggled home and went to bed, where I got absolutely no sympathy from my parents, who assumed that I'd just overdone something or other. I think it was the other they were more concerned with. My bed was soaked, so eventually my mother took my temperature, which was 110 or something. My father, having pointed out that even a horse would be dead with that sort of temperature, relented and called the doctor, who diagnosed pneumonia and I was confined to bed for two weeks.

During this time, I saw a lot of my aunt Carol, who was another favourite of mine. She was prone to strange moods for no apparent reason, but we always got on well. She came to help out in the house I bought with my brother and she loved the constant chaos that seemed to surround us. My brother spent much of his time in Tokyo, where he acted as oriental art advisor for Christies, the auctioneers, so much of the time I had the run of the house to myself (and whoever may have been with me!). Carol enjoyed cooking breakfast for us and she always shouted up the stairs: "How many for breakfast today?"

The house was full of valuables, so my dad suggested we should at least install a burglar alarm and in our absence, we left him with the job of finding the "top men". Christ alone knows where he eventually found them, but find them he did. They were yet another disaster.

John and I had been out for the day and, on our return, we were confronted with literally miles and miles of multi-coloured cables, carefully placed and glued across each and every window pane, up the staircases, not under the carpet but decoratively beside it. There was also cabling around every door and in one room, it went across the floor. I personally could see the funny side of it, but John couldn't. The engineer had also taken the liberty of installing an alarm in my car. This item was supposed to be touch sensitive, but unfortunately it was far too sensitive. Consequently, every time there was the slightest of breezes, the bloody thing would howl and screech at deafening levels. Even a passing pedestrian would set it off.

Everything was now declared totally burglar proof. The only problem was that the engineer had put the bells INSIDE the house and INSIDE the garage, so the only people that would ever be aware of an intruder would be those inside the house. A week later, I had three stereo systems stolen from my car ... on consecutive nights! The bells went off so frequently that we didn't even bother to investigate, so we simply switched the bloody system off. Previously, we had suffered no losses at all.

John suggested to the engineer that pink cable might have been more appealing and that, if went across the centre of every room, it might add to the overall effect. There were already mountainous bulges, which were in fact under-carpet sensors. The clod of an engineer said that we could have any colour we liked and that it might indeed look good. John just exploded, and in his subtle way, told the hapless engineer to fuck off! We were, not surprisingly, never pressed for payment of the account and over the next few days we just ripped the entire installation out.

Then there was my bloody boat, which my father completely took over. Every bloody morning he would set off for St. Katherine's Dock, where it was moored, with a bag of tools, all set for a day's work in the engine room. There was nothing at all wrong with the engines, though after his tinkerings, there was. On one particular day, he set off as usual, but, disregarding the boat, he headed straight for the yacht club, where he cast himself well and truly adrift in a sea of whiskey. He palled up with an American "boat bum" who I spent most of my time trying to avoid. However, after a plethora of whiskey, the pair decided to cast anchor and set off for the unknown reaches of Greenwich. I'd arranged a party that night and had spent the day buying food and booze for the evening, arranging to meet my guests at 8 o'clock at the mooring.

8 o'clock I arrived and so did I, along with my guests, only to find there was no boat. I stood, embarrassed, with eight people, holding bags of prawns and various seafood items, for the nautical theme, plus of course piles of booze. My immediate thought was that the bloody thing had sunk and we all peered into the murky depths for some sign of a mast, or indeed anything.

I decided to go over to the yacht club to make further enquiries. The barman seemed quite disgusted with the entire Harding family. He was also surprised that I hadn't heard of the afternoon's events. Apparently, my dad and the American had set off and, during the course of their "voyage", had drunk the entire collection of booze which was always on the boat.

On their return, the lock was closed, so they left the boat moored just off the mouth of the Marina, merely tied up with a few random knots and bits of rope and string, and left it bobbing about on what is in fact quite a busy stretch of water. They were obviously by now completely out of control but nevertheless they proceeded once more to the yacht club, where they got even more pissed.

The horrible American then suggested that he take up residence on the boat, just to look after things and carry out general maintenance, of which there was far too much going on already! My dad was opposed to this and a furious drunken row ensued. The American called the Hardings capitalist pigs and probably worse things. The American was in his late thirties and my Dad was in his early seventies. This, however, did not stop him from knocking the American unconscious and getting himself a life ban from the club.

But no one liked the American, so eventually my Dad became the marina hero and, due to the public outcry, the ban was lifted. None of this helped my dinner guests who were, by now, freezing at the dockside, awaiting my next move. We all trekked the half mile distance to the mouth of the Marina, where my boat was bobbing about furiously. None of us had a clue as to what to do with the boat as far as "putting it" somewhere a little calmer was concerned, so we ended up eating and drinking on the bloody pier. I was absolutely furious, and so was my mum. My dad had returned home, obviously with God most definitely on his side, in the most atrocious state.

He proudly told my mum of his impressive pugilistic defeat of the American, at which point my mum hit him and sent him straight to bed. She wouldn't go anywhere near the marina for months after that, on account of acute embarrassment.

Things got so bad with my dad's takeover of my boat that he decided to buy his own. It was even bigger than mine, though far more traditional. Its name was Morning Skye. Sadly, he secured a mooring right next to mine, consequently blotting out most of *my* morning sky.

My mum was far more concerned with making curtains and polishing the oak flooring than preparing for any extensive voyaging. My dad proceeded to take the engine to bits and polish every moving part. It looked great: All the brass was gleaming and the vessel was in fine form, but still he refused to venture beyond the marina until one Sunday lunchtime. As he stood proudly at the helm, making final adjustments to the instruments, the engine let out a brief roar, lots of spluttering and the entire lot blew up!!

My father's logic was always, "if it's clean then it must work". Clean it was, but work it didn't. £3000 later, a new and even cleaner engine was fitted. This was never even to have the oil put in, let alone be fired up. Boats, we eventually decided, were not for the Hardings. All we ever did was paint, clean and polish, what fun!

I used to hate weekends at the marina when all the captains' hats would emerge for their day out with their little picnic hampers and their deck shoes and their poxy little boats. Robin Nedwell and I used to spend the odd Sunday down there, choosing to have lunch at the nearby Tower Hotel, get rotten drunk, then go back to the boat and get drunker. Sunday was also a day when people would wander around (not boat owners, just boat lookers) and many were disgusted to see a speechless Nedwell (who was quite a well known "face", due to the "Doctor" series) lying sprawled out on the deck.

N. Twai and John Fisher came down on only one occasion, and Twai suggested we get to grips with the manoeuvrability of the craft by way of a quick turnabout within the confines of the Marina itself. We managed to get into the middle but could find no way back to the mooring position. Big boats have a mind of their own, they don't stop when you think they should and they don't seem to turn in the direction you think you are aiming in, so we floundered about in the middle of the Marina until eventually I had to pay a guy £20 to park it for us.

CHAPTER 8
HERNE-IA

After much deliberation, I bought Herne Place, in Sunningdale, in the summer of 1976. The property had first come to my notice in a minor photograph in Country Life, where I felt it resembled a rambling Italian sort of affair. Of course it didn't, it was Georgian, and in need of a major overhaul.

Not only did I like the idea of "settling down" and opening a studio, I was temporarily in a financial position to do so. My dabbling in antiques had brought some major successes, and there had been profitable spin-offs from my father's business as well. Unlike many musicians of that era, I had eventually succeeded in getting many of the royalties I was due. This was particularly important in the case of the song "Love Is All", from Butterfly Ball. Not only was this a hit all over Europe (being twice Number 1 in France), but it has also been used on numerous occasions as a TV advertising theme. At one stage, I was earning nearly £40,000 a year from that song alone, which in those days was a lot of money.

The owners of Herne Place were Sir Anthony Meyer and Lady Meyer. Sir Anthony later achieved fame for trying to overthrow the Thatcher régime. They were very odd, but likeable, and had endearing qualities. The negotiations which ensued were like no negotiations I have ever since been involved in with buying a property. Every room and the very fabric of the house itself held a special memory for Lady Meyer, so much so that at one point she actually said to me, "Have it! I'd like to further the arts!"

On my first visit, the house was in complete darkness. All the shutters were firmly closed and Lady Meyer seemed unwilling to open them, perhaps for fear of revealing the full horror of what was to come. It was a brilliant summer's day outside, and when she eventually relented, I was stunned. It was like going back in time to a period that one could only dream of. There were pianos everywhere, even stored in the garage. I saw this as an omen to buy. Sir Anthony took no part of the proceedings, preferring to stroll around the grounds "keeping the pigeons down" with his shotgun. He was really of the opinion that his wife was quite mad even to consider dealing with a musician.

I loved that house with a passion, with its beautiful walks and grounds but sadly, as events were to unfold, I would not live there for my lifetime, as I had wished. If only I had met my wife Liz ten years earlier, we would have found ourselves in that magnificent old house and still be there today.

If that had happened, perhaps the course of my life would have been totally different. But as it was, I moved into Herne Place with my then partner, whom, for legal reasons, I cannot name.

Lady Meyer kept in touch throughout my time at Herne Place and still seems interested in maintaining her relationship with it, whoever the owner may be. While I was there, the Meyers' children would occasionally return to Herne Place from far flung places around the globe, just to relive an hour or so of their childhood. Having left Herne Place myself, I can fully understand their devotion to the magnificent property.

Pete York's wedding took place not long after the move to Herne Place. I was best man, but sadly not a very successful one. The stag night was held at Herne Place, which was not in a good state of repair, although it did have the merit of loads of bedrooms and also loads of beds left behind by Lady Meyer. Deep Purple came for the night and, after drinking what seemed to be gallons of alcohol, no one really cared where they slept.

I showed Roger Glover round the house and pointed out the location of the planned recording studio. In order to show him the grounds, I had the idea of utilising some flares which were left over from my boating days and fired them off into the distance, illuminating all eight acres! God only knows what the villagers must have thought, as it must have lit up most of Sunningdale.

I can't remember much about the wedding itself, apart from the fact that the reception was held in the barn of a guy who lived next door to Pete and that Ian Paice refused to stray any distance from his Rolls Royce for fear of someone scratching it. I was way too pissed to drive mine but luckily had the luxury of Merv, my driver, who stayed with me for a few years at Herne Place. Not being in a fit state, I made no speech, and my final recollection is of sliding down the side of my car, after which I passed into oblivion.

Soon after moving into Herne Place with my new partner, I began to become very much aware of the presence of her three children, and, although I quite liked the idea of an "instant" family, it wasn't quite as pleasant as I'd envisaged. I then learnt bits about her past which we won't go into, but which shocked even me. Her husband was by now definitely not at all happy with the situation and my working life as a musician seemed to decline drastically. I was literally too "hot" to get involved with. She had the most furious and dangerous temper and life was not good, but even so, we decided to have a child, partly because I wanted one, and partly to even up the odds a little!

Once Emma was born, and I know this this sounds horrible, my life was devoted to Emma and not to her mother. My mother spoilt Emma rotten and she had the best of everything, while her mother was sort of pushed into the background. Emma had a great nanny, Rosie from New Zealand, and although her mind was poisoned against me, as were so many others, I still thank her for all she did in Emma's formative years. In fact, the two of them are still friends to this day. Rosie now has three children of her own and writes to Emma on a regular basis.

And so the void deepened and I took refuge, whenever possible, with Erica in London. I'd met Erica before Emma's mother, on a night when Pete York asked me to "look after" his then girlfriend (later his wife) Mecki, while he was away working with The Chris Barber Band. Mecki brought along her friend Erica and then began an affair which survived throughout the dismal times at Herne Place.

Erica was in the most awful position, in fact all three of us were. We'd spend many days in London at her house in St. Johns Wood, but when it came time for me to go home, there would always be tears, so now I was getting dramas from all sides. I deserved all of this, because I'd allowed myself to get in such an emotional mess and was trapped. I couldn't sell Herne Place because I loved it and I couldn't move in to Erica's house (which she wanted me to do) because there was a risk that I'd lose Herne Place altogether (not to mention the fact that my parents were now living there as well!)

Christmas time was always the worst. Can you imagine being torn between two homes? Things got so bad that one New Year's Eve, I invited Erica down to Herne Place, on the pretext that she was an old friend. It was the only way I could spend the day with her, so she came, but was terribly upset. The added embarrassment was that various other guests at the party made a play for her, assuming her to be on her own. She slapped one guy round the face, so now I had a mini drama going on within a major one. This all probably makes me out to be a horrible person, and in a way I suppose I was, but these "messes" do happen and I just couldn't deal with it. Neither, eventually, could Erica and we sadly drifted apart, leaving me to do God knows what.

There were constant rows with my partner, some of them, I regret to say, very violent. I broke my hand twice (not helpful for a keyboard player), and on one occasion I was very nearly killed, but we won't go into that.

My father's health was erratic round about that time, and he was rapidly turning into a Mr. Magoo type character. He would drive into central London and not have a clue where he'd left his car. My mother used to ring me up in the middle of a meeting for me to go and rescue him, though

I of course had even less idea than him where he'd left the bloody thing, so sometimes it took the best part of a day to find it.

When we heard the news that my father was seriously ill, my brother John travelled down from Chiswick and we all assembled in a gloomy room in the King Edward VII Hospital in Windsor. The specialists held out little hope for my father and in retrospect, I feel that his death was for the best for him, as he had been an active and intelligent man who could never have coped with the potential disabilities he would have been left with.

My mother and I went to his room, where she kissed him goodnight and I just patted his hand. He never regained consciousness and I was never to see him again. The following morning, there was a call to Herne Place from the hospital and I was given the inevitable news. The doctor just said, "I'm terribly sorry, but your father has passed away".

Immediately, one thinks of all the things one should have and could have done and even said. We had argued a lot and suddenly I regretted it all. Was I really such a horrible person? Probably, on occasion, I had been. I had always been desperate to prove myself to my dad, though I'd like to think that in the end, he was proud of me. I remember when I got the job with Spencer, running to a phone box in Greek Street in London to give him the news before anyone else. How I still miss that man!

We, as a family, were never demonstrative, but on the morning of the news of his death, my mother and I held each other, saying nothing. We were the only ones left and I was now the man of the family ... God help us all!

My father's stories, I must say, inspired me to try to do as much with my life as he had done with his. Although we were never particularly close (in those days it didn't seem the done thing), I was always in awe of him and his ability to rectify the most horrendous of situations. He was far more adventurous than me. At the drop of a hat, and sometimes in the early hours, he would decide on a trip to Wales, so we'd all pile into the car and set off. He had a great "I'll do exactly what I like when I like" sort of attitude, but then of course he could well afford to.

He knew various farmers dotted around his land in Wales and would think nothing of "knocking them up" in the middle of the night. He was always welcomed by them with open arms. I think a career in music was the last thing he had in mind for me, though I'm sure he had a bit of fun during the early days.

During my schooldays, he became a great favourite with the senior staff, who, like me, were inspired by his charisma, and he was invited to hand out the prizes on sports days and other such occasions. Sadly, I was never the recipient, but just to watch him centre stage from the back of the throng was enough for me. My childhood was incredibly happy, an experience I was sadly not able to give my own daughter, although now we get on famously and are at last the best of friends.

I sought sanctuary from my troubled domestic situation in a pub called The Red Lion, which lay in dangerously close proximity to Herne Place (at the bottom of the garden, actually) and became my centre of operations. There was a team in there like I've never met in my life, before or since. Amongst the crew, we had a dentist, a doctor, a future lawyer and an eventual plethora of musicians.

I'll start with Alan Kidd, the dentist. Alan was, and still is, a very tall chap, quite similar in looks and outlook to John Cleese. Every single night, Alan would come in for his obligatory five pints or thereabouts, just to see what was going to happen. Most nights, something did.

It was obvious that he was going to be my dentist. He also didn't mind if I dispensed with the standard dental mouthwash and replaced it with a bottle of Chablis. I think I became a bit of an embarrassment to him, so it was eventually agreed that I should have my treatment during the hours that the surgery was closed.

On one occasion, I was sitting in the waiting room with the normal groups of people you get in waiting rooms, including one really elderly lady. Alan walked into the room and announced: "I'm ready for you now, Mrs. Hampstead", to which I of course had to make a ribald remark, much to the annoyance of Alan (though to the amusement of the other waiting patients). Alan explained, while I was in the chair, that Mrs. Hampstead was 98 and had only come in for a filling! I asked, "Was it really worth the bother?", to which his response was that her teeth were in much better shape than mine, so I should shut up.

Alan drove an old VW at the time, and on one occasion he broke down on the M4. For assistance, he called into the Operations Room (i.e. The Red Lion) where one of the other regulars was an AA man, Dave. Dave's forte was drinking a pint of beer down in one go, not using his hands. He'd clench the pint pot with his teeth and drain the contents. Very impressive it was too, though prior to Alan's phone call he'd performed rather too many demonstrations and was, quite frankly, pissed. The trusty and reliable AA man leapt, or rather staggered, into rescue mode and drove off, lights flashing, in the traditional AA van.

Some time later, Alan appeared in the pub looking as white as a sheet and ordered a large brandy, before unfolding the saga. Dave had hitched

Alan's VW up to his van with a rigid bar and set off down the M4 towards Windsor. It was a windy and rainy night and at some point, the VW had flipped over, leaving Alan upside down in the VW with sparks flying everywhere from the gradually disintegrating roof of his car. He hooted and shouted (why he shouted I'm not sure) to try to attract Dave's attention, to no avail. They both amazingly arrived back in the Red Lion car park intact, albeit Alan was upside down. When they both walked in, they didn't speak. However, it was clear that Alan could have quite happily throttled Dave (by now a sort of beetroot colour) on the spot.

I had a similar experience with Dave. I'd arrived home from the pub pissed and decided to drive round the grounds and look for Spud, my trusty gardener. Herne Place had two entrances, a main one and an entrance from Bedford Lane, which was on the corner of the grounds. I was in an Aston Martin and, after driving about in an aimless search for Spud, got stuck in a marshy area close to the Bedford Lane entrance. I revved and revved, but the more I did so, the deeper the tyres sank into the mud. Eventually, the mud level had reached the bottom of the door.

So it was back to Dave, who wouldn't be available until the pub opened, so I sat in the house just looking at the Aston in the distance, slowly sinking even further down into the mire. I finally called him and through the bottom gates came the hopeful-looking familiar yellow van. He set up what to me looked like a very complicated and unnecessary winching system which was wrapped round a tree, connected at one end to his van and the other to the Aston. When he was all set for the operation to commence, he began revving up the van. After a while, it was clear that he was now also stuck in the mud. The heavy duty wire cord, which did in fact look very strong, had snapped, the tree remaining sturdy and unmarked.

I now had an Aston Martin AND an AA van stuck in my garden. Dave called the AA night line and an even bigger van was sent in order to tow us both out from the Bedford Lane entrance. The new driver, aside from causing total chaos and a huge backlog of traffic in the small lane, then proceeded to knock both sides of my entrance wall down, destroying the front of his truck, which was now buried in a mound of bricks and mortar. To his credit, he did eventually get us both out. I never did find Spud and I never did live that one down and neither did Dave. One wonders if the RAC might have been a better bet.

The landlords at the Red Lion came and went at a pretty alarming rate. One guy was so creepy that he apparently instructed the barmaids to serve me first whenever I walked in. There was no cigarette machine in the pub at that time, so he made sure there was always an ample supply of Rothmans reserved exclusively for me, as I was such a heavy spender (and smoker).

The longest lasting landlord was a guy called Doug Whiting who, like me, was a lunatic. He'd stay open late at the drop of a hat. If the mood was right, he didn't want it to end and quite often it didn't. He had mates in the Flying Squad who were substantial drinkers and instigators of many a late night. Our little local police station (which was more often than not shut) was manned by one officer with a push bike. His name was Martin and he'd often go on midnight reconnaissance missions to catch a "late drinking pub". Of course The Red Lion, which was about half a mile away from him, was always a dead cert for a "nick". He walked in at around 1 a.m. one morning, looking very officious. Unfortunately for him, it soon became clear that he was outranked by most of the late drinking offenders, so he put his helmet on the bar and joined in.

One of the barmaids took a shine to me. She lived on the Wentworth Estate just up the road and was working in the pub in college holiday times. I had bumped into her a few times at other local pubs and bought her drinks and chatted. She took this all far too seriously and letters started to arrive at the house, declaring her undying love, etc.

One night, she called the house from a local hotel, The Berystede, and asked where on earth I was. She'd called at a very inopportune moment, as my "partner" was in the room when I took the call. Anyway, she'd announced to her entire family that we were engaged and her father had gone ahead and booked the banqueting suite for an engagement dinner. I knew nothing whatsoever about this "engagement" and was at a total loss as to what to do, but the phone calls persisted, so I had to own up to the problem.

My "partner" eventually spoke to a very irate future mother-in law, who was having none of it, so I had to go to the hotel to resolve the situation. I rang Paul Trimmings, an ageing Del-Boy type and a really great guy, and he said he'd come with me as he, coming from Wentworth himself, knew the family quite well. We met in reception, where I put the whole problem on Paul's shoulders and said that I just couldn't deal with it. He went in and explained the situation, at which point there was a bit of an eruption, with the whole family up in arms and shouting abuse at the "pop star with the big house". The phone calls continued well into the night, culminating with a call from the "mother-in-law", apologising profusely. It turned out that the daughter was in fact genuinely mad and that this exact same saga had happened on previous occasions.

I, at that point in time, considered myself "retired" and was intent on devoting the rest of my life to nothing but fun. This did not fit in at all with the agenda of my "partner", with whom relations were by now at an irretrievable low. Drinking had become my only solace, as my mind was in total turmoil. My life consisted of going to the pub, getting wrecked and going to sleep.

After a few years of this chaos and the most horrendous rows, I'd had enough and bricked the bloody house in two. I honestly got builders in and constructed a wall right down the middle, spanning three floors. I ended up living in the cellar. But things were about to look up. One night, on a visit to the Red Lion with my medical friend, Dr. Mike, I bumped into Liz. I will never forget that night. As we walked in, I saw Liz sitting in the corner with a friend. I immediately said to Mike, "I'm going to marry her." Mike replied, "Oh no, more trouble", and left.

I didn't have the confidence to approach Liz and introduce myself, so got someone to go over and invite her and her friend over for a drink. She declined. I couldn't leave it at that and kept saying to my mate, "Go and try again ... and again ... and again!" I felt like a teenager.

Eventually, her friend came over and Liz was sort of forced into it. I didn't think I had a hope in hell, as everyone was swarming around, trying to do the same as me. I finally managed to get a word in and asked, "Would you like a drink?", but she declined. I persevered and somehow or other we got onto the subject of what she did. It turned out that she worked for EMI, selling studio tape, which of course was perfect. At least now I had a reason to ask for her telephone number with a view to buying tape for my studio. It took me a while to summon up the courage to make the call, but I did it in the end and we arranged a lunch in London to discuss my "order". From before we even spoke, I was besotted, but it was to take many months before a relationship developed.

I continued to frequent the pub, which was was full of characters. Hardly anyone was called by his / her real name. For example, there was a guy called George, whose real name was Peter. We all called him "Labels" because of his obsession with designer labels. George appreciated good music and told tales of his nights in Richmond, where the Yardbirds would often play. At that time they had Eric Clapton on guitar and for George, Clapton had himself become a bit of a "label", so he added him to his list of trendy things to like or buy. He was a poseur of the first order and, like me, had come from the wrong side of London and set up home in Sunningdale, which he felt was the ultimate achievement.

I must admit that I felt I was in the country, although I suppose we weren't really. It was very green and expensive but that's about as far as it went. George, however, took to wearing the entire Burberry range and was equipped for any sporting activity, though he took part in none. Every Friday night he'd call in for a couple of pints while he waited for his Chinese or Indian take-away to be ready. Rarely did it rest at two pints and without fail he picked up a stone cold take-away, blind drunk, and went home for the standard Friday night ruck. His wife just wanted him to be in the house. He said to me she wouldn't care if he was dead or alive, as long as he was in.

George was only in his forties when he suddenly contracted a mysterious illness. There was no cure and George died. Shortly before he was admitted to hospital, I bumped into him one Sunday morning at the newsagents at Sunningdale station. He was carrying all the tat newspapers, The People, News Of The World, Sunday Mirror. I saw this huge pile of tits and bums and asked why he read that shit, to which he replied, "Oh, I go round the corner for the 'heavies'". A poseur to the very end.

Then there was my gardener, Spud. In fact, he was far more than a gardener. Possessing a mind full of totally useless information, he'd keep everyone amused for hours. He had no desire for luxury of any kind and had a caravan in the paddock which was a total tip. There was a horse trough in the paddock and in the winter, however cold it was (I even saw him breaking the ice), he'd wash in the open air and shave in freezing water.

Sadly, he'd fallen in love with my ex-partner and was beside himself when the time came for her to leave. She, of course, had no time for him whatsoever and just used him as a source of information as to what I was up to. Then came the suicide attempts. The first attempt he planned was to lie on the ground in the garage, so that when she came back to the house, she'd run him over. It was après pub and he was pissed and prepared to lay down his life for the woman he loved. The morning came and, to his disappointment, he was still alive and looking up at the sump of her car. His error was that he'd lain down lengthways instead of sideways, so she just parked and didn't even notice him.

Attempt number 2 was to take an entire bottle of sleeping pills on top of about 26 bottles of Guinness. Once more, he woke up, but told me that it had been the best night's sleep he'd ever had.

While the days passed, he planned what he thought was the ultimate suicide. One of Spud's habits was to sit in his caravan and play "You Don't Have To Say You Love Me" by Dusty Springfield. His proud boast was that he could drink an entire bottle of wine before the record finished (which he could, I saw him do it).

So the suicide was eventually planned, taking the form of shooting himself. He had a shotgun which he normally used for rabbits, though on this night it was for his head. He had left the pub in a solemn mood and gone to the caravan to play a bit more Dusty Springfield before the moment arrived for him to do the deed. Once again, in the morning, he was alive and mowing the lawn. What had happened was that he was so pissed that, as he put the gun to his head, he rolled off the bed and just blew a huge hole in the wall of the caravan.

He gave up after this and tried to adjust to a new life with Liz, who had moved into Herne Place with me. Now, of course, he also fell in love with Liz, but this was a little more understandable. To this day, when we visit England and it's time to say goodbye, there are tears in his eyes and I confess in mine also. He's a lovely chap. From what I've written it might appear that he's a fool, but he isn't, he's very well read, has a unique logic, and on occasion comes out with some remarkable stories .

Spud should really have an entire chapter, or perhaps an entire book, devoted to him, because he's one of the last remaining eccentrics that I know. One weekend, Liz and I decided on a weekend break on the River Thames. My studio manager, Brian Adams, fixed it all up for us and it was strange then, and still is strange now, that whenever we decide to have a "break", it always costs around £1000. Most other people seem to manage a month's holiday, all inclusive, for less than we pay for a night.

So we assembled a crew, which consisted of Mark from Sark and Spud! We set off for Reading on a Friday afternoon to collect what we had been told by Brian was a very desirable craft. He claimed that a mate of his had done him a special deal, which may have been true, but the deal didn't seem to have filtered down the line to us. We were presented with this awful wreck of a thing, much like Spud's caravan afloat. We loaded it up with provisions for the weekend, mostly beer and wine, and were given instructions by the very apprehensive owner.

He asked if we were familiar with the ways of the river, to which Mark replied, "Oh yes, we're all seasoned waterway travellers". The owner's concern seemed somewhat alleviated, until we asked him to point us in the right direction for Marlow. His brow furrowed visibly as he saw Mark fumbling with what were, to him, totally alien controls. He insisted on travelling the first mile with us before finally leaving us to continue our adventure alone, completely convinced, I'm sure, that he'd never see his boat again.

As soon as he was gone, the corks popped and the ring pulls released their familiar gassy sound and the serious drinking began in earnest. We'd arranged to meet my mother and Brian at a restaurant called the Compleat Angler in Marlow for Sunday lunch, and wrongly assumed that we had ample time to get there.

We hadn't travelled very far when we were faced with our first unanticipated obstacle: a lock. I did have the experience to know that boats don't just stop, but unfortunately, Mark didn't. As he searched for the brakes, we crashed into the end of the lock, much to the disgust of the lock keeper, who eyed our motley crew with some suspicion. Mark had, by this time, donned a captain's hat, just to add some authenticity and indeed instil some confidence in all of us. For all the good the hat did, he might as well have chucked it over the side.

We knew nothing of speed regulations or whether one had to "drive" on the left or the right. It soon became apparent that it was not a free for all, as we had at first suspected, and that there are indeed speed limits and you did have to keep to one side. We, of course, ignored all these rules and careered from one side of the river to the other, insults being hurled at us through loud hailers as we went. Then we passed a bunch of very keen-looking fishermen sitting peacefully on the river bank. Suddenly, all their rods dipped into the water in unison, and we realised that we had somehow got entangled in all their lines. They were not in the least bit happy, so we pulled hard on the throttle and sped past, probably taking a rod or two with us. The wake from our craft caused such a wash that water lapped over the keener fishermen's waders, leaving them with boots full of Thames water as well as buggered fishing rods.

Night time was closing in on us and, as we approached yet another lock, it was virtually pitch black. We were ordered by the lock keeper to travel no further, as we had no navigation lights. We did have white lights, but apparently you have to have coloured ones. We did, however, have some toffee wrappers (Liz had eaten all the sweets) in all kinds of colours, and suggested sticking whatever colour may be required over our white lights, but this was deemed unacceptable.

I pleaded with the lock keeper to let us through, but he would have none of it, so there we were, stuck in a bloody lock for the night. I decided the best course of action would be to leave the boat and set off in search of a local hostelry and have a decent dinner. It was Halloween night, so there was a great deal of revelry going on. We trudged across muddy fields in complete darkness, a bit like in that film "The Blair Witch Project". By the time we arrived at what seemed like an acceptable pub/restaurant, we were all soaking wet and covered in mud, which did not go down at all well with the landlord. There were bunches of balloons festooned all over the pub and, as Spud by now was so pissed, he lurched around bursting them with his cigarette. Along with not being welcome in the pub, we were now causing complete havoc and destroying the jolly little evening that the landlord had intended.

Spud announced that it was far too posh anyway, so we set off across the fields for pastures new. We finally found a pub that would serve us, so you can imagine what that was like! We got something to eat and an awful lot to drink, after which we set off back to the lock, where even more was drunk. We were running out of space within the dismal craft, so empties were beginning to be thrown out of the window. In the morning, Liz was disgusted to find cans of light ale, Guinness, lager and wine bottles bobbing all around us. She set about clearing up the lock before the guy arrived to let us out.

The morning developed into quite a pleasant day, weather wise, and we set off, after a huge fry-up, further downstream, or was it up? It was Sunday, the traditional day for the dreadful boating types to take their little boxes on water out for a spin. They wore their captain's hats in all seriousness, and their deck shoes, fuck knows why, as their boats were mainly made of fibre glass. We were behind a little plastic tub being skippered by a Mr. & Mrs. Perfect, out with the kids for their Sunday jaunt. Mind you, at least they knew how to make their boat stop, which we still didn't.

As we approached yet another lock, the "perfect" family was intent in getting into it first. I would have none of it and it was a case of full steam ahead, until we collided with them, knocking them completely off course and causing them to miss the lock entrance altogether. We ground to a halt by crashing into the end of the lock as per usual and the "perfect" family slipped in behind us with looks of total disgust. They said nothing, but they didn't need to, the looks were sufficient.

It was now starting to look highly unlikely that we were going to make Marlow for lunch, if at all. We did actually make it to Marlow, but the worst was still to come. Apart from Liz, who seems always prepared for any eventuality, we were all unshaven, dishevelled wrecks. Spud was the first horror to jump ashore and tie the "African Queen" up on the bank, and we could just about make out the horrified stares from the staff within the restaurant. It wasn't long before bow-tied waiters came running down the manicured lawns, waving their arms in disgust and ordering us off the property.

It was futile to try and reason with them, as we did look a disgrace, so not only did we not get to have lunch with my mum and Brian (which was probably just as well, as she'd have been appalled) but we also had to make our way back to Reading to drop the bloody boat off. So off we set again, foregoing any thought of lunch, to get the absurd boat back to its rightful owner. He was more than bloody welcome to it!

The weather had taken a decided turn for the worst. The heavens opened and now it was pissing down with rain. We endured a couple of daft lock procedures, before, to cap it all, the throttle cable broke and we found ourselves floundering about in all directions, unable to manoeuvre. Mark, being a bit of a DIY expert, figured out that if we all took our belts off and utilised a bit of old rope, we could make a link to the throttle control. Someone would have to sit at the back of the boat (whichever end you call that) and tighten the tension to give us speed.

I was not at all happy at this stage, so suggested it should be Mark who sat out in the pouring rain and pulled on the combination of belts and rope to make us go along. I was also more than a little pissed and Spud didn't even come into the category of capability at this stage, so it was left to Liz to steer. I retired to what was, for want of a better word, my cabin.

I don't know how long passed or how much water we had covered, but I was rudely interrupted from my slumbers by another problem which no-one seemed capable of dealing with. Spud was in a coma, so there was little point in rousing him, so I assembled myself as best I could and went to the "steering section" of the boat, the front bit. Liz was in a panic, because the contraption of belts and rope had snapped and we were once again floundering atop the murky waters of the Thames.

From time to time, we bumped against a piece of land which was in fact the garden of a waterside resident, so I suggested throwing a rope onto the obligatory manicured lawn, thus securing the boat until we could evaluate the situation further. A huge stake was therefore bashed into the lawn and the boat was secured. It wasn't long before what looked like an old colonel and his even older-looking colonel wife came marching towards us.

They spoke in that upper class twang which even educated people find hard to understand, in fact they just made upper class noises. These were the original upper class twits. It was, however, more than evident that they were very unhappy with the situation. By this time, so was I. I couldn't be doing with the strange noises which emanated from their mouths, but still did my best to explain our predicament reasonably and politely. In fact I was even expecting, in view of my very reasonable behaviour, an invitation into the house for a resuscitating brandy, or at least a cup of tea. I persevered for some time trying to translate their strange noises, until in the end I gave up and told them both to Fuck Off.

Immediately, the shout went up: "Daaaaaaaaaaaahling, caaaaaall for the powlice!" So we, or rather Mark, set about making repairs and, if indeed the police ever did come, we were long gone, even though Liz then had fears of the River Police giving chase. Liz is always prone to panic. Miraculously, we reached Henley, where there was a training session in progress with several of those long thin things with about twelve guys rowing.

We blasted our way through the lot of them, the wash in our wake throwing them into all kinds of mayhem and the guy with the loud hailer bawling at us in very un-Henley language. "Bollocks" was our response, as we ploughed on like inept Vikings, Mark soaked to the skin but refreshed by a continual flow of brandy and lager, ferried to and fro by me.

Even when we reached our destination, the worst was still to come. Spud was standing, or rather wobbling, at the front of the boat, as if returning victoriously from an Atlantic crossing, when suddenly, he disappeared. We all knew that Spud couldn't swim and there he was, gone. Oh, for fuck's sake, I thought, now the bloody weekend's ended in a drowning incident.

We all ran round the boat looking for a sighting of Spud. Suddenly, he bobbed up, so Liz, desperate to assist, grabbed one of those round things that are supposed to keep a drowning person afloat. She seemed to be having some difficulty in lifting it and it turned out, on closer inspection, that they were actually made of concrete and were purely for decoration. She hurled this thing at Spud, just as he seemed to be "doggy paddling"away and doing pretty well. It struck him firmly and fairly on his head and he sank again.

"Oh fuck", shouted Liz, "I've killed him!"

What seemed like a long time later, Spud resurfaced on the other side of the boat, a bit bruised and battered, having been keel-hauled several times, and we managed to pull him aboard and plied him with some little needed brandy. He sat bemused in the cabin with his Long Johns on, until eventually the familiar Spud laugh came back to his blue face. Only we could have done this. We had managed to turn a pleasant weekend on the Thames into the Normandy landings.

Spud was well-read but not well dressed. Once, I was sitting in a restaurant with Zak Starkey (of whom more later), when Spud parked his pushbike outside on a visit to the off-licence, where he always stocked up on cider for the weekend. Zak saw him first and said, "There's Spud, get him in". I obeyed, at which point the staff rushed up from all directions, saying, "You can't bring him in here!". I said, "He's with us, he comes in or we go", which seemed to solve the problem.

But Spud did have the occasional triumph, for example the day when Rod Stewart made a surprise appearance in The Red Lion one Sunday lunchtime, causing some consternation amongst the barmaids and a few other regulars. Spud had often regaled us all with tales of his time with Rod, but we hadn't believed half of them. There was therefore even further consternation when Rod came over and said, "Hi Spud, how you doing?", before engaging him in conversation at some length. Spud called me over and said, "This is my new boss, do you know Eddie?"

Rod looked me up and down before replying, "Yes, I'm afraid I do". I wasn't sure how to take that, so after a brief hello, I left Spud and Rodney together, with Spud loving every minute of it. Afterwards, he came up to me and said, "Showed all that lot, didn't I?!"

During the separation dramas with the my ex partner, I got a writ one morning, summoning me to the High Court in the Strand. It was signed by Spud and witnessed by ... guess who. It was a case brought against me for demanding with menaces the keys for my own house from Spud. I thought we'd make a bit of a day of it, so I got together a crowd and we set off for the court. We all went to the Wig & Pen pub, got pissed and headed into court for the hearing, which was a bit of a farce.

I had to get lawyers and whatever comes with them to defend me. Tony Barton shouted out "Hang 'im!" and we were overall a pretty raucous bunch, which didn't go down too well with the judge, or whatever he was. Predictably, I lost the case and had to pay damages and costs and everything else that goes with losing a court case, so, a few thousand pounds lighter, we went back to The Wig & Pen and got slaughtered. I didn't speak to Spud for a year after that.

I then acquired a new neighbour, who had bought the Manor House across the road from me. His name was Clive Brandy and he managed a singer called Iris Williams. I could write an entire volume just on this phase of my life. Clive was to have a big effect on life in Sunningdale for a few years to come.

My first encounter with Clive was when he arrived in the pub to introduce himself to the community. He was a big man with a big voice and in fact everything he did was "big", though it turned out that he didn't have "big" money. He marched into the pub and demanded "champagne, not council house rubbish, the vintage stuff!" The landlord at the time, Gerry Pile, had no vintage champagne on the premises, so Clive despached him to the off-licence to buy several cases. Gerry, of course, could see the makings of a fantastic customer, so off he went.

At the end of the evening, Clive announced that he had no money with him so would it be possible to put it on his slate, which of course he didn't have, as this was his first ever visit. He had such a demanding and authorative voice that it was written down immediately. Clive didn't return to the pub for months.

Shortly after Clive, the comedian Jim Davidson arrived. Jim and Clive were great friends and between them they managed to bring about even more havoc than was already going on. Clive, Jim and I became mates, and there were no boundaries to our drinking, inside or outside of opening hours. It's hard to know where to start, but for the moment I'll concentrate on Clive. He, like a lot of us, had arrived in Sunningdale and felt he was in the country, so set about turning his grounds into a farm. He bought hundreds of chickens and a huge number of rabbits with a view to supplying all the local restaurants with fresh produce. He had so many animals that they were racked up, cage upon cage, three or four tiers high, encircling the perimeter of his grounds.

Clive, of course, had no idea whatsoever about farming and very soon became plagued by rats. This was a major problem, because the rats were starting to outgrow the rabbits and in fact became so big that it was actually quite frightening. Even Clive became a bit concerned, so started to have shooting evenings in order to keep the rats down.

The rats would cross the lane between Clive's house and mine in a virtual sea and honestly, traffic was beginning to stop to let them cross. Sadly, they were crossing into my grounds and my mother was terrified of mice, let alone gargantuan rats. They never actually penetrated my house, but it became so bad that my mum rang the council to get a health inspector round. Clive was not at all happy about this, but I think he was more than a little relieved when they closed his farming activities down.

Actually IN the kitchen he had a pig and a very loud cockerel, which he'd named Garth. This creature, for some reason, only had one leg. One night, I went round to Clive's with Peter Gosling for a shooting night, but Peter was so horrified by what he saw that he made his excuses and left.

Prior to all of this, I had installed, at great expense, a 24 track studio in Herne Place. I'd managed to find the most expensive carpenters in the universe to do the control room. They did a magnificent job... but for £18,000! The very first project was with a band which Pete York had formed, called "Pete York's New York". There was nothing new about them at all, in fact they all looked and were quite a bit older than me. They were basically a jazz band, which I felt was doomed from the off, and indeed it was. I guested on the album but my contributions were NOT jazz.

Anyway, Clive saw the studio as a very handy workplace, as it was within walking distance of his house, so it wasn't long before Iris Williams was recording there. I in fact wrote and produced an entire album for her, of which I am still very proud, but sadly it was released on President Records which is better-kept secret than MI5, so it was condemned to total non-exposure.

Clive had negotiated the President deal for Iris with the label's boss Eddie Kassner. He was a guy who never paid anyone until they asked, and even then you would only get a fraction of what you were due. I was present at the negotiations and they were hilarious. Eddie Kassner was Jewish and Clive made all the wrong remarks. On perusing the contract, he noticed that it was not a world deal but a universe deal, so he asked for Saturn to be excluded from the contract.

He was given a meagre budget but, thanks to synthesisers, I managed to pad it out with an "orchestra". Clive was always demanding a bigger budget from Kassner, but of course this was futile and during one fruitless telephone conversation, he ended by saying to Eddie, "Talking to you, I now realise what gave Hitler his inspiration". Oh God!

Clive thought that I should be back on the road and suggested we get the Spencer Davis Group back together again. I started recording with Ray Fenwick and Zak Starkey and we did a couple of tracks to get the ball rolling. Then Clive set off for Los Angeles to meet up with Spencer.

I was never quite sure what happened at the meeting but I do know that it did not result in the SDG reforming. Clive had checked into the Beverley Hills Hotel and invited Spencer over. Spencer is a little eccentric and, having arrived in his 1967 Mini, told Clive that the Beverley Hills Hotel was a rip-off and that it might be best that they eat somewhere else. Clive was happy to oblige but couldn't fit into the Mini (this gives you a bit of an idea of how big he was), so it was the hotel for lunch after all.

Spencer did come over to England and stayed at Herne Place, where we played over the tracks. Zak fucked up the entire situation in a fairly major way. Zak was very young then, but could match any of us drink for drink and beyond. On that occasion, I had suggested that we should stay sober at least for one night.

Zak said he would only drink orange juice. He started off well enough, but was eventually seduced by a bottle of brandy. He said he would just have a splash in the orange juice. As time progressed, I noticed that the orange juice had gone brown and by now he was in fact drinking neat brandy and rapidly getting totally out of it. Now Zak could get a little tricky when pissed and this night was no exception. His response when Spencer played one of his new songs was, "You must be fucking joking, that's total shit!"

Spencer was not amused and replied, "If your father was here now ..." So it was a total disaster and the next day Spencer left. I mentioned this episode to Spencer quite recently and he said that all he could remember about his visit was that he got lost in the garden!. Clive summoned Zak to the Manor House and gave him what he considered to be a serious talking-to about his behaviour. It of course made no difference, as both Zak and I were hell-bent on self-destruction.

One of the most embarrassing moments I can recall with Clive concerned an Argentinian harp player whom he managed. That's harp as in the big between your knees harp, not Mick Jagger-style blueswailing harp. Clive knew that I had various contacts within certain record companies and he asked me, or rather told me, to fix up a meeting with one of them.

I already had an appointment for myself with Bronze Records, a heavy metal label starring the likes of Uriah Heep. Clive saw no reason why his harpist wouldn't fit in. We arrived at Chalk Farm, where the offices of Bronze were located, and went in to meet the label manager Robert Lemon. Clive took over the situation and my meeting became irrelevant. He informed Robert that he had a harp player extraordinaire. I guess that much was true. Robert explained that they only held A & R meetings once a week and that today was not the day. Clive would have none of this, and demanded an A&R meeting on the spot. Robert gave in and we went downstairs to get the little Argentinian and his harp, all wedging ourselves into the lift: an enormous harp, an enormous Clive and me.

He set the thing up in the corridor and proceeded to play "Stranger In Paradise" to a totally bemused group of A& R men. He played the harp like most people shoot a bow and arrow, i.e. the melody moved in the right direction but it was never quite spot-on. I went and hid in the toilet while Clive attempted to convince Robert and all the others what a discovery they had on their hands. I really don't know how Robert talked his way out of it, but I think he got around it by suggesting, "Let's go to lunch". Now that was another problem.

When we sat down to lunch, the conversation was obviously about the music business. On the next table there was an American girl who just happened to be a composer, so Clive immediately got us (me and himself) involved. I was subsequently bombarded with cassettes of the most awful songs, an attack which went on for some considerable time before she gave up.

Clive's finances were in a total mess and he had regular visits from the VAT man. In fact, these were so regular that Clive's ferocious guard dog became quite friendly with the inspector, although he never seemed to take a shine to me (that's the dog, not the VAT man ... well, either of them, actually). The VAT inspector was at a bit of a loss, eventually commanding, "Mr. Brandy, you have to get your books in order". Clive's reply was, "Samuel Pepys couldn't sort my books out!" Invariably, the VAT man was subjected to Clives's hospitality, which generally came in liquid form. This had the result that the VAT man would get completely pissed and spend the rest of the day swimming and drinking round the pool.

Jim Davidson, Clive and I would have the most outrageous lunches at The Thatched Tavern, a great little pub / restaurant which was in Cheapside and therefore conveniently just down the road from us. These lunches went on for so long that, on occasion, we stayed on for dinner as well. Clive never paid; that duty always seemed to be down to me or Jim, though it was Clive who did all the ordering.

When the waiter came to ask if we'd like an aperitif, Clive would always order a case of Chablis, "just to be getting on with". Jim hardly ate anything, but there was never any wine left at the end of the meal, so then it was on to the port and the brandy. In fact, that was how Clive got his name "Brandy". It wasn't his real name (I never knew what that was), it was just given to him because of his liking for that particular drink.

The journeys home from the Thatched Tavern could be very disturbing. On one occasion, as I took Clive home in my Aston Martin, we drove right across a small grass roundabout and then straight across a T junction, where I missed the "Little Chef" by inches. It certainly sobered Clive up, so when we got to his house, another bottle of Chablis was approached. Steven Stills was staying with Ringo Starr at Tittenhurst Park and, for some reason, Stills was really taken by the Little Chef, where he had breakfast most mornings, presumably because it was the nearest thing he could find to a genuine American diner.

Liz was very much on the scene at this point, although the other demon hadn't yet moved out, because before that could happen, I had to raise a considerable sum of money. One night, Liz, Jim, Clive, Iris Williams, I and our friend Dr Mike and his wife Sue all went to a trendy Chinese restaurant called "The Jade Fountain", which was very good but also very expensive. We took up, as you can imagine, a very big table, where Clive took immediate control and set about ordering. He cast the menu aside and ordered a "job lot" plus, as usual, a case of Chablis. This was unceremoniously placed beside the table, still in the bloody case! The "job lot" turned out to be more than the entire restaurant could possibly have eaten, and I remember a mountain of spare ribs which Clive attacked like a starved animal. His teeth were not in peak condition and, as he ate the ribs, his front teeth demonstrated a kind of lever action, much like a cat flap!

Every Sunday morning, we would have a shooting party at Herne Place. Only clay pigeons were shot at, but it was nonetheless a very risky business, as we'd all start drinking at 9 am. Jim was a keen participant, as was Paul Trimmings, though he only came for the booze and one time nearly blew his foot off, not being sure whether the gun was loaded or not. We were banned from crossing the courtyard by my "ex" because it was visible from her kitchen window and she did, after all, have a Court Order. Jim, however, completely ignored this and walked through regardless, shotgun broken across his shoulder. Eventually, a padlock was put on the gates, so that put paid to that.

We had a barbeque once, not an intimate gathering (there must have been about 200 people there). On that occasion, my "ex" took her Court Order to its ultimate extreme and demanded that a rope be erected to divide the main lawn into half, her half and my half. Can you believe this? It's true! I had to have a special barbeque made for this event, one which was capable of roasting an entire pig, plus steaks, a mountain of sausages, pork chops and all the other requisites for a barbecue. On the booze front, we had three dustbins (new and clean ones) in which we mixed up the most evil of punches.

A guy named Dean Tompkins, who owned The Belvedere, was in charge of mixing the punch. He put everything he could think of into it, brandy, port, whiskey, gin, vodka, every spirit you can imagine. Bear in mind he had three entire dustbins bins to fill up. It was a bit of a shock to see several people (who I actually knew) passing bottles of booze, plus steaks and pork chops, over the fence to take home. That's how to exploit your resident decadent musician. The weather forecast for the evening was not good, so I also hired, at the last minute, a huge marquee. The forecast was wrong and not a soul entered the bloody thing all night.

More now about our closest friend at Herne Place, who was Ringo Starr's son (and currently drummer with The Who and Johnny Marr), Zak Starkey. Zak was very young when we first met, maybe only sixteen or seventeen, but we got on straight away and our friendship has now survived for nearly three decades.

In 1976, I met a Mike O'Donnell, who was running the recording studio at Tittenhurst Park. This mansion had formerly been the home of John Lennon and had then been passed on to Ringo Starr, and was about a mile from Herne Place. I had at that time formed the band Axis Point, along with Charlie Whitney, Rob Townsend and Charlie McCracken. We were looking for somewhere to record outside London, so Tittenhurst seemed ideal, especially for me!

We spent about a month at Tittenhurst recording our second album and, during the course of this, became friendly with Mike. Ringo had gone on holiday and left Zak in Mike's care. During this period, the three of us went out for a lunchtime of madness, not entirely planned by Mike but induced by my good self. It was at The Thatched Tavern and the teenaged Zak rounded his meal off with copious amounts of tea (which was all right) laced with brandy (which wasn't). The outcome was that he threw up all over Mike's car, while I slunk off and left them to it.

Following this inauspicious start, Zak and I would bump into each other in various pubs and eventually started working together on my "Wind In The Willows" project. At one time, there was even talk of him joining The Spencer Davis Group, and Zak and I recorded a couple of tracks which now appear on my solo album "Just Passing Through".

Despite that initial incident, Zak and I became great friends and, as he was living alone at the time, in a cottage in the grounds of Tittenhurst Park, Liz would bring our dinners to us, as we were both completely useless at looking after ourselves. For a long time after that, Liz and I sort of adopted Zak. We would go everywhere together and have the most riotous lunches.

Zak's mum Maureen, no longer with Ringo, was in a relationship with Isaac Tigrant, who at the time owned the Hard Rock Café in London. As a result of this relationship, Zak was lucky enough to have a battered old piece of paper in his pocket which said, "Give this man and his friends anything they want!" This was a very dangerous note to give Zak, but he took Isaac at his word and we'd make the occasional foray to the Hard Rock, sweep past the long queue and indeed be given absolutely anything we wanted.

On my birthday, I can't remember which one, Maureen set up a "night" for us, which started when we (that is Zak, Liz, myself and a driver) met up with Maureen and Isaac at The Hard Rock. When we had all had more than enough to eat and drink, Maureen suggested we all go on to Tramp, a club which was very nice but again very expensive. At this stage of the evening, it wasn't entirely clear as to who would pick up the tab. We all went into the restaurant (another one!), where I ordered some reasonably priced wine. Maureen said to me, "You don't really like that piss, let's have some good stuff!" So she ordered the "good stuff" and then more and more and more of the "good stuff", by which time we were all paralytic, including the bloody driver.

It was a celebrity packed night, as the driver later pointed out to me. Personally, I was too out of it to know who was there, but apparently in the restaurant were Michael Caine, Mel Brooks with his wife Ann Bancroft, George Best, and others that I can't remember. Maureen decided to get the whole restaurant to sing "Happy Birthday", a nice thought but a little embarrassing. Still, Maureen did indeed pick up the tab, so thanks to her, it was a night to remember (even though I actually couldn't!).

After Tramp was closed, Maureen had still not had enough fun, so we all went back to her house, where we had even more to drink. By now it was daylight and Liz still had a job to go to, but this idea was very soon abandoned, probably that very day, because our lifestyle did not fit in with the concept of jobs! The film "Arthur" had just been released and I decided to become Arthur; in fact, Zak still maintains that I was better at Arthur than Dudley Moore was. Our lives were totally devoted to fun and indeed, fun is the best thing to have and I don't regret a second of it, no matter how decadent it may appear to have been.

Eventually, Ringo decided to sell Tittenhurst Park, studio and all. He wanted a million pounds for it so, unable to resist temptation, I set about raising finance to buy it. Not only did I consider it to be an historic monument, but also I hoped to generate an income from the studio. When I had the finance in place, I took my mother round to see the property. She said she thought I was mad, but then she usually did. I probably was mad, but the family vetoed the whole idea and another great opportunity (as far as I was concerned) was lost. The building and some ninety acres was eventually sold for around 4.5 million, but the new owner desecrated the whole thing and now it's a gaudy monstrosity.

The other nearby property I nearly bought was Fort Belvedere, which was ludicrously cheap, but again I was vetoed. I lost the opportunity of buying property after property through bad advice, though I feel that my mother's motivation was just to keep the family under one roof.

And so life continued at Herne Place. The studio was doing well and there was never any shortage of cash, so chaos also continued. There was a constant flow of quite impressive clients, including Denny Laine, Rick Wakeman, Sad Café, Mike Rutherford, Brian May, Bruce Foxton, Maggie Bell, Steve Hackett, Donovan, Billy Ocean and many others that I can't remember.

To me, of course, this was absolute bliss. Not only did I have a going concern, I also had musicians to drink with. Renaissance recorded two albums in the studio and the process seemed to go on for an age. They were serious party animals, whose priority every day was to stock up on booze and spend the rest of the day drinking it (and occasionally recording something).

Sometimes, though, my "partying" didn't go down too well. When Brian May was in the studio, working with Chris Thompson, I arrived in the control room one morning with a gun, not intending to shoot anyone but just to mess around with it. I was very pissed and the producer, Stuart Taylor, was unimpressed and stared at me in total horror, as did everyone else. The gun was jammed, so I asked John Acock to pass me over an electrical screwdriver to resolve the problem. Next thing I knew, the weapon suddenly went off. I've never seen guitars and gear packed away so quickly in my life. Everyone ran away and the following day a furious Stuart demanded a refund. He didn't receive one, but the problem was resolved by giving him some free studio time for one of his projects.

Another band, made up from bits of the Climax Blues Band and a couple of other guys, worked in the studio for around two months. Again, it was party time, but unfortunately they were managed by Miles Copeland, who also managed The Police. Copeland was (purely in my opinion, you understand) an obnoxious bastard, who sat in the control room listening to playbacks and giving the band points out of ten for each song. He'd written the points on pieces of card and silently held them up after each song. I thought this was particularly humiliating for the band and told Copeland to Fuck Off.

Whilst the band were a bit dubious about my remark, I think they respected me for saying it, because he deserved it. He said to me, "On whose authority?" I replied that I owned the fucking place and indeed he left and not a word was ever mentioned again. Copeland also managed Renaissance, but never showed up to any of their sessions.

Rick Wakeman was my best customer. Not only was he a lunatic drinker but he booked the studio endlessly. He was a very early riser and would arrive for work at around 8.30 a.m., when the first thing he'd demand would be a pint of port and brandy. We both used to go to the pub around 9 a.m., where he'd have his port and brandy and a couple of pints of lager to steady himself for the day. By lunchtime, I'd had it and had to go to bed to recover, but Rick stayed the course way into the evening, when we'd all end up back in the pub for more. Every night he'd order a gargantuan

Chinese takeaway, which very rarely actually got taken away hot.

He was on the brink of marrying Nina Carter, a serious error of judgement, as far as I was concerned. Rick held parts of his stag night at Herne Place and other parts at The Camberley Football Club, of which he'd somehow become chairman. We had to make special arrangements with my ex-partner to gain access to my Billiards Room for part of the stag celebrations. Rick of course got slaughtered (by booze, not by my ex-partner) and stayed the night. Nina, however, persevered with him and the marriage went ahead.

The actual wedding was, to me, like a showbiz nightmare, in fact I'd never seen anything like it before, nor wish to again. Nina prepared the guest list and it fell to my secretary to contact everyone with their invitations. There were hundreds of people that Rick and Nina probably didn't even know, but were public "faces", and this was very important to Nina. As far as I was concerned, the most awful person at the "do" was the model Jilly Johnson, full of bullshit about how beautiful she looked for her age.

Brian Adams had bought a huge firework affair which lit up to say "CONGRATULATIONS RICK AND NINA". Needless to say, Herne Place Studios got the bill. Nina's friend Jilly Johnson arrived in a poxy helicopter with an awful poseur twat of an escort. Unfortunately, the chopper landed on the bloody fireworks, the end result being that the message read: "CO..G..TN...S ICK & NA". Money well spent.

As the guests arrived for the "do", they were all captured by a hired photographer to have their photo taken with ... Rick and Nina, of course. They handled their wedding like a publicity campaign. Thank Christ "Hello" magazine wasn't around at the time, otherwise it would have been even worse. The climax of the evening was the band, which featured Kenny Lynch (a guy who would go to the opening of a door), Rick Parfitt, Denny Laine, myself, Rick, and a few others. I do have a photograph of this, which captures the full horror of the event.

And so they were married. I can't recall a honeymoon, I think Rick promised this would happen later! Next, they appointed a chauffeur, an essential item for Nina, and even more essential for Rick, who had a three year ban running at the time. The incident which had led to the ban went as follows: The police opened the door of his Rolls and Rick fell into the road. When asked for his name, he replied, "Oscar Peterson", then passed out. They had a Range Rover and a Rolls Royce and someone to drive them, so Nina could sit in the back. As you can tell, I didn't have the utmost respect for Nina, but I always did for Rick, in spite of his very showbizzy outlook.

The drinking at the studio continued at a furious pace. During one session with Rick, his lips actually went blue and he looked most unwell. He did confess to not feeling on top form, but still managed to continue playing, seemingly unaffected. What a constitution.

Around this time, Jim Davidson started hosting the most extravagant of parties and it was at one of these affairs that I met Keith Emerson again, and I suppose my desire to perform again was re-kindled. Jim had set up a huge marquee in his garden, within which was a pretty good-sized stage. A very big PA was set up (Jim owned a PA hire company at the time and I think he must have used most of his stock on those evenings) plus a Hammond organ and Jim's own band for the basic backing. Everyone joined in, Denny Laine, myself and Keith. They were great evenings and we'd all shout out requests. Bear in mind that the repertoire consisted of "America" and "Rondo", plus anything else anyone requested, and as ever I was impressed by his virtuosity. Jim was in complete awe of Keith and to this day insists on using bits of ELP on The Generation Game!

My own wedding to Liz finally happened on February 2nd, 1985. At long last, all my previous relationship problems had been sorted out, but unfortunately there were troubles of a different kind ahead. As Liz had previously been married and her parents were Catholic religious maniacs, we could not get married in a church of Catholic denomination (not that I wanted to anyway, but it seemed that rules are rules). Her parents completely disowned her and to this day I have never met either of them, which I still find quite upsetting.

Liz went through the most awful times, especially with her mother, who at one point threw "holy water" (probably bathwater) over her in a Catholic fit. She said that Liz would burn in Hellfire and that the marriage was doomed from the start and had no possible chance of lasting. That's strange, because twenty years on, including the years prior to the marriage, we are still together and happier than ever. Her parents, on the other hand, appear to live in abject misery and hardly speak to each other.

Whenever we sent them Christmas presents, they were simply returned. On one occasion, they both arrived at our house and I saw these two strange people talking to Liz at the mouth of our drive. When I asked who they were, Liz replied that they were strangers who were lost and were just asking for directions. This was what her mother had told her to say. Liz had in fact invited them in, but it seems that it was beyond the pale for a Catholic maniac to even clap eyes on a non-Catholic who was married to their daughter. I have no religious beliefs one way or the other, but I accept that people have the right to believe in whatever they like. What I cannot accept is their interfering with others (extreme Devil-dodgers).

Anyway, I've never met them and, 20 years later, still have no desire whatsoever to do so. I explained this situation to an aunt of mine recently, who initially took a more conciliatory approach, saying, "But they are family whether you like it or not, and I'm sure it'll all work out at some point. It's good for families to stick together". I explained some of the history, the lost strangers, Holy Water etc. "Oh, I see," said the aunt, "fuck 'em then!"

After we'd solved the problem of finding a substitute father to give Liz away, in the shape of Tony Barton (star of Coronation Street, Emmerdale Farm, Grange Hill and the Stones Bitter adverts, also a comedian), the wedding was held at The United Reform Church in Camberley and was conducted by a Reverend Long. It seemed that part of the deal was that a contribution had to be made to the church. Rick donated £500 (his cheque bounced) and I made a similar contribution, to have part of the roof restored.

The Reverend Long seemed a nice enough chap, even though we had to go to a few meetings with him, during which he did his best to convert me to a faith. This of course was a wasted effort on his part. Rick, however, was in due course converted, though I think he only went along with it because Nina probably wanted to meet the Pope or an Archbishop or two to add to their celebrity roster. Rick still believes (I'm not quite sure in what), but I suppose he has his reasons, so good luck to him.

I, however, still do NOT believe. It's hard enough to get through the average day as it is, let alone find the time to moon about in search of a God who I don't think anyone has ever actually met. But, come the day, if there is someone or something, I don't think I'll be very polite after all the shit I've been through in life.

The night before the wedding, I had stayed over at Rick's house (repaying the compliment) and was forbidden to have anything to drink at all. In the morning, my best man John Fisher arrived at Rick's house to make the journey with me to the church. John, like me is (in my case was) a professional drinker and had absolutely no chance of facing the oncoming ceremony sober. Rick and Nina had already left and, while we waited for the car to arrive, John finished off virtually a bottle of whiskey and I did serious damage to a bottle or two of wine. For the short journey to the church, John also had a hip flask, from which he took frequent swigs.

So we arrived, feeling suddenly sober as we took our places in the church. Liz appeared shortly after, not late as tradition dictates, and the Reverend Long bent down and whispered to me that she looked absolutely beautiful. Of course, to me she always did and always will.

Now Tony Barton, the "stand in father", was not renowned for his generosity, in fact, to be frank, he was fucking mean! Stan Boardman, another comedian, once stayed with Tony for a few days and told me that Tony turned the gas off every time he turned the bacon over. As the service began, the question was raised, "Who giveth this woman...?'" At that point, Jim Davidson decided to add some extra contributions of his own to the service and you could hear him shouting in the background: "It's the only fucking thing he's ever given away in his life!"

As Tony Barton retaliated and things seemed to be starting to get a little out of control, the Reverend Long said to me, "Well, I suppose these occasions should be a little joyous". He didn't have a clue as to just how joyous it could have got! I particularly remember Tommy Boyce, the guy who wrote a lot of the hits for The Monkees, being present in the church. He sat in the pews wearing a massive white stetson and looked more than a little out of place. Then it was on to the reception, well, more like a gig, really, as I'd invited lots of musician friends along, such as Rick Wakeman, Keith Emerson, Denny Laine, Spencer Davis, Pete York, etc., etc., with a view to us all having a "jam", which of course we did! Spencer unfortunately had to leave with Pete York, as they had a show to play elsewhere.

The reception was handled by a dear friend of ours, Dean Tomkins, who owned a pub /restaurant called The Belvedere, which was situated just behind Fort Belvedere, one of the many places I'd very nearly bought. This just happened to be up the road from Herne Place, so, as you can see, in those days we didn't travel far outside of our little community. Dean made a fantastic effort for us and the food and catering were exceptional. I put £2000 behind the bar, just to get things rolling, which they certainly did. I have a feeling that Dean himself probably contributed the same, as he was enjoying the day so much. Many of the people who came that day said it was the best wedding they'd ever been to, and as for the cabaret ... well, you couldn't have bought it even if you'd wanted to.

That night, completely out of the blue, the Pike turned up! I hadn't seen him since the days of Hardin & York, but he volunteered to take up his driving post once again and take me and Liz home to our cottage, complete with all the wedding presents. We invited him in, but the Pike was not blessed with diplomacy and, after a few drinks and a lot of reminiscing, I felt it appropriate that he left. That's not unreasonable on someone's wedding night, is it? But would he go? No, he bloody well wouldn't, so as a last resort I said, "Well, I'm off to bed", a good enough hint to anyone under the circumstances, but obviously not to the Pike.

So off I went I went to bed. Liz tells me that she was quite anxious to join me but the Pike said, "Don't you want to know what's in that great big box?'" Of course, at that precise moment in time she didn't give a monkey's what was in ANY of the boxes. Still, thinking it might precipitate his departure, she went ahead and let him open it. This whetted his appetite to find out what was in the rest of the boxes, so they sat there until God knows when and opened the lot. Meanwhile, I'd drifted off to sleep and didn't see Liz until the morning, so thank you very much, dear Pike.

The following morning, I woke from my sort of coma and went to visit my mum, much to the disgust of Liz. After all, there was still the early morning bliss which might have been observed, but that's what I did, sorry. Mum was by now living alone at Herne Place, all 32 rooms of it. Suffice to say that my action did not go down well at all.

And so married life began, though initially it seemed to be little different from my un-married life. Not that I was still a womaniser, in fact, from the day I met Liz I can honestly say I have been 100 percent monogamous, even though, as most couples do, we've had many turbulent times to endure.

On with the madness. There was a time when I had a white Bentley on loan for the weekend, I suppose with a view to buying the atrocious thing. In the late sixties, it was sort of acceptable to have a white Rolls or Bentley, indeed I had a white Rolls, but by the mid to late seventies they had become "wedding cars". Anyway, I brought this thing home and Liz initially refused even to get in it, though I managed to convince her to go as far as the local shops, just to see what it was like. We parked right outside Bottoms Up, the wine merchants, where I went in and ordered my booze for the forthcoming week. It was, as usual, a hefty order so a guy was appointed to load the stuff into the boot. I paid the bill, we got back into the Bentley, I switched on the ignition and ... nothing.

After a few abortive attempts at starting the bloody thing, faces were beginning to appear at the window of Bottoms Up, wondering what on earth could go wrong with a Bentley. Embarrassment was setting in, as well as a raging row within the car. I then remembered that there was a re-set switch in a panel just below the steering column. You just lower a flap, press the red button and in theory the electrical system is fully restored. It worked, but as I had no intention of buying the car in the first place, and as I didn't want to face the owner on Monday morning and tell him I didn't want it, I spent the rest of the day trying to sell it on to a third party. And who was the ideal man for a horrible flash brash white Bentley? Why,

Paul Trimmings, of course. He came round on the Sunday afternoon and bought it on the spot. I was saved!

But the saga didn't end there, because on a nightly basis, Paul would proudly swing the monstrosity into the pub car park, which made me begin to think of what to do to add a bit of amusement. I bought some thick red tape and one night, while Paul was drinking, I and a couple of other regulars stuck a big red cross on the passenger door.

Paul had a discreet rendezvous in London that night (I suppose the white monster must have impressed someone) and eventually, off he set for his trip, oblivious to the fact that the car now resembled a posh ambulance. Apparently, there was much hilarity on the M4, as passing cars and their passengers were seen by Paul to be roaring with laughter at him, which was not the effect he had had in mind at all.

He reached Hammersmith flyover before a police car pulled him over, which was all he needed. Not only was he driving a white Bentley ambulance, he was also over the limit. The policeman took him round to the passenger side and pointed out the evidence for Paul to see for himself. He of course knew immediately who the culprit was, but for the moment it was more important to blag his way out of his present predicament.

While the policeman pointed out that Paul was not wearing his seatbelt, the reek of whisky on his breath somehow went undetected. Paul acted dumb and said that he'd just bought the car and that he had got confused by so many switches and knobs on the dashboard. The policeman drew his attention to the fact that the safety belt was, as per normal, adjacent to his right shoulder. Paul replied, "Well, no wonder I couldn't find it!" He wasn't sure what adjacent meant! The next day, I got the telling off I was expecting. Luckily, we were such good friends that even he saw the funny side to it (plus he hadn't been nicked for drunk driving).

Paul then went into the clock business, where he foresaw unlimited fortunes coming his way. I don't think they did, because, for a start, he set up his showroom with the most unfortunate of addresses, Emperor Clocks, Trumps Green. He eventually re-located to Ascot, as his customers were finding it hard to tell their friends they'd bought a clock (a very nasty kit form reproduction grandfather clock) from Trumps Green. It did not have the sound of distinction.

While at Trumps Green, he had a double fronted shop, but the two parts were not linked together, so he decided to smash the wall down himself and turn the two shops into one. He'd told me of his plan, so I decided to ring him and pose as a planning officer. Paul fell for it, hook line and sinker. I started off by introducing myself in the manner of an obnoxiously officious character, as indeed most of those guys really are. I said, "I understand that you are carrying out unauthorised work at your premises".

"No, what are you talking about?" responded Paul. In the background you could hear quite clearly the thumping and crashing and obvious sounds of bricks and masonry falling everywhere. His voice and tone were becoming more and more irate. He shouted that the government was ruining the economy and knocking all the incentive out of every go-ahead person in the bloody country. "No wonder the country is in such a bloody state", he roared. "It's people like you..."

"Fancy a drink, Paul?", I interrupted. I'm sure anyone can imagine what he then called me. He shut the shop, we went to the pub and all business was cancelled for the day.

Paul's birthday came around and he rented a pub/restaurant for the lunchtime bash. It was the Belvedere Arms, right next door to Fort Belvedere, the Mr. & Mrs. Simpson house. His family were there, who were drinkers from the major league, but such a funny bunch. His brother Derek would just drink himself to a total standstill and stand there quietly singing and on occasion pissing himself, though his sister was fairly normal and reserved and usually left these gatherings at the right moment. I, of course, never did.

His other mate was a guy we all called "Bollocks". This came about because one night in the pub I'd asked him if he'd like a drink and he just looked at me and said, "Bollocks". Of course, I went to the bar and asked for "a pint of bollocks please", after which he was forever known by everyone in the area as Bollocks. It must have been a little difficult for his wife, who only came to the pub with him on a Sunday lunchtime, when everyone would cheerfully say, "Morning, Bollocks! What are you having?"

At the birthday bash, there was enormous drinking, before, during and after the lunch, and singing had started in earnest. Another of Paul's brothers was an Al Jolson impersonator, in fact a very good one, who would ramble through the Jolson catalogue and always bring tears to Paul's eyes during his rendition of "Sonny Boy". The songs were getting merrier and a little hysterical, at which point, for some unknown reason, Paul took his false teeth out and hurled them into the open fire. He instantly realised the error, but they were irretrievable and went up with a quick roar. Luckily, the rest of the day involved only drinking, so teeth weren't necessary. He went to Alan the dentist the next day and ordered a new set, but they never looked quite right. He took on a sort of Archie Andrews look and his s's became a little whistle when he spoke.

Paul's long-suffering wife and her mother lived in a large house in Wentworth and were both remarkably normal, verging on elegant in comparison to the brash Paul, who had started his career re-cycling chicken shit! He had a chicken farm in Kent, initially only producing eggs. Somehow, he felt that there should be some way of making money out of every aspect of the chicken.

He had thousands of chickens, but his staff couldn't pack the eggs quickly enough, so he approached a local mental institution, thinking he'd get cheap labour, which he did, although this had a very serious downside. He'd gone off for lunch one day and left the new employees packing away. Paul's lunches were long affairs and he was a big man. During his absence they must have got bored, because an egg fight ensued, meaning that when he eventually returned to the site, he was faced with the makings of a ten ton omelette.

My friendship with Paul continued until the day he died, which was very sudden. One night, he came to the pub as usual but wasn't his normal heavy Scotch drinking self. Even the landlord bought him a large one (some say that it was the shock that killed him, as the landlord was notoriously mean, considering the huge wads of money that were being thrown across the counter).

Through the letterbox one day came a letter announcing a clearance sale at Holloway Sanitorium. The items that interested me were various implements connected with snooker, as I now had a full size table and was looking for an antique scoreboard. At the Sanitorium, the table, as you can imagine, was in a pretty poor state of repair, but the scoreboard looked as if it had hardly been used and, bearing in mind its location, it probably never had. I bought it, along with a cue rack and various other bits and pieces.

When I got back to my car, there was note stuck under my windscreen wipers from someone purporting to specialise in paint stripping, by hand. A superb finish was guaranteed, it said. Round at Tittenhurst Park, Ringo had had the entire pine staircase, library and panelled rooms, doors etc. restored magnificently, and I was aiming for a similar effect at Herne Place. I rang the guy up and he gave his name as John Mansfield. I actually had someone called Keith Mansfield working in the studio at the time but didn't make any connection between the two, especially as they didn't seem to speak to each other. So, one cold November evening, John Mansfield appeared, dressed in flimsy running shorts and a T shirt. I let that go and gave him the benefit of the doubt.

Having shown him the work to be done, which was quite considerable,

I asked him for a quote. I was expecting one to be delivered in the next few days, but he gave me the price there and then, just £250. I should have put two and two together at this stage, firstly having received his flyer while parked in the grounds of a mental home, and secondly because he looked quite unhinged. Foolishly, I offered him the job, at which point he asked if he could have something "on account". I thought this a bit much but asked what he had in mind. "A fiver", he said.

This seemed reasonable, so I gave him the fiver and he went straight to the Red Lion, where he got as pissed as he could on that amount of money. The following morning, he arrived as promised, but with nothing in the way of tools or equipment, apart from a tin of nitromors and a sheet of glass. Having asked if he could borrow a hammer, he proceeded to smash the sheet of glass to bits and do his best, though not good enough, to grind it into a fine powder. From all around the house I could hear the most awful screams of agony. What he was doing was getting a handful of the smashed up glass and dipping it, bare handed, into a tub of nitromors, before spreading it over the painted pine. This was neither sensible nor practical. Had he been allowed to continue, his hands would have been stripped to the bone, so I gave him a paintbrush.

After a day or so, it was evident that I'd employed a total fool, as he'd made absolutely no progress. He had, however, come up with a masterplan. He arrived with a massive old oil tank which had been cut in half, and proceeded to fill it up with whatever acid you use to strip paint. He dismantled the doors and shutters and began the operation by attempting to put a door into the tank. The door, of course, floated, so he decided to stand on it. This proved potentially fatal and his screams of agony now became even more extreme as he sank dangerously close to his private bits. The skin was literally falling off his legs as he was taken to hospital. After that, he abandoned any further thought of continuing pine stripping as a profession. The door, meanwhile, remained perfectly intact.

Peter Gosling warned me, too late, that I was dealing with a lunatic in the true sense of the word. In the end, I employed the same guys that Ringo had used and they indeed did a magnificent job. On the other hand, you had to be a Beatle to afford them.

Another story unfolded, which involved Gosling and John Mansfield going into business selling re-conditioned pianos. They were not, of course, re-conditioned at all, and Gosling's role in this charade was to play tunes to prospective purchasers on the notes that actually did work. Gosling told me of a time when they had managed to sell one of them, and were all set to deliver the heap, which was mounted on a trailer attached to

144

Mansfield's beaten-up car. As they travelled to the delivery point, they both became engrossed in conversation. When they eventually arrived at their destination, they had the trailer, but sadly not the piano, which had long since fallen off. They re-traced their journey and eventually found the piano completely smashed to bits, surrounded by a police cordon. Once again, this spelt the end of another business venture.

Some other notable residents of Sunningdale were Diana Dors and Alan Lake. I struck up a fairly immediate friendship with Alan, as he was also a lunatic (in the drinking sense) of the first order. Diana was far more reserved, though Alan was terrified of her. When he got out of control, which was on a pretty regular basis, one word from her would turn him into a lamb.

Alan and his mate Leapy Lee (a singer of little note, who had made a dreadful record called "Little Arrows"), had been involved in a scuffle at the Red Lion, during whch a guy was stabbed. Anyway, Alan spent some considerable time in the nick, but, on his release, was straight back to the booze in a major way.

They had two sons, Gary and Jason, and Gary would occasionally drive the family car (a blue convertible Rolls) down to the pub in search of both mayhem and women, despite the fact that he was under age for drinking, driving and sex. On one occasion, he entertained the entire saloon bar by screwing a girl on the back seat of the Rolls, roof down, after which we all gave him a round of applause and went back inside.

One night, I invited Alan and Diana round to Herne Place for a drink, even though Diana had warned me that Alan really shouldn't be drinking at all. She said that he'd be quite happy with tonic water, as he was on a course of tablets called Antibuse. It was the most disastrous of nights, during which Alan, assuming I was his confidant, kept taking me aside and asking for a "quick slurp'", by which he meant whisky, brandy, gin, vodka or anything else that was around. In one room, I had a drinks area with a decanter that played a tune every time it was raised from the table. Yes, I know it sounds naff, but I eventually sold it for £2800! The decanter was filled to the brim with Remy Martin and, as Diana and I sat in another room, we'd occasionally hear this little tune start up, which made it obvious (to me) that Alan was on the brandy.

Soon, Alan was pissed and started to get out of hand. As he invariably got aggressive when drunk, I tried to lure him to the pub, where I could dump him, but he was having none of it. Eventually, Diana sensed that all was not well (it seemed to take her a long time!) and, after a few sharp words from her, Alan took on the air of a scolded child.

Diana later broke into what was then modern day pop music and featured in a video with Adam Ant. Karen O'Connor, daughter of Des, was also in the video and later recorded a tragically bad version of "I Want To Be Loved By You" at Herne Place. I didn't personally meet Adam Ant but, according to Diana, he was a "nice boy but a little light in the brains department". After Karen O'Connor had recorded the song, which was supposed to have been sung in a sexy way, it was clear that it was 100% crap, so I decided to get an old friend of mine down to the studio to do the job properly. She certainly did a good job, but the record was never issued, because she suddenly became a royalty expert and her demands precluded any possible release.

Every Sunday lunchtime, the Lakes (Diana and Alan) would come to the Red Lion and order the hugest Bloody Marys anyone could have ever seen. Quite soon after I met them, Diana became very ill, and was eventually diagnosed with cancer. The ironic thing about that was that she had a spot on breakfast television devoted to weight loss, and every week she'd take to the scales and announce that the pounds were just falling off. Little did the public know that she had terminal cancer and was actually dying.

So, of course, she died and Alan really was a lost soul. In spite of their age difference, I guess Alan must have had very deep feelings for her and within a year, he was also dead. I was sitting in the office at Herne Place when I heard a very loud bang (they lived just across the road but still quite a distance away), and a while later a policeman friend of mine, Charlie, came round to tell me that Alan had just shot himself. Apparently, he had blown half his head away with a shotgun.

CHAPTER 9
THE MADNESS CONTINUES

Another character from that era, briefly mentioned before, is Mark from Sark. This gentleman's name was Mark and he came, in fact, from Sark, so that was convenient. Mark spent his days flitting from pub to pub, purely "to promote his business" (so he'd maintain). He did, however, end up blind drunk pretty well every night.

I first met Mark on a visit to The Red Lion, where he was promoting himself as a picture framer. At the time, I had a plethora of posters from my touring days which I wanted framed, so I gave him his first big order, which was for around 50 frames. Surprisingly, he did a good job, so I went on to re-frame more and more pictures. In fact, it reached the stage where I was having everything in sight framed, so I thought it might be a sensible idea for me to buy a part of the business and get my stuff framed for free. Well, that was my thinking, but in practice, of course, nothing ever works out the way you plan it.

Mark was complaining that his small workshop was too cramped to cope with the workload and asked if he could build himself a shed in the grounds of Herne Place. I happily agreed to this and off he went, with my money, to buy all the materials. Old railway sleepers and tons and tons of wood were delivered, as Mark erected what was more a small factory than a garden shed. Luckily, it couldn't be seen from the house.

He then needed (of course) some new equipment, so some massive machinery was delivered. At this stage, he told me that he obviously had no electricity supply and, as many of the new gadgets were electric, asked whether he could connect up to the mains in the house.

After the structure had eventually been completed, he suggested a "launch" party. I, of course, bought all the booze, although some of his "clients" did bring along the odd bottle to congratulate him on his/our new venture. So far, Mark had invested nothing in this, apart from an old machine that looked like a relic from Noah's Ark. Then there was stationery to be printed, most of which was used for calculating lengths, widths and sizes of frames. I can't actually recall receiving a penny back from the venture, but at least I had the advantage of getting everything in the house framed (when he could fit it in!)

There were various disasters and complaints, largely due to the fact that Mark would work in the afternoons, after heavy lunchtime sessions in the Red Lion. One customer wanted an abstract print framed. It was brought to the "factory" carefully wrapped, but when Mark started work on the project (after a drinking session) he unwrapped it, but then forgot what to frame. Inevitably, Mark ended up framing the wrapping paper and throwing the print away. Somehow, he convinced his client that it did in fact look quite nice. Well, the frame did look fine, so amazingly, the customer went on to hang a bit of framed wrapping paper on his wall.

After a year or so, Mark decided to buy his own premises and go it alone. I'd got the whole thing going in the first place and introduced him to countless customers, yet he pissed off leaving me with a "factory" I didn't want, a pile of empty bottles and an even bigger pile of off-cuts. Still, I was never short of kindling wood.

He bought himself a property in Byfleet, in which there was not only space to work, but also a large showroom downstairs. As he was matey with all the arty and crafty people in and around Sunningdale, he launched the business with an art exhibition. Unfortunately, he advertised the opening a little too soon, as he had not finished painting the "gallery". The artist arrived with his collection, only to find a half-painted room in which even what was painted wasn't quite dry. Mark had the cheek to ask the artist if he wouldn't mind finishing off the painting (which he did!).

The grand opening came to pass and everything looked all right, but the paint (on the walls) was still not dry, in spite of the fact that he had put blow heaters on full blast the night before. The artist's pictures were now stuck to the walls and, because the paint was drying, when it came time to remove the works, Mark was left with about 60 squares of nothingness.

To give credit where it's due, Mark did end up with a successful business, but he's one of those types who get bored as soon as a project is up and running. So he shut down shop and went into the guttering business with another chap, sadly from the pub where Mark always ended up in his worst states. Thus, "Southern Gutters" was formed and with it came more disasters. They struggled along, talking people (like me) into having their iron gutters replaced with white plastic new ones. At least my house was white, but others weren't.

After a few months of trials and tribulations, they secured a contract with the local district council to replace all the gutters down one side of a very long avenue. In order to achieve this, they set to at an early hour and by late evening, after having thrown several lumps of discarded iron guttering through the roofs of and onto the bonnets of parked cars, they'd finished and went off to celebrate their as yet unpaid jackpot.

The following morning, the council rang to say that, whilst they'd done a very good job, aside from all the insurance claims for damaged cars, they'd re-guttered the wrong side of the avenue, and that therefore no payment would be forthcoming. All the gutters they had replaced were gratefully accepted by the owners, though many refused to pay, as they'd not asked for the service in the first place. And it got worse: The council now insisted that they re-gutter the correct side of the avenue, so the job turned into a 100% loss.

Mark eventually bought a farm in Devon, got married and had more children than anyone, let alone him, could possible cope with. The marriage predictably ended in divorce. Prior to the marriage, which didn't actually seem to last very long, considering how many children they'd crammed into it, I'd met the Mrs Mark to be in the pub one Sunday lunchtime. As had become a regular habit, Mark always joined us for Sunday lunch, but on this occasion, my wife Liz had only prepared lunch for four people. These included Tony Barton (comedian, actor and star, in his mind, of Emmerdale Farm, Coronation Street and even Grange Hill) who also came to lunch every Sunday. Liz rang the pub because we were late as usual and told me that lunch was ready. I explained there would now be five of us, which did not go down at all well.

I went home as a sort of forward party to resolve the situation, but Liz would have none of it. An enormous row erupted, at the end of which I threw the entire lunch in the bin and went to bed. Mark and his now fiancée (she had only been his girlfriend at the start of the lunchtime session) arrived in the drive and entered a desolate kitchen. Liz had also gone to bed in a different room, salvaging what she could of a lunch for herself, but I had burst in and thrown her lunch, plate, knife and fork, the lot, out of the window. The cutlery, plate and all, was left sticking up from the grass for days, before one of us gave in and brought the debris in.

Anyway, Mark hovered round the kitchen, obviously sensing that all was not well. "Helloooooo", he said, hesitantly. I opened the bedroom door and shouted at the top of my voice "FUCK OFF", before hearing timid steps on the gravel and then a car cautiously driving off.

Amazingly, an invitation to their wedding arrived which, whilst I felt it was all a bit sudden, I agreed to attend. I lent them my Bentley for the day as a wedding present, though I omitted to tell them that it had a steering defect and wouldn't drive in straight lines. Still, the driver managed to manoeuvre them to and from the church without a hitch.

After the wedding, we went on to the reception, which was the grimmest such event I'd ever experienced. The catering consisted of an apple and an orange and a huge chocolate cake, but there was ample booze, so I of course simply got pissed. There were waiters wandering around with trays of champagne and when one passed me, I took the whole tray from him.

My daughter Emma had come with us, as it was her weekend to stay with me. Of course, she had no interest in the apple and orange (neither did anyone else) and wanted to get stuck into the chocolate cake (I preferred to stick to the champagne). Emma was used to getting her own way and would not have it that she had to wait for the cutting of the chocolate cake, which was also the wedding cake.

When I'd had enough of the wails and the screaming and went to ask for a bit of cake for my daughter, I was told that the bride hadn't yet cut the cake (which really wasn't that much bigger than a Jaffa cake), so I'd have to wait. This I was not prepared to do, so I just went over and cut it myself. At least I pacified Emma, but probably, by doing so, put a bad spell on the marriage, which I astutely felt was doomed anyway. Then there was the standard procession of guests being presented to the bride and groom. I was a bit wobbly by now, and when it came to our turn to wish them all the best for the future, I said, "You must come round for Sunday lunch some time!". The bride gave me a look like thunder and I never spoke to her again.

One day in the Red Lion, there was a guy in the public bar telling the barmaids that he was the writer of the theme of the children's TV series "Magpie". This man turned out to be the aforementioned Peter Gosling, who worked on childrens TV and we did eventually end up becoming mates. I suppose he felt on pretty safe ground in the pub. I mean what were the chances of the real writer (which was me) being in the saloon bar?

My involvement in "Magpie" had come about through Spencer Davis. Spencer had been at university with someone who was to become the producer of the show. He presented us with the most dreadful piece of shit , which I flatly refused to sing. His demo was sung in an Etonian accent in the style of Flanders and Swan.

However, Spencer asked for a day or so to come up with something perhaps a little more current. I wrote the song overnight. The lyrics were a nursery rhyme, so it didn't present too much of a problem. We recorded it at Thames TV in Teddington straight to stereo, no overdubs, straight off and done. It was after that that the problems evolved.

At first, "Magpie" was just a pilot show which I assumed would only run once. How wrong could I have been? Fifteen years later, it was STILL on and being shown twice a week! Even though Spencer and I were not at this stage on particularly good terms, he did ask if I was getting good royalties for "Magpie". Of course I wasn't. The song had been registered in his name and everything was going to him.

Eventually, I offered Ray Fenwick a third interest in the song if he could sort things out with Spencer, which he did. Firstly, there were all the back payments to be recouped, plus a sync fee for the band. I had [...] much money would be involved, but it turned out to be a bloo[...] I'd given a third away!

Even so, we weren't out of the woods, because various people p[...] claims as writers who had literally just been in the room when we recorde[...] it. One guy who came up to me and said he wrote it had neither been in the room, nor did I know him! If only I'd phoned Spencer myself in the first place it could have been settled. He still points this out to me to this day.

Peter Gosling, the man in the pub, was yet another "ghost writer" of "Magpie". In Herne Place, there was a vast cellar, where one room was full of bottles, most of which I threw away into a skip. After all, it could have been anything, but Peter, undeterred, offered to drink some of it. I took the cork out of a bottle, which was marked as 1914 Port. We proceeded to drink an awful lot of it, after which I didn't know if it was night or day. I honestly didn't know who I was or where I was or who anyone in my house was.

The doctor was called, and the following day he sent me to London for a brain scan. Brain scans were and probably still are pretty impressive affairs, as are the bills. I was sent by Dr. Mike, my doctor from Sunningdale, to Harley Street to one of those surgeries that are a bit like the Dorchester. Having been led into the inner sanctum, I was stripped to the waist and a massive syringe was plunged into my forearm. It was like one of those things mums used to ice cakes with.

I was then inserted into a mini submarine affair with this bloody syringe still hanging out of my arm. The nurse said that she now had to leave the room, as it was about to become radioactive or something. For fuck's sake, I thought, I was only pissed! Red stuff still poured into me from the syringe and I was then in communication via a microphone and headphones. It was actually quite similar to being in a recording studio!

Over the intercom, they explained that I would probably start to feel hot and perhaps become nauseous. In fact, I glowed like an electric fire with all three bars on and almost threw up. Then the submarine started to turn and lights were flashing. It was becoming a bit like a Disneyland ride. In the end, all the results were okay, though when I asked Dr. Mike if I could have a copy of the scan and the picture of my brain, he said nothing.

Every client in the clinic was in a pin-striped suit or extremely well dressed. They didn't look ill at all, but I suppose they must have been. Then again, perhaps they were the doctors, but if that was the case, there were no patients, except for me. I left the premises still glowing like a traffic light and never did drink much port after that.

ested that I should I have a complete medical check
...ng of appointments all over London at the most
...ve clinics he could find. It was like a sort of "service"
... give cars. At my first port of call, I was wired up to a
...ine, which told the doctor what was working within
...On the first run-through, it appeared that nothing
...it thankfully, on the second attempt it seemed that it
...ble to function, for the time being, as a normal human
being.

My next call was to a heart specialist in Wimpole Street, who asked if I drank and smoked. I said I did both, admitting to a daily consumption of perhaps a litre of wine (which was later to vastly increase) and forty cigarettes. He said that the wine was okay, so long as it was a good one, but that I should cut out the cigarettes. This, of course I already knew, but I still had to pay about £300 for the information.

Before long, I was at St. Thomas's hospital, where I had in fact been born and, the way things progressed, was about to die! Once again I was stripped down to minimum clothing, in itself an exhausting process, and I was wired up to yet another machine. The contraption was a tread board, which gradually gained momentum the longer you stayed on it. It started off at quite a pleasant pace but, as it was a tea break for my nurse in attendance, I ended up at a sort of gallop. Liz was with me, but neither of us knew how to stop the fucking thing and I didn't have the sense to step off it. In fact, I couldn't, because I was strapped onto it. I ended up feeling far worse than I had in the first place, which had been pretty okay.

I didn't make the next appointment and, as Waterloo station was only over the road, we both went home. I could have actually run home, the amount of miles I must have travelled on that bloody machine.

On my rare visits to Sunningdale now, I always drive slowly past my "home of regret". There is a little Wendy House off the paddock with name plates of all the Meyer children, but it now lies forlornly battered by the weather. For many years, the windows were boarded up and the paintwork was neglected. It is true to say that nothing in life is truly freehold, we are all merely guardians for future generations, who could never have as much love and respect for that house as I did. I put so much hard work and anguish into that house and now, even though restored to its former glory and divided into about 18 apartments, it is a house that for me will always have a heart. It is one of my biggest regrets that I didn't hold on to it.

During the last years at Herne Place, Denny Laine returned from Spain where he'd bought a farmhouse and was trying very unsuccessfully to renovate it. I think he finally gave up when parts of it started to fall down around him. I hadn't seen Denny for years, in fact not since the Wings playback session for Red Rose Speedway, but he soon slipped into the mayhem that surrounded Herne Place and anyone who visited it.

I thought I'd gone through a fair few disasters in my time but Denny was first division. On (very unwisely) leaving Wings, he simply bought himself everything he wanted, for example a music shop in Weybridge, a boat, the standard Rolls Royce, a Ferrari and a Range Rover. Over a very short period of time, he'd lost the lot. Here's how:

His first error was that, when buying property, he'd only pay the deposit and have not a thought of any repayment on a mortgage. This applied to the house in Canada, the house in Laleham and the house in Spain. Sounds great doesn't it! The Range Rover he simply abandoned on the roadside in Spain and never had a clue what became of it.

Denny's a great guy and we'd laugh ourselves into hysteria as he told me these stories. He had no regard for money whatsoever, and this was reflected one day when he got a royalty payment on account for £1000 or so. I was short of cash when he came into Herne Place and suggested we all go for a drink, so I said to him, "Den, I'm a bit short at the moment, lend me a grand". Obligingly, he reached into his pocket and gave me the whole lot without a second thought. I didn't really need the money at all but I thought, what a great guy, he just doesn't give a shit.

At one stage, he decided to sail to Marseille for an unspecified length of time, have his Rolls delivered there and live on the boat. He had a roadie, Terry Draper, who was a great big bear of a man, though soft as pudding. He and a couple of other guys were to sail with Denny on the voyage to Marseille. Denny stocked the boat with provisions and even had the foresight to buy life jackets before they all set off to Dover for the voyage.

They arrived early in the morning and all went to the local "greasy spoon", where they had huge "fry ups". A very heavy mist fell on Dover, but the boat was equipped with radar and all the other bits of modern technology, although sadly I don't think either the crew or the captain had a clue how it all worked.

Anyway, they set off into a blanket of fog. Visibility was nil as they sailed through the day into the total unknown. The English Channel can be a bit choppy on occasion and on this day it was really rough. The full English breakfasts didn't stay where they should have for very long and they all went pretty green. Denny suggested that they should wear the life jackets, but they were nowhere to be found. It became obvious that Terry Draper, who was a huge guy anyway, had trebled in size, because he was in fact wearing all of them!

They sailed for a day and a night and, as the mist cleared, Denny could see land. "We're there", he pronounced. That much was true, but "there", sadly, was Dover. They'd sailed all that time in circles and ended up right where they'd started from.

Much later, they did in fact manage to get to Marseille, but then the problems really started. The engine blew up and Denny was stranded for months on end, waiting for a replacement to be shipped over from the UK. However, he did have somewhere to live and the Rolls had been delivered without a hitch. He had a few thousand pounds wired over from England, just to be getting along with, and took everyone out for dinner. For some strange reason, he'd put the cash in a brown envelope in the back of the car on the shelf behind the passenger seats.

On returning to the car after the very alcoholic dinner, they all set off for the moorings but noticed that it was freezing cold in the car. Denny had the heating on full but it made no difference. Then they all realised that the back window had been smashed and the money was gone. This was not a problem for Denny; he simply sent for more.

This tale ended with the boat being transported back to England (the engine never did arrive) on one of those huge low loaders that require police escorts. But by now, funds were running low and even the royalties from "Mull Of Kintyre", which were very substantial, (he co-wrote it with McCartney) were not sufficient to cover his lifestyle. In the end, he was declared bankrupt, but even that didn't seem to bother him overly. The big problem was that his royalties were now the "property" of the bankruptcy court, who granted hims the minimum amount per week for survival.

While at Herne Place, Denny recorded an album (I wrote a song with him, called "Twist of Fate"). A photo shoot was arranged at Herne Place for the cover, and in fact Liz is one of the girls in it, but it was released by President records, which meant that he needn't have bothered to record it in the first place.

The nights at Herne Place were getting totally out of control. I would go to The Red Lion (now a pretentious restaurant called Red's) and, after closing time, I would invite the entire pub back for more drinks. One night, I quite frightened myself with the excess. The house, all 32 rooms of it, was full of people I didn't even know, and this kind of carry-on was actually to continue until the day I left it.

CHAPTER 10
HOW TO LOSE A MILLION

One night, I was having a quiet meal with Liz at The Jade Fountain, the trendy Chinese restaurant in Sunningdale. Centre stage in the room, there was a rowdy table of maybe a dozen people.

The table comprised Brian Adams, Nigel Wright (a record producer) and others that I did not know. I had met Brian many years before, and more recently at Midem, when I went there with Zak, Tony and Liz. The first time I'd met Brian had been on a charter flight in Germany. At the time, he was managing the band Quatermass. The passengers consisted of various musicians and their respective managers, including Fleetwood Mac, Quatermass, Hardin & York, The Nice and I think the Jeff Beck Group and a few others I can't remember.

Everything started out okay, as the pilot was a liberal minded chap who announced after take-off that there were no drug regulations in the sky and that everyone could now smoke and drink as much as they wanted, which of course we all proceeded to do, until suddenly the plane sort of flipped over.

This was pretty frightening stuff, but, being a fatalist, I just sat and waited for what I thought was going to be the final bang. The pilot eventually corrected the plane, but things were clearly not as they should be and we had to make an emergency landing. Mick Fleetwood was particularly affected by this experience and, apart from actually pissing himself, charged up and down the aisle shouting and screaming and adding more horror to the predicament.

The plane landed, repairs were carried out and, after a few hours, we were invited back on board. The pilot took us all to a room and gave us a talk on how safe the plane was and how he wouldn't take off again if there were any doubt in his mind. After all, he said, "I'm a family man". He didn't manage to convince Pete and myself, however, and we took a regular BA flight to the destination, though all the others gave it another go!

So there we were in the Jade Fountain and, as the customers thinned out, I re-introduced myself to Brian, who was at that time running a recording studio at Shepperton Studios for Gary Numan and was also managing Denny Laine after his departure from Wings. We got talking and the subject of my own studio came up. Brian explained that he was not happy with things at Rock City, the studio owned by the Numan family, and suggested he come and take a look at my studio with a view to managing it for me. This appealed to me no end, as it would leave me and Liz with far more time for having fun. That was as far as the conversation went that night, but the following morning, Brian turned up with his office desk and just settled in!

I was a bit taken aback, but admired his front, until he suggested that we should become partners. This was all very well, but partners, as I know them, normally have some kind of joint investment, whereas Brian made none. What I'd effectively agreed to was simply halving my profit, even though Herne Place was already ticking over quite nicely with John Acock as virtual resident engineer. Brian, however, set about changing everything, starting with joint signatures on the company cheque book and bringing in his own staff.

Brian had an overwhelming personality and socially was great fun. On a business level, however, it was not to work out. Suddenly, we had a secretary, who Brian knew, and another engineer, Nick Smith, son of Norman Smith, who had engineered most of the Beatles' early recordings. Nick was another refugee from Rock City.

Immediately, there was a huge surge in outgoings. Brian said he couldn't operate on under £500 per week (eventually raised to £750), though he did kindly say that I could have the same! There was also "petty cash", which seemed to run at £100 per day, plus fresh fruit for the bands every day. Now I've never known a band to eat a bowl of bloody fruit during sessions.

Looking back, I cannot have been mentally stable to hand over 50 percent of what I owned outright to a virtual stranger. But we continued on that basis. To be fair, Brian did do a lot of work sorting out my tangled domestic life, and he did help me to rid myself of my Ex for good, though of course it was down to me, and only me, to raise the money to pay the settlement. Brian was the intermediatory between the two of us, as it was now impossible for us to communicate on any level at all.

As Herne Place was mortgage free, I had little trouble in raising a substantial sum of money, all of which went on the settlement. The loan was on the condition that I took out a pension plan at a cost of a further £750 per month. Brian then proceeded to organise garden parties which far exceeded my own in excess. Now we had hundreds of guests instead of just scores attending these "do's". I hardly knew a soul and at times, it looked as though Brian was basking in the glory of what was actually mine. Well, I'm sure he was. Liz and my mum would stand in one of the upstairs rooms and look down on the floodlit grounds with the swarming mass of people none of us knew.

There were also enormous bills coming in, such as £8000 for laundry in the first year. Then Brian decided that we should expand into other areas, such as getting involved in a bloody football club via Rick Wakeman, who was the chairman. I mean, Camberley football club does not have the ring of success, does it? Brian wanted me to invest in this doomed venture, but I declined, so he set up a syndicate in the pub, whereby fifteen people would each put in £1000. Some did, and of course never saw their money again. Then he wanted to purchase a pub in Egham, which again I declined. He was spreading himself so thinly that he didn't have the time to devote to any single venture efficiently, and consequently Herne Place went into a financial decline.

As Herne Place was the only stable source of income, he started to make crazy desperate cash deals with even crazier no-hope musicians and standards deteriorated rapidly. There was the odd occasion when Liz and myself would take a week or so off. God only knows what happened in our absence. I think the final straw for me was when Brian appointed a tape operator for the studio, which was hardly necessary, since there was already another guy just to put spools of tape on the machines, which were only three steps away from the engineer anyway!

During empty weeks, all the staff were obviously paid and I found myself with Sally (our secretary) knitting and John (the tape operator) reading his book in the garden. So, obviously, the whole thing fell apart in an acrimonious way, leaving Liz and me to run things alone. Unfortunately, by this time things had got into such a financial mess that it was all but hopeless, so we decided to sell the whole bloody lot.

Brian would argue that he did do some good for Herne Place Studios. Well, he could have, but the natural human instinct of common greed got in the way. On the other hand, he did help me out a lot in my personal life, and I suppose everything comes at a cost.

Liz and I set up a meeting with our accountants in Wimpole Street to work out how to salvage the situation. We were advised that, with our assets as they were there was no problem at all in doing whatever we liked, so we did! We found a 16th century monastery in nearby Chobham which was on the market for £450,000, which on the face of it seemed quite safe to buy, though we wanted time to give it more consideration. We also owned the cottage where my mother was now living, which was on the boundary of Herne Place.

Then there was a guy who had started a garage locally and was after a loan to keep him afloat. Our accountants told us there was plenty of money, not only for a loan, but also to buy the business and leave him to run it! Our London lawyers, another high profile company, co-operated with the accountants and somehow or other it came to pass that we now owned the monastery as well. Without consulting us, they had exchanged contracts on our behalf. Liz went through some figures and explained to me that they were £250,000 adrift on their calculations. Of course, I had every faith in top London lawyers and accountants and so assumed that she was mistaken. She wasn't.

So we were now the owners of The Ford in Chobham and moved in, which we would never have done, had they not exchanged for us. Herne Place was now empty, and not selling. My mother was in the cottage and I was left with a massive bridging loan from the bank. At this stage, we were approached by a company specialising in nursing homes who wanted to convert Herne Place into one. Negotiations began and a figure was agreed. The deal was complex, but it did mean that I would retain an interest in Herne Place and in the nursing home itself. This would have been the ideal solution. I could then have "retired" again and had a substantial income from Herne Place.

Liz was offered a partnership as well, plus a substantial income as a director. We were paid a large deposit, but the whole deal was dependent on obtaining planning permission to open a new entrance. The directors of the company who had made us the offer, and who already had several homes dotted around the country, were confident that planning permission would be approved. Of course it wasn't, and they'd lost their first deposit, as their option period had expired. Another deposit was paid and another option period agreed upon.

Meanwhile, I was getting pressure from the bank to clear the bridging facility. The second option period expired and there was still no planning permission, so we had no option but to put Herne Place back on the open market. Now the house had begun to show signs of wear and tear, as it had been empty for so long, plus squatters and thieves were nicking the fireplaces, doors and shutters and even some of the smaller trees!.

We were therefore forced into selling The Ford, with which we had no difficulty. It had four acres, a swimming pool and tennis courts. The interior was magnificent, having been restored by an American gentleman with impeccable taste. There was a sauna, a massive jacuzzi and many of the rooms were oak panelled. The house had seven bedrooms, a luxury Smallbone kitchen, and was just perfect in every respect.

So now we found ourselves having to move back to Herne Place, all due to pressure from the bloody bank. We raised a million pounds, though when the lawyers sent us our final statement, after legal expenses, accountancy fees and various sundries, we came out of it with exactly £1. The accountants offered us £1800 to compensate us for their bad advice, but we didn't even accept that. We did, however ask our lawyers to sue the accountants (what's the use of an accountant who can't add up?), but they wanted a further sum of money on account of further action, even though they themselves had been party to the cock-up. We just dropped the whole thing in total disgust.

We split the £1, added a bit to it and both got pissed. Who wouldn't, having just lost £999,999? But ... we still owned Herne place.

There were, of course, some adventures during the days spent at Ford. At the front of the house was a wall, a 16th Century wall in fact. I'd continued to frequent The Red Lion, though now it was necessary to drive there. Despite this, I continued to drink at my normal irresponsible pace and at closing time I invariably drove home.

On one occasion, I must have had far more than I'd realised, but still managed to reach Ford Lane, where the house was situated, fairly intact. I saw the house looming up far too quickly and the car (yes, another bloody Rolls Royce) suddenly came to a jolting halt. I knew what I'd done but thought that, if I got inside the house and went to bed really quickly, I'd wake up in the morning and everything would be okay. I woke up early the next day and of course, nothing was okay. I'd driven right through the 16th Century wall and ended up on the front lawn.

I walked to the end of the bedroom (it was a very big bedroom, big enough to park a plane in), and there below me was the sight I had dreaded. The bonnet was piled up with bricks and mortar as far as the windscreen and the grill and the entire front was totally buggered. I called the garage (the one we nearly bought!) and the guy came round to assess the damage. "Not a problem," he said. Well, it looked a bloody major problem from where I was standing. Anyway, we were off to Japan in a couple of weeks, so it seemed like a painless time to have the car fixed.

The reason for us going to Japan was that I'd recorded a "New Age" (which was, I think, only just becoming a trend) album for a company called Beggars Banquet under the guidance of Nick Austin, a quiet but slightly peculiar chap. We had a meeting with him, during which he outlined his company's plans for the future. He was going to have his own satellite channel, Landscape, and he'd also have his own satellite to broadcast from. I thought this was more than a little far fetched. I mean, Wandsworth, which was where his offices were based, didn't seem to have much in common with Cape Canaveral. But The Landscape Channel did, in fact, eventually appear on British television every morning for a while.

He also planned to go into the manufacture and distribution of Nuclear fallout shelters, do-it-yourself ones. He was into Bio food in a big way and even had plans to start his own vineyard, which he did! Whether or not the wine was any good, or produced in any great quantities, I never knew, but somewhere in Sussex sits Nick Austin sampling his new vintages.

He obviously got so pissed that he omitted to send out royalty statements on a regular basis. Now I find that the album has been re-released on the Voiceprint label with me credited as only the performer and not the writer and producer, which of course I was. Nothing "New" there, then.

I had no real interest in New Age music at all, but the idea was tempting and, as I've always enjoyed doodling around with melodies on the piano, it seemed like a fairly easy way to secure a reasonable deal. I hired in a Bosendorfer full grand for the sessions. That instrument was a joy to play, it kind of wrote things itself.

I had "in stock" a lot of unfinished melodies from over the years and decided the best way to approach the album was to utilise these and improvise in the empty spaces. Now there is a certain time required to fill a CD, so we developed a system whereby the engineer had written out on large cards the words STOP, START and KEEP GOING. I'd start playing the melody and if it seemed to be running short, he'd hold up the "KEEP GOING" sign at the control room window, and if it seemed to be going on a bit, he'd hold up the "STOP" sign. I know this doesn't sound like peak creativity, but it did reach No. 1 in the Japanese New Age charts!

Then, one of the themes was used for a Japanese whiskey advert. I think the brand was John Brown, a sort of play on Jim Beam. So they invited me to go to Japan for a three-week tour, playing solo piano. Flying to Japan on a non-stop flight is no mean feat if you're a hardened drinker, and I managed three hangovers on the outbound journey and arrived in Tokyo so pissed that I'd become sober again, if that's possible.

I played at the strangest of venues, where the backstage catering was raw fish and whiskey. I don't like raw fish and I don't drink whiskey, so a supply of red wine had to be substituted. One show was in a park, where they'd mounted a grand piano on a raft that would float around and, in theory, reach all areas of the audience. It did actually work, with the help of ropes and pulleys, but there was an added problem. As I'd largely improvised the whole thing, I obviously couldn't remember exactly what I'd played, so I had to get a guy to go through the whole album and write down note for note exactly what I'd done.

I was absolutely "stuffed" without the music, but as it was a windy day on the lake, my sheet music was blown all over it, leaving me to invent entirely new themes on the spot, until small boats had gathered up the missing music and a Japanese lady was sent out to my floating stage to hold it in place for the rest of the performance.

On the tour with me was an acoustic guitarist who took his New Age work very seriously, so seriously that he's vanished into oblivion. He was in Japan with his wife, and they had some strange ways. They refused to touch money (which is a complaint I'd never had to deal with before) and every time they actually came into contact with money, they'd scurry off to the loo and wash their hands immediately. They were the same about door handles and, in fact, anything that was not their own. I thought that Marigolds might have been the answer.

So myself and Stephen, the acoustic chap, were invited to do a radio show and discuss our music in depth. Steven was interviewed first and went into the most extraordinary stories I've ever heard. When asked about his inspirations, he talked about things like pebbles on the beach, sunsets, waves lapping on the shore, sand between his toes, etc. When I was asked what gave me my inspirations, on the other hand, I answered, "the £5000 advance, and if he spoke the truth, that was his inspiration as well!" After the tour, they sent some journalists over to England for more "in depth" interviews so I can't have offended anyone too much.

Liz, however, did. We had an English tour manager and one evening he took us all out, record company and all, to a restaurant in the mountains. We were seated at a huge round table and it all started off in a civilised manner, with lots of bowing and polite sips of Saki (or, in my case, piggish guzzles). I don't recall what Liz was drinking but, whatever it was, it went straight to her head and she started, for some reason, telling the filthiest jokes imaginable, most of which she'd heard from Jim Davidson, so you can imagine the content.

As she launched into these jokes, I of course knew what punch lines were coming and just thought, "Oh no, surely she won't keep the end bit in." She did. I could see mouths dropping open and the only hilarity came from our tour manager, who was beside himself. We drove back from the mountains in a sort of tour bus with TV and everything in it. Caruso, our tour manager, was pissed and was trying to tune in the TV for us as he drove at breakneck speed through the narrowest of roads. It was a terrifying journey and, as we sped through one narrow street, the sides of the vehicle having about one and a half inches of clearance, I said to him, "Let's hope no-one puts their empty milk bottles out".

The anti-money touching squad had a trip planned the following morning to Kyoto and intended to leave promptly at 8 a.m. Liz asked if she could join them and they half-heartedly agreed. Liz was up and dressed (amazingly) and in the lobby at the appointed hour, but they'd gone. Later, they explained to me that they felt Liz had been a total disgrace the night before and preferred to be alone.

I did make one tourist trip with Liz to the Emperor's Palace but it was shut that day! So, with Japan "done", we set off for home via Hawaii for the honeymoon we had never had. This was another disaster, because on the first day, Liz got burnt to a frazzle and couldn't be touched for a week, even by a sheet! There were many places of interest in and around the islands, but I plumped for a trip to Pearl Harbor, which was not the most romantic of outings. I found it absolutely fascinating and moving and in fact, I think Liz did as well, apart from the row we had there, which nearly equalled the invasion itself. Waikiki Beach was like Blackpool, but with surf boards and mahogany coloured muscle bound oafs.

After Hawaii, we set off for a week in Los Angeles, staying at The Beverley Hills Hotel. This is really "pose city", but I love the stupidity of it all. There's a huge pool area, around which lie starlets and lots of very old, though well-preserved, failed starlets. No one actually gets into the pool, which is probably wise, as it would probably become a sea of Max Factor, though water wings would not be required, due to the copious amounts of silicon around.

Liz, of course, dived straight in and while she was "butterflying" around, I noticed that she'd lost the top of her bikini during the dive. I said nothing and she knew nothing until she pulled herself out of the water. We're not very good at posing either!

Spencer came to visit us and we arranged to meet in the Polo Lounge, which is the centre for the mega pose. There are guys with totally obvious wigs and women with even more obvious tits and high heels, which to walk in must have necessitated the skills of a circus entertainer, but I loved it! I had a pee with Charlton Heston and was most disappointed when he spent a few moments adjusting his wig before striding through reception as if he'd just parked his horse.

Anyway, Spencer ordered a "bar snack", which took the form of half a bloody lobster, which at $98 was one hell of a bar snack. As for me, I went to check out some of our old haunts like the "Riot House". This was in fact the Hyatt House, which in our day was the ultimate rock & roll den of iniquity but is now in fact a very Quiet House. The Whiskey was still there on Sunset, but nothing was quite as it had been in the 60's and 70's.

We were now in the 80's and ended up in The Roxy. There was the obligatory shopping trip to Rodeo Drive, lunch at the Beverley Wiltshire and that was pretty well LA done this time around.

Upon our return to the UK, my mother and Uncle Mac decided that they'd meet us at the airport, which was a tradition that went back to my very early days with Spencer, and a tradition with which Liz was not familiar. Quite frankly, as nicely as it was intended, I always found it more than a little embarrassing. In the early days, for example, there'd be The Small Faces, a dapper little bunch with whom we'd been touring, all heading off in their taxis to God knows what excitement and debauchery, and everyone else all doing the same, except for me. Instead, there would be my mum and her little Yorkshire Terrier, Uncle Mac and my dad, all there to meet me and take me home to a chicken lunch. I don't know why, but it was always fucking chicken. On our return from the Japanese trip , plus Hawaii and Los Angeles, we were obviously very, very tired. I'd had the damaged Rolls repaired and the guy who repaired it said the least he could do was pick us up from the airport in it. My mum, meanwhile, had hired another one and had also decided to pick us up.

So there we were at Heathrow, two Rolls Royces (sorry to harp on about these bloody things but that's just how it was) and not knowing which one to get in and who not to offend. We eventually opted for the one with the garage guy, while my mum and Mac got in the rented one and passed us on the motorway every now and then, giving us horrible glares.

Now I knew what was coming, but Liz didn't. It was late afternoon, and when we got back to The Ford it was early evening. My mum wanted tea immediately and to sit down and have every detail of the trip outlined to her. Liz was like a zombie, walking in and out with trays of tea and of course the obligatory sandwiches. Then Mum asked what we'd bought. This was fatal, as we'd bought Kimonos, which are fairly complicated affairs to get dressed up in. Nevertheless, we were forced into it, so now we had Liz teetering around in her little Japanese block shoes, several sizes too small, and dressed in her complete regalia, trying to serve a traditional English PG Tips tea ceremony. But worse was to come. We had made holiday videos and Mum wanted to watch all of them there and then. There I was, looking like the King of Siam, with Liz in her Madame Butterfly gear, watching footage of all the concerts I'd played until around 3 in the bloody morning.

One Sunday lunchtime at the Ford, all had gone fairly well. We'd had the normal English mega lunch, plus several bottles of red and a couple of bottles of white and were still relaxing at the dining room table when there was a ring at the door. For some reason, I'd had a camera put at the front door. In fact, there were cameras all over the house. This had started off as being a monitor system for the studio (yes, I had another 24 track studio at The Ford!) and it just got sort of extended around the house.

We were feeling pretty mellow at this stage and, on glancing at the monitor, I noticed that we had a horse at the door. I said to Liz, "There's a fucking horse at the door", to which she merely replied, "Don't be so bloody stupid, how much have you had?" But when she looked up, there it was, a bloody great horse, apparently ringing the door bell. I opened the door to find a mate of ours, Jim Collins, who was separated from his wife and had custody that weekend of his daughter who, it turned out, had fallen off the bloody thing and was covered in mud and manure. He had called on us as a last resort to salvage the situation. His ex-wife had dressed the kid up in a white tutu and Jim had rented a horse, which was even more stupid, for her to have a trot round Chobham. Now she was covered from head to foot in God knows what. They both came in and Jim and I got even merrier while Liz washed his daughter's clothes.

By now a few hours had passed and Jim was not on peak form, and neither was I. We all decided that it was time to take the horse back to the stables and for Jim to make his way home as best he could. We walked into the front garden and the bloody horse had gone. Jim said, "But John Wayne always ties his horse to twigs and it's always there when he gets back!" Yes, but Jim's horse wasn't.

We searched the grounds and there was not a sighting, not even in the pool, into which we feared it might have fallen. Finally, Jim asked Liz to go with him to the stables and own up to the fact that he'd actually lost their horse. When they reached the stables and confessed all, the guy told them that the horse had found its own way back, arriving minus the saddle and all the other bits required to make it go along. Jim got a bill for £300 extra to cover the costs.

Then there was the day that a friend called Drunken Duncan called me to say he'd just become the rep for a gadget that would change the world, namely a fax machine. Of course, at that time no one knew what such a thing was or whether it would catch on. I bought one, but it was pretty useless, as the only other person who had one was the company that sold it to me. I went to our bank manager, Barry Evans, a man who polished his shoes at the bottom as well as the top, but he declined the offer of a fax machine, not having a clue what it was. It was, however, with fantastic speed that these things caught on, and I had one of the first! Well, it was the second. Drunken Duncan was so pissed when taking the first one back to the depot after the demo that he dropped it and it smashed to bits.

Next, I decided to take up fishing, a fairly quiet sport, Tales of the Riverbank and all that, although my system was even less athletic than that. I bought a row of fishing rods and placed them along the banks of the river that ran at the bottom of our back lawn and carefully took all the lines up to our bedroom (Mission Control), where I could then fish from the peace and tranquility of bed.

In the morning, I had a bumper catch of the most amazing fish I'd ever seen. They were bloody huge. I took the hugest one round to my mum to gut and do all the things that you have to do before cooking it. It was so big that she had second thoughts about dealing with it but eventually it was prepared for the oven with about two pounds of roe as a side dish. I have to say it was the best fish I'd ever tasted, but so it should have been. It turned out they were Koi Carp and were being bred by our nearest neighbour as an investment. Apparently, they can run into thousands of pounds for a good one, but we were eating them, occasionally with chips and tomato ketchup!

One night, while I had a band in the studio, I caught the biggest monster fish to date. When faced with it, none of us knew quite what to do. The most sensible suggestion, I thought, was to throw it up in the air, hoping that the "landing" would kill it. It was far too huge to thump with the traditional lump of wood. Suddenly, my fishing rods were found thrown up onto the lawn. The neighbour had taken to coming into the garden late at night, in an attempt to spoil my sporting activities and preserve his prize fish. He never actually said anything, but every time I put the rods out, they'd be strewn in all directions within a couple of hours. So that was the end of that particular hobby.

He did make one complaint, though. We had two ducks, and his wife knocked on the door one evening to complain about the quacking. Now there was an abundance of wild ducks up and down the river who also quacked on a fairly frequent basis, but for some reason they took exception to the quacking of our two "domestic" ducks. How they had managed to differentiate the quacks was a matter for conjecture, so the lady was summarily dismissed. Shortly afterwards, our ducks mysteriously disappeared. I can only assume it was a "tit for tat" arrangement they'd come to for the deceased carp.

The neighbours were typical country types with brogues and tweeds, like the boating set transferred onto land They were glad to see the back of us and we were equally glad to see the rear end of them. I suppose we didn't make a lot of effort to fit into the community. We continued to have very noisy late night bashes, and music carries a long distance in the still of night. Despite our love of music, we did make an exception at Christmas times and had a large sign on the front door which read, "Carol Singers Fuck Off", which meant that we were never bothered by them.

A memorable evening was when we decided to have a "dinner party". This is the sort of thing which we normally hate and do our utmost to avoid at all costs. However, our dinner party was not quite like any other, devoid of the usual idle chit-chat and "What do you do?" kind of conversation. We all knew what we did, namely drink heavily and at all times. Careers, mortgages and pension plans for the future were all irrelevant in our household.

The cast was mixed. There was a pilot friend of mine from school days and his wife (he was flying the following morning for a very well known airline), Paul the clock emperor and his wife, Dr. Mike and his wife, myself and Liz. I can't remember the food but I can remember the intake of alcohol. There was not a moment of boredom as there usually is on these mundane occasions. Why the fuck do people have dinner parties when none of them gives a toss what the other person does nor even really cares if they were to die the following afternoon? I've been to a few where the other guests certainly didn't care if I did! But still they do it, and sometimes they spiral out of control, in which case you're pretty well guaranteed to find an absolute bore amongst the gathering, along with the "know alls" and the aggravating wives flashing their cheap rings and dodgy Rolex watches. Then you get the couples (the Howards and Hildas) with matching Cartiers, who constantly play with their noses making sure you get a bloody good look at the watches. It's like those people who dress their twins up in identical clothes. Their other topic of conversation is usually "And what car do you drive?". I mean, who gives a toss if we'd walked, flown or swum to their bloody boring evenings.

As you can see, we don't like dinner parties, nor the people who attend them. Anyway, our soirée staggered on until about 7 a.m, when it was getting light. I had two decanters, one containing Port and the other dark Sherry, but I'd forgotten which was which. Paul and the pilot reckoned themselves connoisseurs and set about differentiating the two. The result was that they'd drunk both decanters and still were not of the same opinion, but shared the common complaint of being legless.

The pilot, who had better remain nameless, had a flight at 10 a.m and his wife, also pissed though not quite so badly, was getting edgy and insisted they make tracks straight to Heathrow! We had had a snowfall during the night and, as they left, Richard, suddenly hit by the fresh air,

166

fell flat on his face in the fresh snow.

Finally the guests straggled off into the early morning and I straggled off to bed. When I got up and went to the door to get the newspapers, there was the impression of Richard, still fresh in the snow, together with a few handbags strewn around the pathway. During the course of the day, the respective owners returned to collect their sodden belongings. Richard, meanwhile, had flown to Tokyo that morning. Lord help his passengers!

Several people lost their jobs and some became very ill as a result of socialising with us. I heard from a musician friend recently who claims he had to undergo a liver transplant as a result of two months at Herne Place. But then again, I, too suffered later in life when I was diagnosed with cirrhosis of the liver. As a result of this, I no longer drink, and in fact many of my fellow survivors don't either, Zak Starkey being an example. Both he and I were on a head-on collision course with certain death as a result of alcohol abuse.

I think Liz was becoming a little discontented with the constant partying and decided it was time that at least one of us "grew up" and became a little more responsible. I was not to be the one. Liz started a gardening business and named it "The Garden Workshop". As we had enough garden machinery to service a small nursery, it seemed like a reasonable idea, as long as I was not involved in any way. She employed two of the most inefficient guys you could hope to find, and that was after a long search. You see, these problems befall us in whatever we do.

There was the senior partner, Geoff Lloyd, who had been the gardener at Herne Place, taking the place of my beloved Spud, and the junior one, Robert something or other who knew even less than me about the garden. He couldn't even cut grass in a straight line, which is something the Sunningdale/Chobham set are very particular about. They do not want their lawns to look like the Grand Prix circuit.

To give Liz her due, she did everything she could to salvage a rapidly sinking ship. There are several examples of their magnificent inefficiency, such as the time when we were away and there was a drought in the UK. They just couldn't think what to do, when of course there was a bloody river running through the garden! During the terrible storms in England in the late 80's, when trees were down all over the country and gardening companies made an absolute fortune chopping up the debris, they failed to remember that they had a chainsaw and declared themselves marooned for the week.

During our trip to Japan, we had a call from Geoff, asking if we could bring back (in our hand luggage?) a new gearbox for the Mitsubishi pick-up truck we'd bought for them. I would have thought that Mitsubishi were fairly well represented in the UK!

Being cheesed off with my repaired Rolls, I decided to trade it in for another one. I'd noticed a very nice Silver Shadow for sale in a garage in Sunningdale and thought I'd arrange a test drive. On a trip into the village with Liz, I casually announced that I was thinking of changing the car. For some reason, probably because things were going so badly at that moment in time, she went bloody mad.

I stopped outside the garage and we both, Liz under protest, went in. The atmosphere was tense, to say the least, so I thought, "Oh fuck it, I'm off". I left Liz in the garage and proceeded to walk home. She hadn't noticed that I was missing when the guy came out with the keys, so she was kind of stuck with going through the routine on her own. By now, the heavens had opened, leaving me with the prospect of a 3 mile walk back to Chobham. But I was fuming and there was no stopping me from this stupid gesture.

The rain was torrential and I was dripping wet and must have looked ridiculous striding up the road. The only cars that did go past were driven by people I knew, and they all stopped to ask if I wanted a lift. I told each and every one of them to fuck off. Isn't it bloody marvellous, the times when you really want to be on your own, all the bloody do-gooders turn up from nowhere, but they're never there when you actually need them!

Then, I heard the familiar whooshing sound of a Rolls Royce approaching from behind. It was Liz and the guy from the garage on their test drive. The guy said, "Isn't that your husband there?" but Liz replied, "No, I don't think so", and the buggers swept past. Now I was madder than ever. They reached a roundabout and returned along the same road, proceeding to pass me again! The guy said, "I really am sure that that is your husband", so this time they turned round to come and pick me up. They glided up alongside a now dripping and ringing wet me . Liz lowered the window and they both peered out in anticipation. "FUCK OFF!", I shouted, and Liz said, "I don't think it is him after all." When I reached home, I went straight to bed and we didn't speak for the rest of the day.

Our days in Chobham were drawing to a close, largely due to the bank, which virtually forced me into a sale. As things turned out, we could have stayed there and probably still been there today. It was just that they panicked and that, in turn, panicked me. It was all quite unnecessary, as the day after we sold The Ford, Herne Place sold as well, so we now had to find a new home in some haste. Our next move took us to Ascot, but it was not intended to be a permanent move. We bought this new "footballers palace", mock Georgian; in fact it made a mockery of anything that was truly Georgian. However, it was a new house and we felt it would be very easy to sell at the drop of a hat.

This didn't stop me going to great expense installing yet another recording studio! But it was around the time of the big property collapse in the UK and we lost a fortune ... again.

CHAPTER 11
NEXT STOP FRANCE

A property developer friend of ours, known affectionately as Charlie Bubbles, due to his liking of champagne and, well, anything alcoholic actually, had a mate at Thames Television who wanted to use our house as a location for a couple of days, filming a detective series. Charlie had another favourite tipple which springs to mind. He took a liking for rum, but would only drink Cockspur, which he'd elegantly renamed Cocksucker. The barmaids in our pub were well adjusted to these quaint terms. He'd walk up to the bar and order "Two large cocksuckers, please."

Charlie Bubbles had already donated his house for a few days, though sadly the scene they shot there involved blowing all the front windows out! All damages were of course paid for, and no doubt Charlie Bubbles added on a few extra thousand here and there.

By now, being at a loss as to quite what to do, we decided on a short break in France to visit my brother John, who had had a holiday home there for about 30 years. During our alcohol-sodden sojourn in France, we bought a property in even more haste than usual. At first, I thought this was one of my finest blunders and my mother cried when she came over to see it. There were literally just four walls. It had no roof, no sanitation, no electricity, in fact it had absolutely nothing at all, but such is the peril of buying anything when you're pissed, which I most definitely was.

So we unloaded the "footballers paradise" on some unsuspecting ... footballer, I guess, and moved to France. The house we'd bought was in such a dire state that we stayed at my brother's holiday home for the first few months while the builders made the cottage part of the house habitable. It was then our intention to have the main part of the building restored and move into that. We had enormous problems with the builders, both linguistically and financially. The first "quote" was for £250,000, which came as a bit of a shock, though as things transpired it was, in fact, accurate. At the end of the day that was about what it cost, although doing it in stages sort of reduced the agony.

So there we were, cut off from our friends and family and totally alone. Next door lived a madman, I mean a total madman, whose drinking habits spurred me on to an even greater intake, meaning that things were soon totally out of control. His name was Fernand, and he was a painter and decorator, though totally incompetent at both. Fernand spoke not one word of English and my French was schoolboy French and pretty useless, but it's an amazing fact that drunks can communicate in any language when pissed, which is what we did.

He introduced me to the local watering holes, until finally I found one I liked and went on to spend much of my time there. Fernand had his painting and decorating jobs to cock up during the day so I was thrown in at the deep end on my own, which must have had an effect on my French. In fact, I probably speak French with a builder's accent, as it was a pub frequented mainly by builders. I didn't even bother to unpack my studio and music took a back seat for a very long time, apart from the nights of chaos at Fernand's house, when I would entertain us all on his very out of tune piano.

A welcome visitor arrived in the shape of Denny Laine, who came over to stay for a few days and ended up staying a few months! Denny has a lot of gypsy in him and he was used to the bohemian way of life. I was most certainly not, but we had some great times together, and it was Denny who finally got me to occasionally leave the bars and actually see part of the area. Fernand one day suggested we should all go canoeing, which sounded ominous to me. However, Denny convinced both Liz, her daughter, my daughter Emma (who was over on holiday) and myself to go. To this day, I still wish we hadn't.

We all set off in convoy, following Fernand and family along a precarious mountain road, which worried Denny more than a little, as I was driving a right hand drive Jeep, leaving Denny nearest to the edge. The road became even more dangerous and I decided I'd had enough and stopped at the next roadside inn we came across, leaving the Buissons, (that is the Fernand family name) sailing on.

He came back looking for us and I gave him the best bollocking I could muster in my limited French. I think he got the gist of the fact that I was definitely not happy. After a bottle of wine or two, he'd convinced us all to carry on, as it really wasn't that far. Now we were all driving along a very dangerous road, very pissed.

We arrived at the site where you pick up the canoes and were presented with waterproof containers, into which to put all our valuables. I was told there was no risk, but at that stage it looked very fucking risky to me. So we all assembled in our little flotilla and set off down the stream. I was in a canoe with Denny and we'd loaded it up with beer and cigarettes as he paddled us along. He said to me, "You have to admit this is quite pleasant, but don't let on to the others that we're actually enjoying it!"

I had to admit it was quite pleasant. I had my beer and was smoking fags as big-breasted topless German girls were passing us, coming from the opposite direction. They were going very fast and it made me wonder why they were in such a rush. It all became very clear further downstream, when we reached what appeared to be the "edge". By this, I mean the stream/river, or whatever it was, just stopped and we found ourselves thrown over the edge into rapids. The Buisson family somehow managed to become suspended in mid air between two huge rocks and I, Denny, Liz and daughter and Emma just went cascading over the edge.

All our supplies were lost and we all suffered cuts and bruises. The Buissons, however, fared far worse. Fernand lost his teeth, his watch, car keys, and very nearly his entire family and subsequently spent a week in hospital suffering a minor mental breakdown, not that he had very much to break down in the first place.

When we got back to collect our vehicles, Fernand had the added problem of no ignition keys, but there was no problem finding a likely lad to break into his car and start it up. My suggestion was to smash the windows, which would have been no use as he couldn't have started the car anyway. So we set off, Fernand straight to hospital and us home. That episode put a temporary but not permanent stop to my exploration of France. I was making lots of forays back to the UK around this time, as I could not adjust to the French way of life, so I suppose my life was pretty uninterrupted, the only inconvenience being that I had to get on a plane to go to the pub.

The building work continued at some pace on the French property and it seemed that every time I returned from England, another terrace had been built ... on the instruction of Liz. We actually ended up with five! It was never clear to me then, or now, where all the money came from, though a lot came from my family's estate, and still does.

During these "wilderness years", Pete York would occasionally offer me the odd TV show or concert in Germany. I recently watched a clip of a TV show we did (I'm afraid I can't remember where or when), which was based around drummers. Pete was recording a series called "Superdrumming" specifically for German TV and wanted to incorporate some Hardin & York material, plus of course use my mate Zak, who has the ultimate lineage as far as drummers are concerned. In fact, indirectly, it was probably Zak who got me the job as I was, to say the least, a bit of a hazard, especially when in the company of Zak. However, the H & Y formula fell into place like it was yesterday. Even though I was bloated with booze, it sounded great.

There was another TV show, which I think it was in or near Munich. It featured an opera singer, Placido something or other, plus Jon Lord, The

Spencer Davis Group, Elkie Brooks and Joe Brown's daughter Sam. I hadn't seen Sam since she was crawling around the floor, and in that time she'd turned into a great singer and songwriter. Her mother Vicki had sung on many of my productions along with Margo Newman, the long-suffering wife of Tony Newman. I sang "Gimme Some Lovin'", which I did, I might add, a lot better than Steve Winwood did at the Queen's Jubilee concert in the grounds of Buckingham Palace.

Elkie Brooks was a total and complete pain in everybody's arse, complaining about her hotel and pretty well everything else. The rest of us were at The Hilton in whatever town it was. "Placido" was wonderful, though apparently very ill, I was OK and also very ill and Sam was brilliant, though at that time with little dress sense. She wore a flouncy dress with army boots, or whatever the young considered trendy at that time.

I arrived on the set with what I thought was a spot on my chin. It turned out to be a cyst, but Jon Lord reckoned that if I gave it a good squeeze, all would be resolved, so I did. It had become so huge that even the make-up girl refused to touch it and Liz had to do cosmetic repairs for my TV appearance. Back at the hotel, I took Jon's advice and gave it a good squeeze. The result was quite sickening. There was a gargantuan explosion of puss and God knows what and the entire mirror in the bathroom was obliterated. As a result, I nearly fainted.

Aside from these brief excursions. I was pretty well entombed in France, although I still maintained a property in England, where my mother lived. A highspot came when I decided to stage "The Wind In The Willows", an album I'd recorded with Zak Starkey and an all star cast, live. I'd met Liz shortly before the recording of the original album began, which must have been in late '82 and early '83. As I said before, I'd decided to marry her before we'd even spoken! As the songs evolved, I'd "twisted" the lyrics in a way that would relate perfectly to the development of our relationship. Some people have figured this out, but not many! There are lots and lots of hidden clues for the attentive listener.

The logistics were frightening and it must have been the best part of a year in the planning stages. I'd contacted all the guys I knew to boost the keyboard section, because on the album I'd layered everything myself, so obviously more keyboard players were necessary for the live show. I tried Keith Emerson, Alan Price and Rick Wakeman, but all were working elsewhere, so Pete York suggested Jon Lord. Now Jon, although a nice guy and sincere at heart, is not renowned for his reliability, so I didn't hold out much hope that he'd even make it to the first rehearsal. In fact, he actually made all seven of them. On secondary keyboards I had Don Airey to pad out all the complicated string parts. He must have put an awful lot of effort into working out his various parts, since I had absolutely nothing written down and he worked everything out from listening to the album. His playing and performance on the two live shows were exemplary.

Along with Jon Lord on Hammond, it was one hell of a cast list, which included Graham Bonnett, Ray Fenwick, Donovan, Maggie Bell, Ray Ravenscroft, Tony Ashton, Zak Starkey, Steve Richardson, Joe Fagin, Val Mckenna and me. This is now available on DVD and, as it catalogued my early days with Liz, it is something that I'll always be very proud of. I'm glad it's preserved on film for ever, as so much blood, sweat and tears went into the work from the day of conception.

The rehearsals took place in a cricket school located behind The Red Lion in Sunningdale. Knowing the ways of musicians, I felt it would be easier to run an open tab behind the bar. The plan was that we (Pete York and myself) would pick up the bill after rehearsals. Pete was not in the least bit happy about this when he saw that the bill came to £1800 just for the alcohol! The show had by now turned into a Hardin & York production, as it was Pete who arranged the filming deal.

Had we had the foresight, it would have been good to have filmed the entire week's work, as it contained some of the best performances I've ever heard, particularly from Graham Bonnett. Ray Fenwick was, as ever, note-perfect and helped me enormously in putting the final touches to the arrangements. On the night, Ray played the main theme in the most moving way I've ever heard him play, giving it his all as if every note was torn from his body. It's a lovely melody and he played it magnificently. Ray must be the most underrated guitarist in the world.

Zak added the backbone of the rhythm section and, aside from a small feature of himself and Jon Lord, Pete was happy to fill in. Zak had also been conscientious in his preparation work and added some great new touches. As ever, he played superbly.

The two shows took place on the 14th and 15th of June 1991 in Freiburg, Germany. We all stayed in a lovely hotel overlooking the Alps, which was an idyllic setting for an idyllic moment in my musical career. We all arrived a day early, so Liz and I decided to host a big dinner for the entire cast and crew. Pete arrived a little late and was absolutely horrified to see us all in the restaurant eating and drinking as much as possible, envisaging another huge bill. He needn't have worried, though, as I paid the bill. As a way of thanking all those great musicians for joining me for shows that meant so much to me, it was the very least I could do.

Tony Barton, the comedian and narrator for the show, had a trick which entailed getting a scrap of brown paper, licking it and sticking it onto oil paintings, giving them the appearance that they had been ripped. In the restaurant, there were oil paintings hanging everywhere, so he attached his piece of brown paper onto the painting nearest us. When Pete York saw this he went completely mad: "Oh, for fuck's sake, you've only been here a few hours and now look what's happened!" Tony pulled the paper off and Pete, having performed his totally unnecessary tantrum, felt pretty stupid.

The shows themselves were great fun despite my anxiety. The piece was something I had never done before and I had fears that either nobody would turn up or that, even if they did, they wouldn't enjoy it. There were no introductions, just Tony Barton narrating the story. Prior to the first show, from backstage, I heard the mumbling sound of people taking their seats. Gradually the mumbles grew louder and louder until, when it was time to take to the stage, we were confronted by a packed house (both nights). What a relief!

After Tony's preamble, the music began with us playing the main theme. The sound quality was wonderful and, as I was playing piano alongside Zak, the power was also quite awesome. What a year it had been. Getting all these guys together and to suddenly see them all on the stage was, for me and Liz, very moving. Putting this whole thing together, plus writing and producing the music itself and at the same time beset by problems and dramas that were the most daunting I'd ever faced in my life, this lifelong ambition had now become reality. The first melody ended to rapturous applause (which took me back a bit!) and from then on I felt we had a winning concept. Indeed, each song was received better and more enthusiastically than the last. There was an encore, for which I decided on "Gimme Some Lovin'" as a wink to Spencer Davis, who had, in so many ways, put me where I now was.

I'll never forget the end of the first show. When I came off stage, Liz hugged me like she never had before and we both, for that brief moment, shared an enormous sense of achievement and relief, which overwhelmed us both. It was a moment of real love, as Liz knew what each and every note and lyric meant and that it had documented and in many ways cemented our relationship.

We recorded and filmed both nights' shows and the best was spliced together for what has now become both a CD and a DVD. The next thing I would like to do is to stage the show in London, but sadly, poor old Tony Ashton is no longer with us. To find a replacement for him is next to impossible, because he turned "The Wild Wood" into his own song.

Now that he has passed away, I miss Tony Ashton terribly. He was a true one-off and a wonderful person. Shortly after our return to France, Tony decided to pay us a visit, together with his wife Deborah. I had, I feared, miscalculated the make-up of the house party, which was to be my dentist Alan and his wife Deborah, along with their son Timothy. Alan had previously been a captain in the Army, so I was concerned about his compatibility with the ill-disciplined Ashton. As we set off to pick them all up from Montpellier airport, my doubts about such a strange combination suddenly hit me: uh-oh, is this going to work? Tony swore like the best of troopers, while Alan and his wife were very quietly spoken.

They became aware of each other in the arrivals lounge, where they were to meet for the first time. Tony instantly christened Tim as "Silly Bollocks", Deborah as "Debs" and Alan as "Al", which immediately broke the ice. Both Alan, his wife, and indeed Tim, still have fond memories of dear old Tony, who had perfected the art of coming across as a befuddled buffoon, which of course he was not. He was actually a little bit of a social climber, though not at all in a offensive way. He was the nicest guy you could possiby hope to meet.

I have many happy memories of Tony, from the day he worked on "The Butterfly Ball" at the Albert Hall and went on to sing on both Wizards Convention albums. Also burned into my memory was the night we played at the Harrogate Opera House to an audience of four people. Hardin and York were supporting Ashton, Gardner and Dyke, who were at No. 1. at the time with "Resurrection Shuffle"). We offered to give the entire audience all a lift home, as there were more musicians on stage than there were members of the audience!

When Zak and I were recording the first album of "Wind In The Willows", Zak struck up an immediate rapport with Tony. In return for my giving him free studio time, Tony performed the song "The Wild Wood" for me. In fact, he performed the same song on the DVD version but by then, his lyrics bore no resemblance to the ones I'd written. For his own compositions, he chose such illuminating titles as "The Pope's A Poof" and other such meanderings. He was hopelessly drunk, but still the most affable of guys. The Red Lion, as ever, was largely to blame for this condition.

The Ashtons' stay in France was interesting in the sense that I really got to know him well and realised just how bad his alcohol problem was; mind you, mine was not too good at that time either. Amazingly, Tony was a very "sporty" guy, who played tennis, swam and was happy to take long walks, totally the opposite to myself. His diet, however, was a revelation. Basically, he just didn't eat! He ate raw fish fingers, by which I mean still frozen solid, and his main meal was generally a cup of Bovril. An occasional gastronomic treat would be a bar of chocolate, though he'd give most of it away to any children who passed by.

At one point, shortly after his success with "Shuffle", he was declared bankrupt, even though Tom Jones had recorded a version which, I believe, reached the top ten in America. At the hearing, the judge asked inquisitively just how Tony had managed to get through virtually a million pounds in a year or so. Tony's reply was: "I had a fucking good time!"

I did many tours with Tony in various combinations and he was a great piano player in his own style, which occasionally didn't adapt to whatever else was going on but was still a winner. A story which springs to mind concerns a time when we were in a small town in Germany, where a number of street artists were performing. Some were playing violin and others were playing guitars, but Tony picked on a juggler. This guy had just managed to get an amazing number of those things they throw about in to the air, when from behind him Tony shouted in a very loud voice: "Oi!". Of course, he dropped the fucking lot. Another time, we were in Avignon, so Tony decided to slip into the French way by buying himself a bird whistle and an outsized beret. He loved hats.

I spoke to Tony several times during his battle with cancer and, despite the fact that he was obviously in a great deal of pain, he still managed to maintain his sense of humour. I think the last person to see Tony alive was Jon Lord. Tony said to him, "I've drunk, I've smoked, I've done pretty well everything unhealthy and now I'm a junkie." He was referring to the fact that he was on large doses of morphine during his last days. Jon was a true friend to Tony and I have the feeling that he helped him out of many a tight situation.

When Tony was very ill, Pete York and Jon Lord organised a benefit concert at the Abbey Road Studios, at which a cast of his best friends turned up to play before a live audience. It was entitled, "The Endangered Species Awards". Liz and I were very shocked to see Tony, who had wasted away to virtually nothing and was very frail; but that night, he gave the performance of his life. I'd never seen him in such fine form and though I don't have any comprehension of the suffering and pain he must have been going through, he was absolutely superb. He played the best piano and Hammond I'd ever heard him play.

Tony died on the 28th May 2001. This was one of the saddest moments I can remember. Why should such a great and talented guy be taken away from us? I was unable to get to the funeral, but Zak went, and of course hundreds of other friends. The funeral was reportedly pretty chaotic, which is exactly what Tony would have wanted. A piper had been organised, but apparently he got so pissed, he was unable to play the bagpipes. Miller Anderson played "Rainy Night In Georgia", which was one of Tony's favourite songs, and also "The Weight", the classic song by The Band.

And so Tony was gone, but his memory will live on. I miss him.

During our stay in Freiburg, Chris Farlowe arrived, as we were to do a few shows with him afterwards. Chris can come across as an aggressive and rude sort of guy, but beneath the gruff exterior lies a heart of gold, although he'd never let you know it.

When Chris arrived in the restaurant where we had arranged to meet, he had grown an awful lot in size since the days when he had had big hits with songs such as "Handbags and Gladrags". But at that time so had I, so I was far too polite to make reference to Chris's enormity. That didn't stop him having a go at me, though. "Christ", he shouted, "There's fucking two of you now!"

He was accompanied by the bass player Gary Twigg, who went on to play with Roger Chapman of Family fame, having been for a while with - er - Olivia Newton John, a phase which lasted until he made some arrangement suggestions, at which point his contract was terminated. Gary is not only a great bass player but also a very funny guy; in fact he's more like Tommy Cooper than Tommy Cooper was (in humour I mean).

When he arrived, Gary was literally laden down with plastic bags, which seemed a bit odd. It turned out that they were full of items, well, junk really, that Chris had bought during their journey from England. Anyway, they both joined us for dinner. The menu was very comprehensive and Chris scoured the pages with interest, finally ordering his "usual", a schnitzel. Gary was still dithering, so Chris advised him: "Don't fuck the man about. What yer 'avin?" Gary had the schnitzel too.

In a way, Chris and I have had parallel lives, in that he was totally devoted to his family, so much so that it sadly precluded him from ever entering into a long lasting relationship of his own. This, as we know, very nearly happened to me. He would recount the most amazing tales of his family get-togethers, which again reminded me of my own lot. I actually have some of his stories on tape, as I filmed the entire making of the Wizard's Convention 2 album, so I shall loosely transcribe some of the funnier stories.

There was the one about Rita the Cigarette Eater, whose fascination was to eat the contents of full ashtrays. Then there was the one about an "uncle", who drank everything and anything. Apparently, on one occasion, a party was drawing to a close and the uncle, still not alcoholically satisfied, drank all the dregs of whatever came to hand. Chris found this a bit much and mixed him a more potent cocktail, which included washing-up liquid and other household cleaning fluids, plus of course a smattering of brown ale. He drank it and said, "Got any more of that stuff, Chris?"

The family lived in Camden, where Chris shared a large house with his mother, whom he idolised. Chris says that, when it got cold, they'd throw their shoes or anything else that came to hand onto the open fire and just carry on singing and dancing. During the course of one of these riotous events, and after several complaints from neighbouring houses, a man came round to complain about the noise at God knows what hour in the morning, accompanied by a very large Alsatian dog, and announced that, if this chaos were to continue, he'd set the dog on the lot of them. The dog was knocked unconscious by Chris's uncle, wielding a brown ale bottle. So that was the first complaint dealt with.

Next, a policeman arrived on his pushbike to make a more formal complaint, and was duly invited in to join the festivities, during the course of which he lost his helmet. When he finally staggered out of the house, his bike had been nicked.

The best story of all concerned the occasion when Paul McCartney visited the Farlowe household. Chris and Paul had been imbibing at some club or other in London and, as Chris had the most amazing collection of records, he invited McCartney back for a musical evening (or by now, of course, morning).

In they went and on went the music full blast. Before long, Chris's mum came downstairs, saying, "For fuck's sake Chris, turn that bleedin' racket down". Then she noticed the stranger sitting in the chair normally exclusively reserved for Chris's uncle.

"And 'oo the fuck's 'e?", she shouted.

Chris explained that "'e" was in fact Paul McCartney from the Beatles, upon which she then changed her accent into that of the queen and said, "Ooh, it's so nice to meet you, Mister Macarfy", before scurrying away, only to return a while later, fully dressed and made up and carrying her handbag. From then on, the chair was known as "Mr. Macarfy's chair".

One day, in Freiburg, I walked into the lobby of the hotel to find it looking as though a coachload of tourists had arrived. It was packed with plastic carrier bags and all kinds of stuff. It's well know that Chris is obsessed by World War 2 and is, in fact, a bit of a historian on all matters relating to that period. During his shopping extravaganza, he'd come across some candle holders which had apparently been presented by Hitler to the more senior of his staff. Chris had purchased a pile of them and proudly brought one over to me and Liz, who were having a quiet drink in the bar area.

"Look at that", he said to Liz. "What is it?", she enquired. "Only the candle holder that Adolf gave to his Generals, that's all!", he said, producing a faded photograph of Adolf, holding indeed an item which appeared to bear some resemblance to the candlestick Chris had.

"But how do you know that it's the genuine article?", Liz asked.

Chris, completely frustrated by these minor details, replied: "Because it's still got the fucking wax in it, innit?".

He had a warehouse in Camden, where he kept jeeps, tanks and all kinds of militaria, even supplying film crews with their props. Zak bought a German general's leather overcoat from Chris, though I never quite knew why. It was about eight sizes too big for him, plus Zak is very politically correct.

The shopping continued on a daily basis. Chris loved furniture and fabrics from the 50's and early 60's, and his own flat within his mum's house was adorned with calypso tables and chairs and lots of those horrible plastic table cloths you used to see, all in the most horrendous of colours. He just loved plastic.

In his bathroom, there was an enormous stuffed swordfish above the bath. One day, en route to a show, he unfolded a blown up photograph of his apartment in its full glory, including a white, ball-shaped television. "Now that's what you call a flat", he said, proudly.

His eating habits were predictable. Every day, he'd go to the canteen of Kaufhof, a German department store chain, and every day without fail he'd have a bloody schnitzel. "Best schnitzel in the world at Kaufhof, mate", he'd say. On a daily basis, like me, he'd phone his mum and go to any length to make sure he called every single day. I've seen him standing in the middle of a freezing cold field, just to make the call to reassure himself that she was OK. Sadly, she died a few years ago and (again like me), Chris was totally devastated.

Say what you like about Chris, he has a great (in my opinion and in his opinion, the best) voice and if anyone has had the pleasure to hear him singing "standards", long before Rod Stewart decided to turn himself into Frank Sinatra, then you will know what I mean. I've never heard a guy sing with so much conviction. It may be genuine or false, I just don't know, but to me it comes across as being from the soul. In fact, for me, Chris is a real soul singer, not in the sense of the grunting and silly noises that are sometimes associated with soul. He's a hard guy to get to know; in fact

I'm not at all sure if I "know" him even now, but he is very sincere and very honest, and this all comes out in his vocals.

He recorded a couple of tracks for me on Wizards Convention 2, and had them to perfection in two takes. He did a wonderful version of "Try A Little Tenderness", which could bring a tear to a glass eye. So Chris, I think you are wonderful.

I did a few other tours with Chris. These were organised by Pete York, but the names Pete gave to the various combinations of bands were more than a little suspect. There were (blush) the "Blue Jive Five", then "Daddy and the Steamers" - can you believe it? Then there was a "Superblues" series, and finally "Superdrumming", which was, in fact, a very tasteful and creative TV series. There are more, but I suggest you visit Pete's website for the full impact. Pete is the greatest of guys and will always be one of my closest friends, but if only he guided his own head!

So there we were, back in France and dealing, once again, with moronic builders. I was never one to become involved with the mundane organisation of these affairs, so it was totally left to poor, long-suffering Liz, who, it has to be said, can turn a house into a home in a day. At any rate, she has done it five times in a comparatively short year span. Liz and I have now been together for over twenty years and still every day together is a joy for me. Yes, of course we have our rows, as any couple does, but she will always be the most beautiful woman I've ever met, though she does get bored with my constant attention! We recently had dinner with Zak and Sarah Starkey, and Zak and I both agreed that our biggest fear was that one or the other partner would be left on their own. It's a frightening thing, this love business!

As for Liz and myself, we can go to the same restaurant week after week, or even day after day, and still find new topics of conversation, even after twenty years, which has to be quite a feat. Should I die first, which no doubt I will, having abused my body with alcohol and cigarettes for far too long, I would want Liz to remain the happy soul she has always been. She is always smiling. When I spoke to Reg Presley of the Troggs the other day, his first question was, "Is Liz still happy?". This is what people remember and love her for, and she has been my inspiration and my life for so long that even when I do depart, I would want her to retain her optimism and happy outlook and never be sad for me. I will love her till the day I die and if there is an after-life, I'll be looking out for my dear Liz for all eternity!

Right, that's enough soppy stuff. Where was I? Ah yes, there I was, drinking again at the local "auberge", when I discovered, to my amazement, that the waiter there was English. Joy of joys, a compatriot! His name was Geoffrey. We now call him "mid-channel Geoffrey", because he's not quite sure whether he is English or French. Despite being 100 percent English, he now speaks his native tongue with a French accent, which can be quite disturbing.

Geoffrey, it turned out, was married to a lady by the name of Angela. Angela is even stranger than Geoffrey and they are indeed the "Odd Couple". Angela, it turned out, had lived about a half a mile away from me when I was in Herne Place, which was a strange coincidence. Geoffrey was quite well connected with some people I knew. He knew Gordon Waller of Peter & Gordon fame, and did some things for the Indica art gallery in Mason's Yard, where John Lennon met Yoko Ono.

Geoffrey can now be seen in the picturesque town of Uzès, which is about twenty minutes from our house, walking around the market wearing what looks like a pizza on his head. This is to give him a French ambiance, the "pizza" in fact being a blue beret, though it's so excessively large, it resembles a flying saucer. We've had people staying in our cottage who have been to Uzès and come back saying that they'd seen this guy, quite obviously English, impersonating a Frenchman with a pizza on his head!

As a result of my innocent drinking liaison with Geoffrey, we eventually met Angela, who in turn introduced us to the ex-pat social life of the area. Out of this came some good, but mostly bad. No, on reflection, I can't actually think of anything good. We suddenly found ourselves part of the "Dinner Party Set", a type of social interaction to which I have always been temperamentally unsuited. Here, all my fears were confirmed, as the participants were totally alien to anything I could relate to.

Angela and Geoffrey had a small gathering on one occasion, but the evening was marred by the music, which was that of the "drum and bass" ilk, played at ear splitting levels, due to the presence of their son. I became so pissed off that I left early, but sadly their dog, "Charlie Brown" insisted on following me on my long walk home. I had covered some considerable distance before it became evident that Charlie Brown was intent on coming all the way home with me, so in the end I had to turn back, just to return the fucking dog to its owners!

Our first invitation to the "sit down and get totally bored" dinner parties was to a house owned by couple of gay guys. I have absolutely nothing against gay guys as long as they don't labour the point, but unfortunately, these two did. Heterosexual guys don't normally go on in graphic detail to complete strangers about what, how, when and where we do or have done it, but these two did and still do. My final attendance was when the two of them danced together, one wearing stilettos.

The Dinner Party brigade in France assembled weekly, and, within the elite, probably nightly. Mainly due to my political incorrectness, we were banished to the weekends, but even that was more than enough. The worst of it was that we had to do "return matches", which meant that, once invited to one, you had to invite everyone back. On one occasion, Liz arranged one to welcome me back from a tour with my musician friends, who, as far as I know, were all real men in the true sense of the word.

I arrived home to find a surprise party assembled, with the obligatory gays and a couple of de-frocked lawyers. It was fucking horrific. One of the "lawyers" (female) repeatedly asked me if I'd take her to bed, until I eventually told her that I'd rather sleep with a tree. Meanwhile, the other one kept spouting on about million dollar bank drafts and Lord and Lady Dumper Truck, who happened to live in the area and we simply MUST meet! No bloody thank you. Still he droned on about all the important society people he knew and how impossibly rich they all were, at which point I interrupted to ask, "Do you know any fucking plumbers?" In this way, I sort of screwed up any social life we might have had in France, but I don't regret it for a second.

The best bit was when this lawyer and his wife said they were well connected within the music biz and mentioned a very dear friend of his, whom I actually happened to know. He was Chairman of MCPS/PRS and we were, and still are, extremely good friends, in fact he is my publisher. As chance would have it, he was coming down to stay with us for a couple of days. I thought it logical to invite the two lawyers over for an evening, because at least we'd all have something in common. As it unsurprisingly turned out, my mate from MCPS/PRS didn't know either of them from Adam or Eve.

Another guy I met was named Leonard, whom I christened "Limonade", French for lemonade! He was a fanatical music fan who imagined himself becoming the Harvey Goldsmith of France. Limonade started to promote dreadful concerts with even more dreadful bands, and at one point asked me if I'd participate. Of course, I declined. He had arranged a poxy synthesizer for the night but hadn't managed to get hold of a stand, so it just lay flat on the stage. Limonade actually expected me to lie on the fucking floor and play it!

He started, at enormous loss, to promote a series of concerts entitled "New Wembley". I only attended one and that was enough. As it was evident that I was not willing to play, he asked if I'd record an announcement to start proceedings. This I did, together with Liz, but we did not take it seriously. He arrived at the house with a cassette recorder, having drafted the most awful script you could possibly imagine for us to read. Being pissed, I decided to make a mockery of the whole thing, so Liz and I adopted a Derek and Clive mode to make the recording. We ignored his dreadful script and instead, took the piss for half an hour, culminating in calling the event a total load of bollocks.

Limonade didn't understand a single word of what we'd recorded, but felt it sounded enthusiastic and so went away happy. This was the sole event we actually did attend and there were, surprisingly, quite a few people there. Suddenly, our "Derek and Clive" announcement resonated around the venue, leaving the French audience totally bemused, confused and ignorant of what we were in fact saying about the crap night they were about to endure.

As the building work continued on the house in France, we were beset with problems on a daily basis. First, we employed a clod of an electrician who re-wired the first section of the house, which included my new recording studio. It wasn't until a couple of years later that we found that he hadn't earthed it. Everything was "live", meaning that it was a miracle that I wasn't "dead". He hadn't colour coded any of the wires, as a result of which no other electrician knew what he'd done and nobody would even attempt a repair. By that time, the original guy had forgotten himself, so it was a case of re-wiring.

Eventually, we found a new electrician with the doubtful name of Aj. He was a strange but likeable guy, who resembled Crusty the Clown from the Simpsons. Aj unearthed miles of cable that was within a gnat's fart of bursting into flames. He also assembled some electric gates for us, together with an intercom system and a video screen within the house. I just didn't want anything to do with the outside world.

On the day that he fitted the camera and remote controls, my daughter Emma was staying with us and for some reason Liz and I had to go to a meeting, no doubt with the bank. Aj took pride in his work and went to extraordinarily boring lengths to explain to us exactly what he'd done, and why. What lead went where was of no interest to us whatsoever, just as long as the bloody thing worked.

So off Liz and I went, leaving Emma in sole control of Aj. He'd got the camera on the gate working and also the screen within the house, and so was intent on convincing Emma that it did work. First, he stood at the gate, his "Crusty The Clown" visage staring at Emma through the monitor, and then he insisted that Emma should go down to the gate and repeat the procedure, so that he could see for himself that his work was satisfactory. Apparently, this process went on for some hours and, as Emma was suffering from a hangover, the look of total despair on her face when we returned was quite a sight to behold.

Other highlights were the builder who claimed we'd only actually paid him for two sides of a three-sided window. Then we had the kitchen floor tiles laid. One tile was raised, meaning that the interconnecting door wouldn't open, upon which the tiler claimed that it was our fault because we'd bought a faulty tile! Then there was the archway we had built, leading from the kitchen to another spare room. We'd bought a door especially for this archway and shown the builders the door and the dimensions, to make sure there was no danger of faulty communication. The builder went on to construct, with great care and precision, an arch that would have accommodated Goliath and bore no resemblance to the shape, size or dimension of the door we intended to fit.

The final phase of the construction/restoration was "overseen" by an English oaf we had found. We felt we might have a fighting chance if we could complain in English, but it was not to be. It made no difference whatsoever. He was a pretentious franglais who rolled his 'r's like Edith Piaf (for which we christened him "Edith") and pirouetted about in fucking pink jeans like someone from an amateur dramatic society pretending to be camp. Quite frankly, he couldn't have got pissed in a brewery. He then slid his "own" architect into the equation. This architect announced that he would need at least three days to get the "feel" of the village, the house and the way we lived, before he could actually put pen to paper. For fuck's sake, we were only building a kitchen and a spare room! With his master design (which Liz had already given him anyway), he was in and around the house with his periscopes, dividers, tripods, biceps and triceps for such a long time that I thought he was making an Ordnance Survey map for the entire village and surrounding areas. In the end, we were presented with a childish daub of a painting, featuring two buffoons waving from a terrace the size of the Centre Court at Wimbledon and a swimming pool overflowing from the terrace in a cascade to challenge Niagara Falls, tumbling into a further pool on ground level. The price of this work of art was £3000! My French mate in the local auberge said he had in fact gone to school with the guy, that he was an arsehole and that £500 would have been too much.

There was no hope. During the building work, we had to go to the UK to visit my ailing mother. While we were there, we received a phone call from the contractor telling us that a wall had fallen down. He was clearly pissed as he told me that the extra cost would be a mere £8000. Now I am not a builder, but even to me, it's clear to me that if you remove all supporting walls, which they did, something has to give. Needless to say, he received his £8000. Another, slightly less expensive shock was waiting for us on our return: John Acock, my engineer, was taking care of the house while we were away. Being super-conscientious, he had spent the week watering our silk plants!

In the end, we settled for the best we could expect and deducted what Liz thought was an adequate sum of money from the final invoice, which in itself changed from hour to hour. Meanwhile, "Edith" arranged, unbeknown to us, a meeting with all the various tradesmen who had worked on the project and they arrived one evening, like a posse, to discuss the problems we felt we had. The loudest of the assembled "craftsmen" was the guy who was supposed to have built the kitchen. We had given up on him, as we never actually even received his estimate, but it was he who had the most to say, even though he'd done nothing and a complete fitted kitchen had already been installed by another company.

The plasterer moaned, though the Chicago plaster casters could have done a better job than he'd done, and another carpenter moaned, though all his wood was stained by cement by the oafish builders. Beams didn't quite meet and he had an obsession with what the French call "chocks", which are supposed to stop the beams from rolling away. In my opinion, if a joiner joins, then there is no need for a fucking chock!

It was clear that we might as well have been arguing with a statue. "Edith" was prancing around like Rudolf Nureyev in his pink jeans and occasionally holding his head between his hands. The electrician was okay (so far, we haven't been blown up) and said nothing. In the end, they all just went away again. As long as they had a cheque they seemed happy, even if it was only half what they asked for. Perhaps it was double what they had expected.

I would never, ever undertake a job like that again. I would certainly never again even speak to "Edith", who was little more than a site manager. He rarely turned up on site, probably too worried about his pink jeans. Right at the beginning of this phase of the project, there was some demolition work to be done. "Edith" had ordered a gigantic crane with a huge lead weight attached to it, to knock down an existing part of the building. What he hadn't taken into account was the turning circle of the crane, which would in fact have resulted in him knocking down half the bloody village at the same time. All the houses around us would suddenly have become bungalows. The crane was sent away, but this was deemed to have been our own fault, so the cost spiralled, as the demolition had to be done manually. Despite falling down on their construction and finishing abilities, French builders are master demolishers.

We had been in France a few years when we invited the Griswolds for Christmas. The plan was for them to drive down from the UK with my mother and all the mini Griswolds. The Griswolds are, in fact, the Blakeys, but they seem to wreak so much havoc that they have become affectionately known to us as The Griswolds.

I had first met Peter Blakey during the time he ran the nursery for Ringo Starr at Tittenhurst Park. It wasn't until Liz and I had gone to Egham, during our last few days in England, to have some fish and chips at a renowned little "chippie" called "Jack's Golden Plaice" that we finally cemented our relationship over a few pickled onions and multitudes of gherkins. We'd always avoided the Griswolds, because much of our courting had taken took place in Zak's cottage within the grounds of Tittenhurst, and we were in fear of news spreading. Anyway, there we were, mid-gherkin, when the Griswolds joined us and we found we got on pretty well. Peter was about to leave the employ of Ringo and had bought a plot of land in Chobham, where he intended to set up his own nursery. This he proceeded to do, with a great deal of success. It is apparent that he has made a good deal of money, which he does now tend to flaunt to the most ridiculous extent.

Everything in the Griswolds' life has to be the BIGGEST and the BEST. Each night, Peter surveys his estate with his dog, which is the size of a small camel (it has 12 pounds of sausages for breakfast) and a torch the size of a medium tree. Chez Griswold, which we now call "Wallyworld", EVERYTHING is BIG. If he buys a packet of crisps, it has to be the size of a postman's sack, and in their house, everything seems out of proportion. It's like the opposite of one of those "show houses", where they put in small furniture to make the rooms appear larger. In the Griswolds' case, the furniture, the dog and even the family are somehow out of proportion, and on occasion it can be quite disturbing. They are very excitable people as well, and there are times that things reach such a crescendo that it's impossible to think. There is Peter, his wife Jackie and their children Sarah, Rachel and Adam, and en masse, they become a frightening ensemble.

We had asked for a few English provisions to be brought down, things you can't get in France, such as digestive biscuits, Heinz Baked Beans, English sausages and bacon, plus of course things that you'd take for granted like Worcestershire sauce, tomato ketchup and mature cheddar cheese. The Griswolds, of course, brought with them enough of all of this to enable us to survive the aftermath of a nuclear war for a good year or so. They really wanted to get festive in a BIG way, so, armed with Bing Crosby tapes and other seasonal festive melodies, they set off. I remember that it was Christmas Eve as Liz and I sat quietly contemplating their arrival. Around midnight, we became aware of a distant drone of "Jingle Bells". We didn't at first associate this with the arrival of the Griswolds, but as the volume grew with alarming momentum, I decided to look out of the window. There was some consternation in the village and lights that were normally off came on as the Griswolds cruised into town with a big red beacon flashing on top of their newly purchased all terrain, all weather condition, go anywhere, any time, do anything four wheel drive Mitsubishi. The car was equipped with more headlights than the spaceship from "Close Encounters" and lit up the entire village. I quickly opened the gates and ushered them in, to avoid further embarrassment.

As Liz switched on the outside lights, we were faced with the entire Griswold family singing "Jingle Bells" at the tops of their voices, and all wearing Father Christmas hats, my mother included, although she did look a little bewildered. Apparently they'd been singing, with enormous gusto, "Jingle Bells" from the moment they'd arrived in Calais, which was some 700 miles distant.

Everyone stormed into the house and the task began of unloading the Mitsubishi. Cases of baked beans arrived in the dining room along with boxes of digestive biscuits, then a virtual pallet load of bacon, along with a mountain of cheddar cheese. The result was like the European Food Mountain. Then young Adam decided to demonstrate to us the various optional extras of the Mitsubishi. The Griswolds, of course, had them all, plus a few more. Firstly, we had a demonstration of the car alarm, which made the most hideous "whoop whoop" sound, like that of an armada of battleships and with a volume to equal them all. My poor mother sat in dazed confusion and Liz told me she had to go and have a lie down.

Then came Christmas Day. The Griswolds had brought with them two videos of films we just HAD to see, so at 8 a.m., we were treated to the hysterics of "Riverdance", consisting of hundreds of demented Irish people stamping about the stage as if they were at the end of a queue for the toilet. During this maelstrom, Liz was attempting to prepare Christmas lunch. Further hysteria broke out when it was decided that the Christmas gifts were to be opened. Wrapping paper and string and sellotape were strewn around in a mountainous heap, as Peter sat on the floor amidst it all and ate an entire box of ginger that he'd been given. In the background, the Irish dancers were still stamping away.

Even our dog Oscar was caught up in the frenzy and in a matter of hours, his entire personality had changed from one of a lovely little placid dog into a demented beast as he charged from room to room. Thankfully, "Riverdance" came to its climactic end. Lunch was served and for about twenty minutes, comparative peace reigned, before Peter suggested they all go for a walk to work off the lunch. He went upstairs and returned dressed like Clint Eastwood in "High Plains Drifter". He had one of those huge (even for him) waterproof overcoat affairs with overlapping shoulder bits topped off with an outsized leather cowboy hat. You couldn't actually see his feet, so as he walked into the distance, he had the appearance of a person on wheels.

Young Adam had a fascination for any weapon of destruction and, on a shopping trip the next day, he amassed a fair old arsenal of dangerous-looking items including a hand grenade and a laser light. Peter bought himself a pistol. Yes, I'm afraid it was a real one! On a visit to our local restaurant, we were seated at a very long table, on which Adam placed some of his more menacing looking items. Beside him on his side plate were his hand grenade and his laser light, which he used to shine into the eyes and faces of other diners. I wasn't aware of it at the time, but apparently these things are quite dangerous. It wasn't good for our image in the locality.

So, being unwelcome in the better hostelries, we decided the next day on a trip to Mcdonalds. This was quite an experience. We went through the "drive-thru" section, where you order through a microphone and pick up your goods at the exit. During the course of the ordering, everyone shouted out what they did or didn't want, with the result that we ended up at the other end with a bin liner full of what must have been everything on the menu. It was such a massive order that the staff actually came out to see what kind of family would order such vast quantities. Liz kept chanting "Pommes frites", of which we ended up with bags and bags full. There were mounds of Chicken Nuggets (which no-one liked or even wanted) but as they had all kept shouting it out, it was written down and prepared.

Finally it was all over and the Griswolds set off for England with the intention of "buying out" the supermarket at Calais. My mother had taken a liking to French salted butter, so she was assigned a trolley which was filled to the brim with the bloody stuff. Bear in mind that she lived alone and only wanted one or two packets. Instead, at the mercy of the Griswolds, she ended up with a fridge full. But having said all this, I must add that the Griswolds have been very helpful to us over the years and have remained one of our few loyal links with England.

Meanwhile, my drinking days were finally approaching their end. Like most alcoholics, I required a major shock in order to kick the habit. One morning, in February 1997, I noticed a small spot in my umbilical area, but thought nothing of it. As the weeks went by, this small spot rapidly grew to the size of a grapefruit and started to cause me more than a little concern. At the same time, purely coincidentally, I developed an incredible pain in my left knee. This pain far outweighed the grapefruit on my navel and became so ferocious that I couldn't sleep, and eventually could hardly walk.

I went to our local doctor, who referred me to a "specialist" (note the inverted commas). This expert X-rayed my knee and pronounced it to be a meniscus problem, which could easily be solved by keyhole surgery. This ensuing operation, though it was indeed keyhole, was sadly performed by an arsehole. He told me that, within a day, I'd be fully recovered and would be able to run, skip and jump, none of which I'd ever felt inclined to do before the operation anyway. The following day arrived, but not only could I not run, skip and jump, I now couldn't walk at all, and the agony had increased tenfold. I returned to the "specialist" (whom I was now calling Dr. Mengele), who informed me that the only sure-fire solution was to fit a plastic knee. In fact, while he was at it, he may as well fit TWO plastic knees.

At that point, I opted to return to a specialist in the UK. By now, I was in a wheelchair and must have looked awful. I think Liz genuinely thought I was dying and, as the pain was so intense, I almost wished I was. I was wheeled onto an aeroplane at Montpellier and then taken straight to the Wellington Hospital in London. The specialist there explained that the operation performed by Dr. Mengele had in fact been totally unnecessary and that, to make matters worse, he'd chipped a bone while performing it! I had scans and all kinds of tests performed before the final diagnosis was delivered: I had crystallization on my joint, which had come about simply due to excess alcohol intake. I, of course, took no notice and carried on drinking as normal, but was booked into the Princess Margaret hospital in Windsor to have my "grapefruit" sorted out.

The night before I checked into the hospital, I hobbled up to London to meet Jim Davidson, who was pre-recording "Big Break", a snooker TV quiz. The moment we got together, the drinking began in earnest. Jim had a small private bar laid out behind the "set". It consisted of a table, stacked with bottles of wine, and a few chairs. I sat there while he did his show and virtually drank the bloody lot, with the help of a couple of other guys. I felt great, no pain whatsoever, and we even arranged to meet up the next day for dinner. I had completely forgotten my "check-in" at the hospital and that one was not supposed to eat or drink prior to an operation.

Jim arranged for a taxi to take me back to Sunningdale, where I was staying with my mother. I even asked the taxi driver to stop at the off licence so I could get a couple of bottles of wine to last me the rest of the evening. My mother was horrified and disgusted at the state I was in when I staggered in, and I finally began to realise that this was all getting way out of hand.

I arrived at the hospital the following morning, still semi-pissed, and was wheeled to my room. The nurse examined my grapefruit, which now appeared larger than ever. Even she seemed impressed by the size of it. I was given a surgical gown and put to bed. There was a full-length mirror to the left of the bed and, as I got up to have a pee, the full horror faced me. I had turned into a monstrous blob of humanity and I just felt total disgust at myself.

The surgeon arrived to mark the incision points on my stomach with a felt tip pen. The proposed operation looked so bloody big that I asked him whether he planned to cut me in half! Later that afternoon, I was wheeled down for the operation. The general anaesthetic was very pleasant indeed. "If only I could have some of this stuff to take home," I thought, as I drifted off. I awoke in the recovery room, still feeling no pain, and was eventually taken back to my room on a trolley. When the surgeon came in to check on his handiwork, he asked me, "Exactly how much DO you drink?" I jokingly replied, "About two acres a day". Unfortunately, he did not share my sense of humour and told me that, as he'd made his incision, he had been engulfed in a flood of red wine, which he described as being like a whale when they do that spurting thing.

The hospital in Windsor led to an accounts department nightmare. I'd ordered a daily paper, one daily paper, the Daily Express, and was given a bill for £10. For several years, they wrote to me in pursuit of their £10 newspaper and must have spent over £100 in postage. Then they even started legal proceedings to recover the tenner. I would not pay £10 for a single copy of the Daily Express, so they started to add interest and then compound interest. In the end, the fucking paper must have been worth about a thousand pounds!

My hernia done and my knee diagnosed, it was now recommended that I should have a liver test. I failed abysmally and was now pronounced as having cirrhosis of the liver, on top of everything else. This meant a seemingly never-ending round of tests, during which I must have visited most of the major hospitals in London and indeed the Home Counties.

The liver specialist explained that, if I carried on at my present rate of alcohol consumption, I would have eighteen months to live ... if I was lucky.

One appointment was made for me at the Cromwell Hospital in London. Arriving at the front desk, I was asked by the receptionist for my credit card. "But you don't even know what's wrong with me yet!" I shouted. Anyway, I didn't have a credit card with me, as I was in fact covered my private medical insurance. She then asked, "Well, do you know anyone else who has a credit card? Otherwise, I'm afraid we can go no further." This is the down side of private medical treatment, just like in America. They don't give a fuck if you're lying on the floor dying ... no credit card, no treatment.

I telephoned my medical insurers, who were told by the Cromwell that they would have to fax confirmation that my account would be settled. They did indeed do this, but I'd had enough and left the bloody hell hole of a place and went back to Sunningdale. A few weeks later, however, I received an invoice from the Cromwell for an operation that I'd never even had. They eventually started legal proceedings until I managed to convince them that I had not even been in the bloody hospital on the day of the supposed operation.

I was sick and tired of all these tests. The total cost was now around £27,000 and even my insurers were becoming concerned. They explained that in some cases within the world of private medicine, you have to be careful, as the hospitals can just go on and on, purely for their own financial benefit. So when a liver biopsy was suggested, I declined and have been fine ever since. I never drank again, simple as that. That's how I stopped drinking and began thinking again.

Life back in France was never dull. There was the time when Liz set off in the Jeep that we had to do some shopping. Realising it was low on petrol she pulled into the nearest garage and unwittingly filled it up with diesel. She did comment that it didn't seem to smell quite the same as usual. She set off for the shops, but after about a quarter of a mile, the vehicle spluttered to a halt. I was, of course, in the local hostelry at the time when the phone call came through from Liz, telling me that there had been a minor error of judgement and that she had blown the jeep up ... nothing serious, you understand.

The guy behind the bar, with whom we were friendly, immediately sprang into action and offered to go with me and tow the Jeep back to the garage to have the fuel tank drained. We arrived at the spot and he set about fixing the tow rope to both cars. I was pretty pissed off at having my lunchtime drink interrupted and therefore told Liz to get in the car with François while I'd get in the jeep and steer.

So off we all set, along a straight main road which led to the auberge. It was a few moments before I realised that there were no keys in the ignition, as Liz had them. The bloody thing wouldn't have started anyway, but it unfortunately did possess a steering lock. Having travelled the necessary quarter of a mile, they turned left into the Auberge but I didn't, well actually couldn't, as the steering was locked. The rope snapped and I just went sailing on along the busy road, having no control over the vehicle. Everyone else thought it was hysterical, but I was terrified.

It has to be said that Liz, far more than myself, tried from the very start to integrate into French village life and occasionally I was dragged along on what I felt were futile forays into what is, to me, a very mysterious culture. On the instigation of Fernand, it was decreed one day that we should all go off "mushrooming" for a morning. The French are very big on mushrooms and so am I, but, as it turned out, most of them are lethal, by which I unfortunately don't mean magic! We set off early in the morning and very soon had gathered together several huge bags of what looked like quite pleasant mushroom things. We assumed, quite incorrectly, that Fernand, being French, would have some idea on these matters, but over a period of time it became clear that Fernand didn't have a clue about anything at all.

Fernand said that we had to take them to the chemist to have them analysed, just to be on the safe side. Liz dutifully took her sacks of mushrooms to the local chemist and we went off for lunch while they were checked. On our return, we were presented with a single mushroom which was safe to eat; apparently, all the others guaranteed virtual instant death. I think Fernand and his family actually ate the bloody lot, which could explain why they're all so odd. On the frequent occasions that Fernand and myself would "fall out" he'd adopt the American "fuck off" sign, which is a raised forefinger. He couldn't even get that right and would raise his index finger at me threateningly.

Our first attempt at a swimming pool was also fraught with problems. Fernand, again, had suggested we used the local village idiot to dig the hole, as he had mountains of equipment that suited all possible requirements. One morning, he trundled into to the courtyard with a digger that was capable of creating a crater the size of a large bomb. He dug a gigantic hole, but, to his consternation, was subsequently surrounded by so much earth he couldn't get the fucking digger out. It looked as if we'd suffered a direct hit from a nuclear missile. In order to get out, he had to fill in the hole again, which left us not much further forward.

On another day, Liz suggested we should have a day at the beach. I've hated beaches since childhood. What do you do when you get there? Build a sand castle and then smash it to bits, sit in a deck chair and get burnt to a cinder or eat a picnic in the most awful conditions imaginable. That's no fun, is it? But Liz took me to a beach which she assured me was the most tranquil one she'd ever come across. There was indeed mile upon mile of total serenity, even though it was a little on the windy side. Liz had prepared the obligatory picnic and set it out on a table cloth as well as she could. Despite the wind, she persevered, but in the end the food was covered in so much sand, it looked as if it had been breadcrumbed. The final straw camewhen two oafs, ignoring the available mile upon mile of deserted beach, started to play football immediately beside us, kicking sand all over us and what little edible food we had left. We packed up and went home.

Every year, the local voluntary fire brigade call with calendars for sale in aid of their charity. The first time I experienced this, I went down to the now "Fernand proof" gates to be confronted by a fireman clutching a huge pile of these calendars. Not knowing quite what to do, I took the whole lot off him, thanked him and took them into the house, shutting the gates behind me. Horrified, the fireman continued to ring on the intercom, becoming more and more frantic. Liz, walking into the kitchen to see this mound of calendars, asked where they'd all come from and who was ringing the bell like a maniac. I explained that a fireman had given them to me. "You fool", she said, "you're only supposed to take one ... and pay for it!"

I have absolutely no sense of direction. It's something of a miracle that I can find my way around a piano. Indeed I'm sure there are those who maintain that I still can't, like the cameraman at The Albert Hall when we did The Butterfly Ball concert and I'd had quite a lot of beer, in fact a very BIG lot of beer. He was sitting beside the piano watching me tuck into what seemed to him to be an endless supply of Becks and said, "I'm surprised you can see the fucking piano, let alone play it!"

On one of our drives back to the UK from France, Liz and I encountered a logistical problem, that being knowing exactly where we were in relation to where we were going. I have always been opposed to maps and anything that would make life clearer, but on this particular occasion Liz insisted on taking a map, one of those that folds out and you never quite manage to get it to fold back into the same condition.

All went well until lunchtime. I hate motorway services, which tend to be full of people who look like they've just walked off the set of the film Deliverance, so insisted that we take a slip road and find somewhere decent. We did in fact find somewhere very nice (though of course, we've never found it since) and, after a very pleasant lunch, tried to find our way back onto the Autoroute ... which we did, though sadly we were now travelling in the wrong direction.

French signposts are confusing, in that they take you to a certain point and then just stop, leaving you to guess whether to go left, right or straight. We followed signs to the best of our ability but seemed, after about four hours' driving, to keep returning to the same spot. We passed through one village so many times I thought that people might start waving at us.

At this point, Liz finally insisted that I consult the map. I opened this bloody thing, which covered France in its entirety. Now France is a very big country, and the map spread out so far that Liz couldn't see the road before her, because the map spanned the entire windscreen. Hysteria now set in and Liz began laughing so much that tears were rolling down her cheeks, with the result that she couldn't see anything at all! I then got pissed off with the map, screwed it into a ball and threw it out of the window.

So now we were mapless, hysterical and completely lost, at which point I suggested we go home and start again the following day. Having only recently bidden our farewells to the housesitters, Liz felt far too embarrassed to take that course of action, so we looked for a garage without a guy playing the banjo on the front porch, and asked for clear directions to point us the right way.

I'm ashamed to admit that we had only managed to get as far as Lyon, which is just over two hours' drive from where we live. The guy in the garage asked where we were headed, to which we replied ... England! Realising he was not dealing with seasoned tourers, he did point us in an English direction and we finally made it to Sunningdale.

***

My mother survived my father by many years. Liz often says that she's never known a son and a mother to have such a deep relationship and she is absolutely correct. My mother gave me support throughout my entire, not only musical career but the career of life itself, and loved everything, well, nearly everything I did. Her criticism was often harsh and we often ended up having rows, but everyone is entitled to their own thoughts.

Her favourite song was "Little Chalk Blue", a little-known item from "Butterfly Ball". She attended the live concert at the Royal Albert Hall and I managed to get both her and my dad and Uncle Mac a box, which I filled with champagne. This was not for my mum, who was allergic to alcohol. What a pity I didn't inherit this affliction. My brother refused to attend the concert and also didn't make an appearance at her funeral. This was so despicable that I am determined never to speak with that man again. She had a lovely and very varied life, and I know that, deep down, she loved every minute from the bad times to the great times. She saw me go from number one to nothing and then back again but remained the perfect Rock'n'Roll Mum!

The ultimate tribute to Mum came after Ray Fenwick and I had recorded a version of "Silent Night". We'd used an entire choir, supplied courtesy of one of my piano teachers, a Mr. Bernard Gare, who lived virtually opposite us in Champion Hill. One Christmas Day morning, he gathered the entire choir and assembled them at the front of our house to sing "Silent Night" for my mother. It would have reduced the hardest of mortals to tears and indeed it did have the desired effect on my mum.

My mother died on the 17th of December in the year 2000, and I don't think I will ever get over the shock of that moment. My friend had left me. I had seen her the night before and I knew she was dying and I knew I would never see her again, but in my mind she is still and will always be with me in all I do in the future.

I was heartened by the people who attended the funeral, my family, whom she strove so hard to bring together in her last months, and Zak and Sarah, who really are two of the loveliest people I've ever met. Tony Barton, with whom my mother had an ongoing feud, also came. He had enormous respect for her in spite of the fact that she never left him alone, constantly nagging him. Our faithful old cleaner Jean was there too. Jean had been with the family for over twenty years and I should not refer to her as a cleaner, since she was my mother's friend and confidante.

I played piano at the church service, as I felt it was the least I could offer to not only a mother, but a friend who had given me life. Mum thought Hardin & York was a deafening row, but still managed to attend a few of our Marquee performances. "Time Seller" was another of her favourites, although she never did see the Spencer Davis Group live. She gave me the hardest of times in my love life, because no-one was ever considered to be good enough for her son. Even when Liz came along, they had their ups and downs and quite furious arguments, but in the end, all was resolved, and very few days go past when she doesn't crop up in our conversation.

From Mike D'Abo through to Jim Davidson (dumping his arsenal of weaponry in her kitchen, from machine guns to hand grenades, brought back from the Falkland Islands) my mother had loved them all. She'd experienced Tom Keylock, the Rolling Stones' minder, and various twilight characters, e.g. Freddie Foreman. I will miss her eternally and no words, certainly that I could write, would ever do justice to such a magnificent woman.

So now I'm an orphan.

CHAPTER 12
ON THE ROAD AGAIN

In the year 2000, Pete York and I decided to do a tour of Germany. I'd finally come out of my wilderness years and, after my medical scare, no longer drank alcohol.

Pete had been living in Germany with his family for several years, so Liz and I flew to Munich and settled into a hotel near to Pete's house, where we set about a week's concentrated rehearsal period. Not thinking I would ever tour again, I had long since sold my original Hammond to the Pretty Things, who had destroyed it in every possible way, but I found a great 1956 C3 through a friend of mine called Don Larkin, who runs a second hand studio equipment warehouse.

By chance, Don had just one Hammond in stock and, of course, no-one wanted a Hammond because very few people could actually play one. But, with my brain restored to more or less full working order, I could. I went down to the warehouse with my daughter Emma, to have a "test run". Don's place is quite disturbing in a way, as it contains masses and masses of studio consoles. This tends to make one think, if all these desks are for sale, surely there has to be a reason?

The reason is, of course, that there are very few engineers who can actually work them and that modern day production can largely be done in a bedroom. Equipment has become smaller and - so they say - more efficient, but for me the finished recordings all tend to sound the same. Samplers were the end of the game and indeed the inspiration. If used sensibly, they can be of assistance with the initial creation of a song (although it also leads to songs sounding the same as one another, thus resulting in artists resorting to recording cover versions of songs that were honed in the old fashioned way, and fucking them up with technology). You won't be surprised to hear that I personally feel that all the sampled shit should be replaced by someone playing the "proper" instrument.

We arrived at Don's place and there before us was the trusty C3. I played it and it sounded magnificent, but the only problem was that Don, for reasons best known to himself, had placed a goldfish bowl, complete with goldfish, on top of the Leslie cabinet. I didn't feel it was my place to move them and Don didn't seem concerned, but as the volume became louder, the poor fish grew blurred and swam about in a frantic manner. Emma, being an animal lover, eventually moved the bowl elsewhere!

I bought the Hammond on the spot and then set about adapting it for my own sound. I had the volume set to "supercharge" and fitted a string bass system for the bass pedals. It's a system I would recommend to any Hammond player and is manufactured in America by a company called Trekk, who are fantastic and can provide any original Hammond parts. There, that would be worth a drink, if I drank.

The next problem was flight cases. The organ was not "split" as, for obvious reasons, many of them were, so I had a flight case made which turned out to be the size of your average garden shed, a roadie's nightmare. The Hammond and Leslie were promptly freighted to Munich and the whole lot was set up in a rehearsal room. Pete's immediate reaction on re-living the volume was one of horror, but he soon adapted and the rehearsals went well, incorporating a virtually new repertoire, plus of course the old favourites, "The Pike", "Deep In My Despair", "Can't Find My Way Home", "Tomorrow Today" and "Candlelight".

It was a winter tour, which is the best time to be in Germany, as they take the onslaught of Christmas very seriously. It was also a very happy tour. Pete and I always get on great when it's just the two of us, although it always seems to go a bit strange when we're in a band situation. Hardin and York were, and still are, in my opinion, a unique and valid proposition, so it was heartening to see the die-hard fans, many of whom have now become friends, still turning out.

Mind you, everything had started out a bit grimly. Liz and I flew from Nîmes to Paris, where we were to catch the connecting flight to Hamburg. We got to Paris, and that's where it all started to go wrong. We had checked in, gone to the departure lounge, proceeded to the boarding gate, received our boarding passes and even boarded the plane. Sadly, the seat numbers we had extended beyond the number of seats on the plane. As it was not a full flight, the stewardess said,"Oh, just sit anywhere you like".

I had an inner sense that said something was not right, and asked, "We are going to Hamburg, aren't we?" "Oh no," she replied, "Hanover". The engines had already started up, but we managed to get off, and Air France tried to rush us to the correct plane which had, by now, of course, left, complete with our baggage.

After much arguing, which is all you need on the eve of a tour, we were given replacement tickets for the next flight to Hamburg, two hours later! But it has to be said we were compensated for our misery with a bar of chocolate, courtesy of Air France, which, for allowing us to board the wrong plane (good thing we weren't terrorists) should now be renamed "Air Farce", or perhaps "Air Chance".

So we arrived in Hamburg to find Pete surprisingly happy. Pete York is not the most tolerant of people (neither am I, which is why the two of us are now nicknamed the Grumpy Old Men) and I had visions of him being in a rage and leaving without us from Hamburg, where he had also flown. But I was prepared for all eventualities; I had bought a new mobile phone, with all the instructions in French, but had not a clue as to how it worked. After lots of button pushing and wrong numbers, I finally got through to our agent in Munich, who relayed the message to Pete, who, by now, I'm sure, was well prepared for the chaos which generally follows me. Also, bear in mind that I was right next to a phone box while I fiddled with my new piece of technology, but I would not be defeated. During all this, I lost my date sheet with all the relevant phone numbers on it, so had Pete left the airport, I would not have had a clue where to go. We were driven by a guy who was either very tired or very stoned to our hotel for discussions about the following dates. Fortunately, we weren't playing that night. The following day we rehearsed, and I was both surprised and pleased that everything just fell into place. That night was the first show in Husum and we played really well together.

The audience was great, as they all were, and again we met such nice people and made some new friends. Some of the journeys were pretty horrific in distance, but every show was a joy to play. I can honestly say that Hardin & York have never once had a bad audience or a disastrous show since we re-formed. If ever we feel that things aren't going too well, one or other of us always comes up with that "something" extra and we invariably finish on a tumultuous note.

Germany was enveloped in Christmas celebrations, and the general atmosphere everywhere was wonderful, with all the street markets and decorations. The weather was fantastically Spring-like, and, as it was so close to Christmas, everyone was in a festive mood. During the course of the tour, we visited some of our old haunts, including the Star Club in Hamburg, which is now merely a marble stone, much like a funerial headstone. The club has long gone and is now a strip joint. We even went back to the first hotel we ever stayed in, the Imperial, which can be found at the top of the Reeperbahn. Every time I go to Hamburg, even now, I make a regular pilgrimage to all the old haunts.

The tour was, for me, very nostalgic. Liz accompanied us and I enjoyed showing her that part of my life, which now seems so long ago. Many of our friends from those days have now departed, though for me their memory will always remain. I think we owe a special debt to Frank Dostel, who initially booked us for the Star Club and indeed the Essen Festival, which really gave the band its big break way back in 1969. Frank was the man who launched Hardin & York into so many different directions. Thank you, Frank!

With my life now being on an even keel, I was able to return to touring on a regular basis. With audiences still very interested in bands from "our" era, the Spencer Davis Group now tours regularly. Spencer, in fact, has two bands, one for the USA and one (ours, the "original" band) for Europe. The European line-up consists of Spencer, me, Pete York, plus our old friends Colin Hodgkinson (bass, late of Whitesnake) and Miller Anderson (guitar, known to me from the days of the Keef Hartley Band).

The earliest jaunt with the re-formed SDG took us back to Germany in 2001. I arrived in Munich, probably an hour or so late, at a completely different terminal to the one on the schedule; however, at least I was in Munich, which is a feat for someone who tends to get on the wrong plane altogether!

After walking from one terminal to the next, I surprisingly found Miller and Colin, but there was no sighting of Spencer. Having finally gotten to grips with my mobile phone, I called Bernie, the roadie, who came and found us. During the course of our "hellos" and the exchange of various musician jokes, we found ourselves on the Autobahn. It hadn't seemed to occur to anyone that Spencer was, in fact, still missing. "S'pose we won't be waiting for Spencer," I pointed out.

We finally arrived at the hotel, which was not only in the middle of nowhere, but also shut. Finally, the hotelier (for want of a better word) arrived and led us into our nightmare for the night. We convinced him to open the bar, which he did under extreme duress, and beers and brandies were served. As I no longer drank alcohol and the suggestion of tea was totally out of the question, I settled for a couple of bottles of water. After an hour or so, a taxi arrived, bearing a most unhappy Spencer. As I had lost a considerable amount of weight since my absence of alcohol intake, he didn't recognise me at all and proceeded to join Colin and Miller at the bar. It was Miller who finally re-introduced me to a stunned Spencer! Eventually, we were shown to our "rooms". Mine was a kind of Colditz cell, with no window, just a skylight, which even Superman wouldn't have been able to open.

However, exhaustion took its toll, and I was soon sound asleep. A rehearsal was planned for the next day, though of course this didn't happen, and it was decided that we'd just add songs as we went along and stick to the "known" repertoire for the first show. Bearing in mind that I hadn't played with the band for some years, the "known" show was not known to me, but we got through it somehow.

The gig was at Karstadt. I was a bit miffed as to why the band was being steered towards playing this kind of venue, because Karstadt is a chain of German department stores! It was a bit like playing a gig at Marks and Spencers. Our concert was in a rooftop restaurant. During the day, it was a kind of cafeteria and in the evening it was an average restaurant, filled with what seemed to be late-night shoppers with the odd music fan thrown in. Many of the customers seemed rather baffled by our presence.

We had to play at controlled volume levels to avoid the "Hands On The Ears" brigade. This was not a rock venue, and, in my opinion, it was one that should have been avoided at all costs. You simply cannot play "Gimme Some Lovin'" or "I'm A Man" quietly. Pete is of the opinion that music does not have to be loud to be exciting. I disagree; with the type of music we play, it HAS to be loud in order to be exciting, otherwise it turns into karaoke and loses its edge. Imagine Deep Purple playing quietly in a rooftop restaurant!

Anyway, we did the show, and it all went fine, though I personally got nothing out of it at all. From then on, though, all the gigs were sold out. Miller was singing really well these days, and Colin was quite stunning on bass. Spencer was able to hold his own; he's a great guy, and I found I could get on with him better than I ever had before. In the early days, I could always talk with Spencer very easily. He was and is open to suggestions and keen on new ideas, and has a good ear for what sounds good and bad.

Frankfurt was great. I'd last played there with Hardin & York in the late 70s, and it hadn't changed a lot since then. Bensheim, Berlin and Karlsruhe were all nice shows but, en route to Bad Aibling, the final show, disaster struck: the tour bus broke down in the middle of nowhere. So there we were, marooned, The driver called for a breakdown truck, as it turned out that the gearbox had blown. The low loader arrived, driven by a guy who just hitched us up to a steel rope and hoisted the bus, with us all in it, on to the back of his low loader. As we travelled along in a driverless bus on top of the loader, we must have looked a pretty dumb lot, so thank heavens it didn't have "S.D.G." emblazoned on its side!

The venue was a huge sort of indoor games complex, and the support band was Them. Now I didn't recognise any of "Them" but the keyboard player seemed to know me, having visited my studio in Ascot. There was certainly no sign of Van Morrison, I can tell you that! As far as I could figure out, their only link with Them was that they were Irish. Their keyboard player kindly offered to loan me his "Hammond" for the night, but he appeared to have built it himself and it was literally hanging together with cables and gaffa tape, so I declined.

After the show, they were all pretty pissed. As Miller walked past their van and saw the bodies lying in disarray, he tut-tutted, "So that's rock'n'roll? Do we want to end up like that?" Hmm ...

After the German tour, it was on to Birmingham, and a bizarre, week-long residency at the Ronnie Scott Club in the city centre. We all made our way separately to Birmingham, largely due to the management's "thrifty" attitude that seemed to persist. Pete went home to Munich for the night, Miller went to his home in Brighton, I'm not sure where Colin went, and Spencer flew straight to Birmingham. I ended up on a flight which landed some two hours away from Birmingham! Organisation at its finest, you might say, but I suppose there was an overall saving of about 50p.

At Stansted Airport, I met up with Liz, who had flown in from France. I was by now very tired and not looking forward to Birmingham at all, as it was not entirely clear how I was going to get there. The train was impossible, as I had four suitcases and would have had to travel into London and then all the way out again, so I got a taxi. Thus, any notion of economy went straight out the window, at least as far as I was concerned, as the cab cost me £120!

In Birmingham, we met up with Spencer. We'd both decided to get there the night before the first show. I was by now pissed off with living out of suitcases and moving from one hotel to another. Also, I didn't feel at all comfortable in Birmingham. After 11pm, the centre took on the air of a battle zone. I'd never seen so many pissed people lurching around. Some had even given up the lurch and just lay right where they fell. So Spencer and I sat in the hotel lounge, both pretty fed up, as we felt it was unsafe to go out.

I was relieved and amazed to see a familiar face from Ascot in the lounge. It was Russ Abbot, the English comedian, who had lived just down the road from me in my Sunningdale/Ascot days. Russ managed to convince me to stick around, as at this point I was really getting ready to throw in the towel and go home. He was in a pantomime just around the corner, and we at least had something in common from the old days.

So off we set to Ronnie Scott's the following afternoon for the soundcheck ... ho ho ho!! There was no Hammond, only a piano - again for reasons of economy. How could anyone play classic Spencer Davis Group songs on a piano or a synthesiser? Answers on a postcard, please. The support band had a little synth which made the worst organ sound I'd ever heard. However, I was simply told it would have to do. The synth was so bad that for the first night I just played the piano. It was intolerable, so for the remainder of the week, and at my own expense, I hired a Hammond C3, and the change in the sound was obvious to everyone. Well, almost everyone.

The dressing room at Ronnie Scott's was atrocious, so much so that I was loath to even hang my coat in there! The sound engineer was reasonably helpful, but the rest of the staff were definitely not. They had a strange attitude that we were staff, less important than a wine waiter. They treated us like shit, but luckily, we will never have to play there again, as it is now a lap dancing club. The audiences, however, were great. Muff Winwood came to one show, fortunately not the first one, and he was very friendly to us all. Roy Wood turned up one night as well. On the final night, Liz and my daughter Emma came up with some friends, and Emma joined the group on stage for "Gimme Some Lovin'". It was a great night, marred only by the attitude of the staff.

A date had been added in Nantwich, which is near Manchester, but this presented a problem, because the organ could not be transported there - it was deemed to be beyond budget! So it was down to a piano again, though this time a very bad one. It was a town hall, and a very full town hall at that, and I felt embarrassed to be playing that heap of shit. The audience didn't seem to mind, though, and the promoter was more than helpful and told me he would have arranged transport for the organ himself had he only been forewarned in advance.

Had I been a member of the audience, I would not have been happy. I think the band should reproduce its sound to the best of its ability. If a fee does not support the cost of a Hammond, then the show should not be done at all. Of course all the fees do support the cost of Hammond, but that's another story altogether. So before any more tours were contemplated, there was much to be discussed.

And so it was that, prior to a mammoth package tour of the UK in 2002, I spoke to Spencer and sorted out the Hammond issue to my satisfaction. We also agreed it would be more comfortable to travel the length and breadth of Britain in my car. In some ways, this was a desperate error, but on the other hand, I grew closer to Spencer and developed a bond of friendship that we probably had never really had over the previous 35 years. Sure, we bitched and moaned, but Spencer, at his time in life, really just wants to enjoy himself - and why on earth not? The error we made was in effectively splitting the band into two "camps", so that towards the end of the tour, atmospheres had deteriorated to levels that I hadn't encountered since I was 17!

Liz and I drove to England on the 10th February, with the intention of having a couple of days' rest at The Castle Hotel in Windsor. The journey from France was eventful and at one point it seemed we'd never get to England at all. We were stopped for speeding near Troyes, where apparently we were approaching double the speed limit! We were hauled off the motorway by two officers on bikes, real "Chips" types who just loved the power of a uniform and "clicky" boots.

We were questioned in a Gestapo manner and I was breathalised, which was a lovely feeling, as, of course, I no longer drank alcohol. After a long debate in French, most of which we didn't understand, we were presented with an on the spot fine of £250 ... the perfect beginning to our journey. Just as that was being settled, another stormtrooper "clicked" into the room with even graver news, explaining to the guy who had just settled the affair that we had been so far over the speed limit that the fine should be £1000 and that our car should be confiscated.

It's at times like these where I start to think, oh fuck it, it's fate and there's really nothing you can do about it. At that stage, I start to become REALLY uncooperative. Liz, on the other hand, goes into Judi Dench over-acting mode and can miraculously summon up crocodile tears in an attempt to salvage what seems to be an impossible situation. Liz explained that we were on our way to England to work and that we really, really needed the car, but the guy would have none of it. The best he would offer was a lift to the nearest railway station, after which we would be on our own. But after what seemed an eternity, Liz's tears had the desired effect and we were released with a mere £250 fine. Perfect.

Arriving in Windsor in the early hours, we settled into The Sheridan Suite, overlooking Windsor Castle. We now had a couple of days of peace and relative quiet, blissfully unaware of the horror that was to follow. After a far too brief recovery period, we set off for the Holiday Inn at Stoke-on-Trent, which was to be the assembly point for all three bands, The Troggs, The Yardbirds and of course The Spencer Davis Group.

Everything was very sociable, as Flying Music, the promoters of the package, had laid on a champagne evening to celebrate the beginning of the tour. This was the first time I'd met the Troggs since the Sixties and I don't think I'd ever met a Yardbird (not that there were many actual Yardbirds left in this version of the band). But it all had the makings of a jolly outing and, largely thanks to the Troggs, it was.

At the first show in Stoke, all three bands assembled for sound checks. Reg Presley saw little point in this procedure, which is in fact quite valid, since anything one ever does at a sound check is normally instantly forgotten by the crew and subsequently bears no resemblance to the sound created once the hall is full of people (which is a totally different environment from a hall bereft of people). The crew, however, were confident, having worked with The Spice Girls (which we didn't find too encouraging). They had gone from the Spice Girls to the Old Spice Men!

As for the SDG, we'd managed to fit in a few rehearsals on previous tours, prior to any of this, so we were pretty tight. The first show went really well. We had a full house, which gave us all a very settled feeling and inspired us for what was to follow. Reg Presley, who was to become the tour comedian, announced on stage on that first night that the tour was being promoted by Flying Music, so called because "our arses don't touch the fucking floor!"

On the 15th, we set off for Llandudno in Wales for the North Wales Theatre. It instantly became clear that Spencer had appointed himself navigator, which was just as well, as neither Liz nor I knew our North from our South. We were in room 327 at The St. George's Hotel and the first obstacle was that the hotel lift was not working and we were on the third floor. I had absolutely no intention of carrying Liz's mound of suitcases up three floors, so we were helped out by a young porter who seemed to possess the power and strength of the Incredible Hulk. In no time, our bags were in the room and Liz was in the bloody bath.

The concert hall was, according to Spencer, a mere fart away, and as it was such a nice day perhaps we might take a stroll to it? Now I am not a great walker, largely due to my knee problem which was, as I've previously explained, alcohol induced. Spencer was soon way ahead of me, oblivious to the fact that I was lagging far behind. Bit by bit we drifted in and the briefest of soundchecks took place. From then on, there were to be no soundchecks at all, apart from the Yardbirds, whose boundless enthusiasm seemed to encourage them to have one whenever and wherever possible.

As we were on the coast, the window sill of our room overlooking the sea was festooned with seagulls, who were constantly pecking on the pane, creating a similar effect to a drum roll. Liz's solution was to feed them a few biscuits, after which, she assured me, they'd be happily fed and fly away. This was a poor theory. It soon became like a scene from Alfred Hitchcock's film "The Birds", with hundreds of the buggers frantically pecking at the window. As the situation was in fact becoming quite alarming, I started to throw ashtrays at the window and was considering something heavier when Liz pointed out that if I actually smashed the pane, the whole lot would be in the room. We therefore had to suffer the paradiddles throughout the night.

The next show was in High Wycombe, a mere 250 mile drive, where we were to play at the Swan Theatre. This was a nice night, because a friend of ours from the Sixties, the Stones' minder Tom Keylock, came to see us. Tom is now quite an elderly chap and I have the utmost respect for him, but I was surprised to see the dismissive attitude displayed towards him by the rest of the band. One cannot blame Colin or indeed Miller, as they'd never met him, but the rest of us had. Tom is a great guy and another good thing that came out of that tour is that Tom, Liz and I forged a friendship way beyond the one I'd had with him in the Sixties. Back then, Tom had put himself out no end to ensure some comfort for us as a band and put Keith Richards' Bentley at our disposal whenever possible (though I'm sure Keith had no idea).

Keith had a wonderful blue Bentley Continental which was a fitted with speakers in the front grill. Tom, in his younger days, would shout commands to passing pedestrians. The ultimate technological improvement to the vehicle was that it would change colour with the beat of the music being played within. I never did actually see this working, but Tom assures me that door panels and the bonnet section did indeed change colour according to the volume.

It was a few days later, at Cambridge Corn Exchange, that Reg Presley launched forth with his theories on life and the evolution of mankind. From the outset of the tour Reg, and indeed all the other Troggs, kept us amused and, on occasion, interested, with Reg himself being the major expounder of tales of the extremely bizarre. He holds ground-breaking views on topics like crop circles, UFOs, eternal life, and the existence of a time machine which, Reg explains, is located somewhere in Italy. He validates the crop circle myth by explaining that birds don't fly across them, only round them, as there is in fact an invisible wall around their perimeter. Eternal life was a little more tricky and was a topic he elaborated on for nearly two months.

The theory goes back, according to Reg, to the days of Jesus Christ who was, in fact, a metallurgist, as a sideline to going around performing the odd miracle here and there. The basis of the theory, from what I could gather, is that gold can be heated to such an extreme that it turns to dust, and by taking a mere particle per day, much like we all take vitamin tablets, it is possible to attain eternal life. Of course, says Reg, there is no-one who has the equipment to perform this operation; well, some people have, but they won't admit it to the outside world, as the system has been bought up by the pharmaceutical industry and, were they to release this magical formula to the public, there would no longer be any need for regular medicine and the general drugs market would collapse. The Royal Family, and indeed all Royal Families, however, are privy to this "dust", which explains why they all live for so bloody long!

I said to Reg, "Well, suppose you did have this dust stuff and you got to the age of 300 or whatever and then became tired of living, what then?"

"It's bloody obvious," replied Reg, "You'd just throw yourself off the top of the fucking Eiffel Tower!" All this, don't forget, is spoken by Reg in the broadest of Andover accents. I'm convinced that Reg believes it all. If he doesn't, he's a bloody gifted comic.

The time machine was my particular favourite. After much research, Reg had traced the said machine to a remote part of Italy and, indeed, had arranged for a camera crew to go and film it. It transpired that film crews were not allowed near it for security reasons, so we therefore have to take Reg's word for it. Apparently, it actually works, but can only go backwards in time. When I asked Reg why this was, his instant response was, "Don't be so fucking daft, the future ain't happened yet, so there ain't nothing to go to!" How silly of me not to have thought of that.

Although it can't be denied that I am a champion smoker (tobacco having replaced alcohol in my affections) Reg Presley is the heaviest smoker I have ever met. The first thing the Troggs did on entering any dressing room was to sellotape over the smoke alarm, and Reg justified his enormous tobacco consumption by using a small plastic filter, which enabled him, he explained, to smoke twice as much, live twice as long and only get half as ill!

On most nights of the UK tour, Reg drove home to Andover from wherever we happened to be, undertaking the most ludicrously long journeys just for the pleasure of sleeping in his own bed. On the rare occasion that he did stay in a hotel, he'd book a morning call but get up a few hours before it was due, just to check that it worked!

In Cambridge, it was my birthday. I was feeling a bit offended because nobody mentioned it (we can all be touchy buggers from time to time), but in the evening, Spencer confounded me by announcing the event from the stage. By now, the bands were starting to become friends, as, after all, we were destined to spend the next two and a half months together. It would have been awful had we not all got on at least in some combination or another.

In Hull, Spencer dragged me along to a radio interview. I hate doing these things, and you will now see why. The guy who did the interview was a complete "turnip", who wasn't sure why we were there and certainly not at all sure why he was. He had a prompt sheet with some scanty information and, having played an old Spencer Davis track, pulled himself together for the first question which was, "So, Spencer, how long have you been in the Spencer Davis Group?" I mean, what do you say, what can you say, what should you say?

Spencer, being the old soldier that he is, responded that he had in fact been in the band from its conception as, indeed, his name was Spencer Davis. This somewhat flustered the "interviewer", who went on to say, "Eddie, when you joined, you were the youngest member", to which I logically replied, " ... and strangely enough, I still am". By now, he was totally fucked and didn't know what to say or do, other than to announce where we were playing that night. Unfortunately, he didn't have this information to hand either, and had to ask Spencer to provide it.

We were only a week into the tour and already quite a major bit of rot had set in between our Mercedes and the tour bus. This resentment didn't seem fair to us, as we had all been given the option of driving ourselves. We had chosen this option and the others hadn't. After-show drinks at the hotel bar were becoming an event for which a strategy needed to be worked out. Obviously, when a group of people stand at the bar, it's commonplace to work on the "round" system, though this was very soon proven to not be the case as far as the band was concerned. Colin had the ultimate solution. He wouldn't even go to his room, but instead would dash straight to the bar, guitar still in hand, which safely eliminated him from getting involved in a buying a round. Initially I found this very odd, and there were occasions when I'd go to the bar for, I might add, a mere glass of mineral water, and engage Colin in conversation. The norm, at least where I come from, is to ask, "What are you having?", but with Colin there was no such luck. I found this not only embarrassing, but also quite deflating, and so tended to sink into a bit of a depression. I'd had such a life of it in pubs, clubs, restaurants and bars and always paid for everything. I just like to see people having fun. Fun was not to be the objective of this tour, at least, not in that department.

I've never in my entire life been to a bar and not bought a drink for someone or other, so when one night Miller said to me, "Isn't it about time you bought a drink?", I was fucking furious and had every intention of getting the whole fucking place pissed; but then I thought, no, I'll play their game, which was a very hard game to play. Spencer knew of my frustration and tended to over-compensate by buying everything for everyone.

On the 22nd February, when we were in York, the city was beset with storms of hurricane force, and in fact the roof blew off the railway station! The staff at the hotel recommended us not to go out that night. The following day, we drove through blizzards, hail, rain and every meteorological horror that God could throw at us, but we made it to Cheltenham, where I was met by my friends John Fisher, John Acock and also SPC, together with his new lady love. Cheltenham was close to the village where Steve Winwood lives, but Winwood stayed very much at home that night.

The system in the hotel bar was that only residents were allowed to buy drinks. This suited everyone down to the ground, as no cash needed to change hands at all. John Fisher, however, would have none of it. He strode firmly to the bar, demanded a round and, on being told that the bar was indeed only open to residents, withdrew an enormous sum of money from his pocket (he always seems to carry a minimum of £1000 in cash) and demanded, "Perhaps this might sway your loyalty to this ludicrous system". Of course, he got his round, after which everyone promptly said goodnight. Liz, Spencer and I stayed behind for a few more, especially as the system had now been shot down in impressive flames.

The following day, we set off on another three and a half hour drive, this time to Chatham. Liz, Spencer and I were the first to arrive at the hotel, and later it turned out that Pete & Co had got lost in the town and couldn't find the hotel. In our car, we had the system of phoning from our mobiles for exact directions and consequently rarely got lost. This system could not work in the "following vehicle", as the batteries of all their mobile phones went flat or were found to be packed at the bottom of cases, as soon as they reached a town. Pete had a German mobile which he reckoned would cost him four times as much to ring from than anyone with a UK mobile. So the rest of the band remained lost, until Pete finally succumbed and telephoned on his German phone.

We were standing at the front desk when Pete's call came through. The poor receptionist was virtually reduced to tears and could be heard pleading, "It's not my fault you're lost!" After replacing the receiver, she said to us, "What a rude man!" "Oh, that'll be Mr. York", explained Spencer.

In Halifax, on the 26th February, a band dispute erupted which was potentially quite serious. I will say no more than that, because it's now water under the bridge. Luckily, the hotel in Halifax had turned out to be a little gem of a place. Halifax is not the most inviting of cities and, having driven through the doom laden city centre and onwards to the outskirts, expecting to come across a "Mrs. Brown's B & B", we suddenly stopped before a huge manor house, which had in fact been used by the Beatles in the Sixties as a secret hideaway. Deep Purple, who were on tour at the same time, were also due to be staying there, but sadly, their concerts had been cancelled because of illness. At least Roger Glover would have spoken to me ... I think.

Well, of course you don't want a complete blow-by-blow account of every gig on the tour, but one place certainly worthy of mention is the seaside town of Torquay. Here, we actually stayed in the hotel that had given John Cleese the inspiration for Fawlty Towers, which was appropriate, because by this time, we were all extremely fawlty ourselves. England is not renowned for its climatic excellence, and Torquay was not at all warm. Nevertheless, Spencer decided that, as were were at the seaside, he would become the ultimate tourist, despite the cold.

He donned shorts, a T-shirt, a pair of trainers and a baseball cap upon which was written, "I Love Hawaii!". The only item missing was an array of cameras around his neck. Liz and I were returning from Harry Ramsden's fish & chip shop when, in the distance, we saw a strange guy twirling about with an ice cream cornet and wearing the most extraordinary garb, considering the conditions. It wasn't until we got closer that we realised it was Spencer. When we reached him, it was clear that he was not a happy chappie. He explained that the reason for his mood was that he'd ordered a "99", which in England is an ice cream cone with a chocolate flake stuck in it.

The price difference between an ordinary cornet and a "99" had apparently spiralled to about 10p. Spencer thought this a disgracefully inflated charge for a bit of chocolate and said to the woman in the kiosk, "Fuck the '99' give me a '98'!" The woman was not at all impressed and pronounced that Spencer was the type of person who gave American tourists a bad name. Spencer then noticed a few telescopes mounted on the seafront and seemed intent on looking at the Isle of Wight, which I'm not at all sure is remotely near Torquay. He said to Liz, "I suppose it'll be a tenner a look, bollocks to it." Ah, how times had changed.

We then walked to the Princess Theatre, into the reception area, where there was the hugest of signs saying "Information". The desk was being "manned" by a girl so young that she shouldn't even have been in charge of herself. Spencer, obeying the sign, asked for directions to the dressing rooms. Of course she had not a clue as to where they were, who we were, or even who she was. The "Information" sign was immediately above her head, so Spencer scanned from the sign to her a few times, before pointing to the sign and saying, "The sign beneath which you are sitting says INFORMATION, so please inform me." The poor girl just sat there looking bewildered at this maniac with the "I Love Hawaii" hat, still sucking furiously on what was left of his "98".

Still receiving no satisfaction, Spencer then leant over the counter and reached for her telephone, saying, "With this implement, you can communicate, so bloody well communicate with someone and tell us where the dressing rooms are!" It must be something to do with the air in Torquay which turned us all into Basils. But nothing worked, and the girl merely stared back gormlessly.

After the show, we were pretty pissed off, not because of the show but because of our "dispute", so we went back to Fawlty Towers, to be confronted by the cabaret. There were a few rows of seats and a couple of pensioners listening to "Just The Way You Are" and other songs which have been demeaned by the sort of acts that perform at such affairs. I just sat there, completely stunned, as the girl singer went through her routine, accompanied by an older guy who seemingly played every instrument at once. He was adorned with guitars and played the standard synth with the standard crap string sounds.

I think I must have been frozen to the spot, as I was still sitting there at the end of their "show". I was even more shocked when they both came over to us and it transpired that he was, in fact, a brass player who had played on some Hardin & York tracks which were recorded at Olympic Studios in Barnes. My only thought was ... there but for the grace of God. They were, in fact, a nice couple and he dashed off to get some Hardin & York CDs for me and Pete to sign.

The following morning, Liz and I woke at 6 a.m, still in despair about the band dispute, and decided to go for a quiet walk while no-one was about. However, it seemed like everyone had the same idea, and, as we walked through the deserted streets, we noticed Pete concealed in the bushes, attempting to make a discreet video (of Torquay at 6 am, presumably). He joined us for the final part of the stroll and we ended up at a newsagents which wasn't quite open, so we waited. I wanted a newspaper, cigarettes etc, and for some reason which still eludes me, Liz bought an umbrella, which to this day has not been opened. It was lucky that there were no shoe shops open between the hours of 6 and 7 am.

On our return to the hotel, we found the entire band in reception, waiting for breakfast to commence. As per normal, the band members had spread themselves around the restaurant. I'm sure the staff must have found it a little strange to see five guys, who were supposedly together, all sitting at separate tables. This oddness is explained by the smoking habit which Colin and I share. Still, the journeys themselves did have some funny moments. Routing was left to Spencer, who undertook the task with a fanatical passion. He knew road names and numbers and every motorway the length and breadth of the UK.

On entering Liverpool, on the day of a football match, we asked a guy stuck in the same traffic jam for directions to our hotel. He said to firstly look out for a pub called "The Yellow Submarine" and then "The Liver Birds", which sounded a little bizarre and also rather doubtful. Before long, however, we did indeed come across The Yellow Submarine (Liverpool should really be re-named "Beatlepool"). Liz, however, was scanning the horizon for figures of the two girls who appeared in the TV sitcom The Liver Birds and therefore missed the massive bronzes of real birds that adorn the top of the City Hall.

The climax of the tour was at the Royal Albert Hall in London, but by that time, the tensions within the band had reached a point where I decided to stay at a different hotel. We stayed at The Gore in Kensington, which gave Liz the opportunity to go shopping (of course): Harrods, Harvey Nichols, etc. Jon Lord and Muff Winwood came to the show, after which there was an abysmal end of tour party laid on by Flying Music. The standard photos were taken of all the bands together, and then of the bands separately. My God, did we (the SDG) look happy! Nobody within the band said goodbye to each other, which, in my view, was a pretty sad ending.

Back at The Gore, The Yardbirds had decided, by chance, to have their own end of tour party, but it was so chaotic that Liz and I only stayed for about half an hour, before saying our goodbyes and going to bed. In the morning, Spencer (and only Spencer) rang to bid his farewells and to wish us both a safe trip home. The tour, which had latterly become something of a nightmare, was over.

On the homeward journey, we of course got lost, even though Spencer had gone to great lengths to give us directions to get out of London and onto the road to Dover. We did eventually reach France and decided to stay the night in Troyes, which was the town where we had been "nicked" at the outset. By pure chance, we found the most fantastic hotel. It was called "Les Oiseaux", situated in a tiny side street. It was wonderful. It gave us time to relax and contemplate the last couple of months of misery. As we lazed in bed, we had just decided that France maybe wasn't so bad after all and that here we were in one of the the most luxurious rooms anyone could imagine, when our ears were attracted by an unusual sound: ... "Bzzzzzzzzzzzzzzzzzzzzzzzzzzzzzzzzzz". We only had a fucking wasp in the room! I have long since come to realise that nothing in life is ever perfect. Far from the hoped-for hours of passion, I spent the next hour or so trying to swat the bastard, which I eventually did, after which I was so knackered that I fell asleep.

The next day we were home, and after all the fuss and crap and bollocks we'd all been through, I immediately found myself missing the other guys. Within minutes, I was on the phone to Miller (who can be a champion moaner). You see, after all the shit, and after knowing each other for a virtual lifetime, we really all have a great deal of affection for each other. As my only true friend John Fisher once said to me, "It is the privilege of true friends to on occasion offend each other".

So now I have come full circle and am back with The Spencer Davis Group. I have come to realise that I have lived a wonderful life and, should it end tomorrow, I could never complain. I've had a superb and loving family and have the love of my wife Liz (I hope!). Spencer Davis opened up a whole new spectrum for me and I owe him a lot. Through him, I've met people who have since become both heroes and friends, both in the musical sense and in my private life, and for this I thank him.

There has been one final thought that has occurred to me throughout the writing of this book. It may well be trivial, and indeed stupid, but in the Seventies, the writer Martin Amis (son of Kingsley) became part of my "circle". He asked me to lend him a fiver, and gave me a cheque in return. It bounced! I understand, or rather, I know, that Martin has subsequently made his fortune, which leads me right back to my original idea for a title for this book: "Ain't LifeA Bastard"!

EPILOGUE
CAN'T GIVE IT UP

It's ridiculous, really. It's summer 2003 and here I am, still touring with the rejuvenated SDG, still doing the rounds of the legendary rock venues of Germany, still loving it.

Spencer has entered the internet age in a big way. In fact, on this last tour, he was on his mobile for the entire three weeks; he'd also sadly brought his laptop with him and was in Multimedia Global Connection mode. He seemed to be "firing off" (as he put it) faxes and e-mails day and night, even in the tour bus, in which he had had his printer installed! In the odd moment of non-communication, he'd play noisy computer games, one particularly aggravating one being "Shooting Cats", which involved a horrible squawking noise every time he scored a direct hit, which was not infrequent. Not for a moment was the laptop dormant.

The shows in Germany surpassed anything we'd done before. Pete York is now working with Helge Schneider, a major star in Germany. Helge's speciality is jazz, so Pete is in his element. Whilst I retain the utmost respect for Pete's quite incredible virtuosity and technical precision, our new Bavarian drummer, Steff Porzel, fits in excellently, and now the band is as solid as a rock, with new songs being written and rehearsed with enthusiasm, for the first time in years.

I can't recall what incidents happened where, but one of the best ones was when I decided to have a "meeting" with Spencer at 3 o'clock one morning. It was clear that he was awake because you hear the clatter of printers and films being watched all along the corridor. On entering his room, I was presented with a sight that was quite disturbing, considering the hour. Picture the scene: Empty wine bottles were piled around the room, Spencer was charging around in his underpants, three phone lines were ringing constantly. The TV was on and another film was playing on his computer, interspersed with global e-mails and faxes flying in as well as flying out. It was like walking into the CNN news centre mid-morning!

Bernie Zylka, our tour manager, who is normally totally organised and efficient, had on this occasion completely lost the plot and the power of movement in his entire body; in fact, not to put too fine a point on it, both he and Spencer were pissed as parrots. Bernie was doing his best to answer all three phones, explaining that we were in a business meeting - at 3 am! Spencer was trying to book himself on a plane/train/bus/taxi and every other known mode of transport to get him to Venice after the tour. My last vision of Bernie that morning was watching him casually leaning, or rather trying to lean, against the wall with a Fender Strat around his neck, while gradually sliding to the floor in a heap of tuneless twangings, with a phone balanced on each ear.

So really, the lifestyle wasn't that much different to that experienced on our first tour of America over thirty years before. The candle has two ends, and Spencer burns both. The schedule was pretty gruelling with only a day or two off, which was a bit of a joke, as on these "days off" we had 400-mile journeys to undertake. We played at The Hamburg Downtown Blues Club, and it was the most amazing reception I can recall; the owner was so pleased, he not only supplied us with a marathon dinner, but also delivered endless supplies of booze. I allowed myself to have some Grappa, which I guess was okay, as, not having had a drink for five years, my liver is now functioning normally.

In Augsburg, in Austria, the mayhem reached its heights, as did the intake of red wine. But then, fuck it, Spencer is happier than I've seen him in ages, so why not? After days of chaos, the tour drew to its close. I left the hotel at 7.30 am and could still hear the clatter of printers and faxes and e-mails and TVs emanating from the Davis room.

Steff is a lovely person and a really great drummer. I personally find it very hard to accept "new" people, especially at my age, but I can safely say that Steff is now well and truly one of us. He takes my song, "Deep In My Despair", into another dimension. He's fucking perfect. I do like to form bonds with people, but it's very, very rare; it's only fairly recently that Colin and I have finally broken down the barriers, whatever they were, and can have a bloody good laugh! For some reason, we never could in the past. And as for Miller, well, we go back beyond history, and that speaks for itself.

Basically, we are just a very happy band, and it shows in the music, which I love as much as ever. Is there any stopping us now?

```
                MR HARDING
EXTRA  WORK IN STUDIO
SHLEVES                                £175
BOXING AROUND SPEACKERS____           £125
BROARDING LOFT___                      £150
BROADING FLOOR___                      £125
BROADING GARAGE WALL____              £125
DOOR TO FUSE  BROAD_____            £55

                TOTAL_____      £755


          mr
        MR HARDING
TO SURPLY AND FIT NEW 5 LEVER DOOR LOCK
TO UNBLOCK DRAINS TO REAR OF HOUSE
                    £155



TO SURPLY AND FIT  2PAIRS SOLID WOODEN GATES

WOOD (4x2_ 6x2  extenal ply  sbip-lap broading )    £700
HINGES+ VANISH                                      £175
POST (4x £80)                                       £320
DIGGER AND CONCRETE                                 £125
LABOUR TO MAKE (3x2 MEN days)                       £450
LABOUR TO HANG  (4x2MEN days)                       £600

                            TOTAL        £ 2370
                  STUDIO                 £755
                  BLIUDER                £155

                            TOTAL        £ 3280
              LESS PAID ON ACCOUNT       £1000
                  TOTAL OWING            £2280
```

Three weeks later, the gates fell off

DISCOGRAPHY
Compiled by Miguel Terol
(All release catalogue numbers are U.K. unless otherwise stated)

A Wild Uncertainty
Man With Money/Broken Truth (Planet PLF 120, 1965)

With The Spencer Davis Group:
With Their New Face On (1968, UA 1192) (CD reissue: Repertoire, 1997 REP 4684-WY)
Funky (1968) (CD reissue: One Way, OW 34529)
Taking Out Time 1967-69 (aka Letters From Edith) (RPM 127)
The Masters (compilation) (Eagle Records, May 1999)

As Hardin & York:
Tomorrow Today (1969, Bell, SBLL125) (CD reissue: Repertoire, 1994 REP 4481-WY)
The World's Smallest Big Band (1970, Bell, SBLL136) (CD reissue: Repertoire, 1994 REP 4482-WY)
For The World (1971, Bell, SBLL141) (LP reissue: See For Miles SEE 41, 1985)
Live At The Marquee (1994, RPM RPM135) (1971 recording)
Hardin-York Live (Repertoire 1994, REP 4459-WY) (1970 recording, previously a bootleg)

With reformed Spencer Davis Group:
Gluggo (1973, Vertigo, 6360088) (CD reissue: Repertoire, 1997 REP 4683-WY)
Livin' In a Back Street (1974, Vertigo, 6499978/6360105) (CD reissue: Repertoire, 1997 REP 4682-WY)
Catch You On The Rebop (Live in Europe 1973) (RPM 150)

As Hardin & York (again):
Hardin & York with Charlie McCracken (1974, Vertigo, 6360622) (CD reissue - Repertoire, 1994 REP4452WP)

With Axis Point:
Axis Point (1979, RCA, PL 30039)
Boast Of The Town (1980, RCA PL 25277)

As Hardin & York (again):
Hardin & New York (1979, Teldec, 624595)
Still A Few Pages Left (1995, RPM Thunderbird CSA 106)

Solo albums:
Home Is Where You Find It (1972, Decca TXS 106)
You Can't Teach An Old Dog New Tricks (1977, ATTIC LAT 1023) (CD reissue - Repertoire, 1994, REP4464WY)
Circumstantial Evidence (1982, RCA) (CD reissue - Angel Air, SJPCD024)
Eddie Hardin & Zak Starkey's Musical Version of "Wind In The Willows" (President PTLS 1078, 1985)
Situations (President PTLS1089, 1988)
Music of the Stars - Aquarius (Birth, BIRTHLP 4)
Wind in the Willows - live, featuring Maggie Bell, Graham Bonnet, Rafael Ravenscroft, Jon Lord, Zak Starkey and others (1992, INAK/BOSE inak 9010 CD;1998, Angel Air)
When We Were Young (1996, INAK 11005 CD)
Dawn 'til Dusk (Voiceprint BP316CD)
Survival (NAGE 19)
Just Passing Through (2000)

Solo Singles:
Driving / Where I'm Going to Sleep Tonight (1971, Decca, F 13252)
Why Does Everybody Put Me Down / Spend Your Money Honey (1972, Decca, F13307)
S'easy / Strange Times (1974, Mercury, 6008008)
Summer Days / Seems I'm always Going to Love You (1975, GTO, GT24)
Good Morning to You / Wayfarers All (1985, President, PT 538)
Red Nose City / Caribbean Nights (1987, President, PT 561)

As Wizard's Convention:
Wizard's Convention (1976, RCA, RS 1085)
Wizard's Convention, vol. 2 (1995, Resurgent; EDEL Germany edel 0029152EDL, Angel Air SJPCD009)
Wizard's Convention, vol. 3 (1997, TDK CD, TDCN-5615)

With Deep Purple
Live at the Royal Albert Hall - "Love is all" (Roger Glover/Eddie Hardin) 4:40
Featuring Ronnie James Dio, Eddie Hardin and Mickey Lee Soule.

Japan December 1999 Polydor POCP-7445/6 [2CD] / Europe/Australia January 2000 Eagle Records/Spitfire Records 0000124 EDG 5034504112421 [2CD; with MPEG] / US February 2000 Eagle Records/Spitfire Records 0000124 EDG 5034504112421 [2CD; with different MPEG] / Europe October 2000 Eagle Records/Spitfire Records (Special Tour Edition) EDGTE 124 [2CD; no MPEG, but extra track] / US October 2000 Eagle Records/Spitfire Records 6-70211-5068-2 [2CD; no MPEG, but extra track]

Collaborations:
Ray Fenwick "Keep America Beautiful, Get a Haircut" (1971, Decca, SKL 5090) (CD reissue: Angel Air, 1997, with 5 bonus tracks. Eddie appears on one of those bonus tracks)
Jake "And In The Morning" (1972, Deram DM 350 - EH vocals)
Keef Hartley Band featuring Dick Heckstall Smith "Go Now"/"You Can't Sit Down"
Ewan Stephens "We Can Give It A Try" / "Queen Of The Good Times" (Decca - EH vocals)
Bo Diddley - "London Sessions" (1972, Checker, 6499476)
Roger Glover - "Butterfly Ball" (1974, Purple TPSA 7514)
Eddie Hardin/Roger Glover as **Natural Magic** - "Strawberry Fields Forever"/"Isolated Lady" (Oyster, 1975)
Sweet "Cut Above The Rest" (1979, Polydor POLD S022)
Renaissance - "Time Line" (1983, IRS, SP 70033)
Chris Thompson "Out of the Night" (1983, Teldec, 625484)
Denny Laine - "Hometown Girls" (1985, President, PTLS 1080)
Iris Williams "Peace Must Come Again" (President; EH - producer, songwriter, keyboards)
Michael D'Abo "Indestructible" (President, 1987, PTLS 1084)
Pete York "Pete York presents Super Drumming, Volume II " (Disc 1) (1989, BMG Ariola)
Pete York "Pete York presents Super Drumming, Volume II " (Disc 2) (1989, BMG Ariola)
Renaissance "Songs from Renaissance days" (1997, compilation, HTD CD 73)
Various artists Maxi-Single: "You'll Never Walk Alone/Messages" (1985, Spartan) (SR 12124)
This was a maxi-single where a massive all-star lineup was assembled in the aid of the Bradford City Disaster Fund. The list of people involved in the recording of this single is immense: Gerry Marsden (from Gerry & The Pacemakers, he was the one who made this very song famous back in

the early '60s), Tony Christie, Denny Laine, Tim Healy, the late Gary Holton (from Heavy Metal Kids), Ed Stewart, Tony Hicks (from Back Door, not the Hollies one), Kenny Lynch, Colin Blunstone (ex-Zombies), Chris Robinson, A.Curtis, Phil Lynott (from Thin Lizzy), Bernie Winters, Girlschool, Black Lace (featuring the late Alan Barton - later with Smokie), John Otway, Rick Wakeman (from Yes), Barron Knights, Tim Hinkley, Brendan Shine, John Verity (from Argent), Rolf Harris, Rob Heaton, Patrick McDonald, Smokie, Bruce Forsyth, Johnny Logan (of Eurovision hit "What's Another Year" fame), Colbert Hamilton, Dave Lee Travis, Rose Marie, Frank Allen, Jim Diamond (from Ph.D), Graham Gouldman (from 10cc, also functioning as producer), Pete Spencer, Chris Norman (both ex-Smokie), Gerard Kenny, The Nolans, Graham Dene, Suzy Grant, Peter Cook, The Foxes, Jess Conrad, Kin Kelly, Motorhead, John Entwistle (from The Who), Jimmy Hennie, Joe Fagan, David Shilling, Karen Clark, Gary Hughes, Zak Starkey (mis-spelt as Zac), Eddie Hardin, Paul McCartney, Kiki Dee, Keith Chegwin, and John Conteh.

The maxi-single contains two versions of "You'll Never Walk Alone" (long and short versions), along with some messages.

Where Are They Now?

John Acock
Lives in Cheltenham and still engineers.
Gordon Barton
Last heard of drumming in Thunderclap Newman.
Tony Barton
Currently apearing in "Coronation Street".
Maggie Bell
Lives and works in Spain.
John Craig
Works on musicals with Tony Edwards.
Mike D'Abo
Successful songwriter and solo artist.
Jim Davidson
Still a major TV star in the UK.
Spencer Davis
Lives in Los Angeles and still tours with the Spencer Davis Group.
Frank Dostel
Has a music publishing company in Hamburg.
Ray Fenwick
Teaches guitar in Lincoln.
John Fisher
Retired
Ian Gillan
Still sings in Deep Purple.
Roger Glover
Lives in Connecticut and still plays in Deep Purple.
Emma Harding
Flourishing career as a solo artist.
Glenn Hughes
Lives in California. Still records successfully.
Denny Laine
Lives and works in Las Vegas.
Jon Lord
Finally quit Deep Purple in 2001.
Charlie McCracken
Working with a re-jigged version of Taste.
Florentine Pabst
Married a doctor in Hamburg.

The Pike
Last heard of at working at a dry cleaners in Englefield Green.
Marlene Pinckard
Lives in L.A. and involved in Real Estate.
Reg Presley
Threatens to retire but never will.
Phil Sawyer
Has a successful career in film and television music
Ian Smithers
Last heard of working at the Ministry of Defence. Lord help us all!
Spud
Works as a gardener for the Griswolds.
Zak Starkey
In-demand session drummer, currently working with Johnny Marr, The Who and, I hear, in line for Oasis.
Rick Wakeman
Lives in Italy and tours with Yes (in between appearing on panel games).
Corinthia West
Was associated with Eric Idle. Worked for Handmade Films.
Charlie Whitney
Has his own studio and record label.
Pete York
Lives near Munich and tours with various acts.
No longer with us:
Clive Brandy, Reg King, Larry Uttal, Keith Moon, Tony Ashton, Hugh Mendl, Carlo Enchelmeier

LINKS

Rare items from Eddie Hardin's back catalogue, plus numerous CDs and
DVDs covering all periods of Eddie's career can be purchased at

www.eddiehardin.com.

where you can also keep up to date with tour news, etc.

OLIVER GRAY assisted Eddie with the writing of this book.
Oliver's best-selling and acclaimed books

VOLUME and V.A.C.A.T.I.O.N.

can be obtained from

www.olivergray.com

VOLUME: A Cautionary Tale of Rock and Roll Obsession
"If you only ever buy one book about the music industry, make it this one" -
Amazon

V.A.C.A.T.I.O.N.: Cautionary Tales of Travelling Without Style
"The 'Never Mind The Bollocks' of travel writing." - ***Mid-Hants Observer***
Available from all good bookshops.

Further interesting links:
www.tonyashton.co.uk
www.spencer-davis-group.com
www.thehighwaystar.com
www.emmaharding.net
www.chrisfarlowe.com
http://members.aol.com/rockinfo/rayfenwick
www.jonlord.com
www.harthouse.u-net.com/trogg.html
www.peteyork.net
www.zakstarkey.com